ASPECTS
OF ENVIRONMENTAL
DISSONANCE

A COMPARISON OF GERMAN
AND POLISH WORKERS

*In memory of my father
and grandfather
whose search for the truth
had a great influence on me.*

CORNELIA MESEKE

ASPECTS
OF ENVIRONMENTAL
DISSONANCE

A COMPARISON OF GERMAN
AND POLISH WORKERS

Lublin 1998

Please address correspondence to:
Helga Berger Blazkova
6501 Red Hook Plaza
Suite 201
St. Thomas, U.S.V.I. 00802-1306

First edition 1998

ISBN 83-908526-5-9

Published by:

**WE WYDAWNICTWO
EKOINŻYNIERIA**

ul. Głęboka 29, 20-612 Lublin, Poland
tel./fax (+48-81) 743-61-79

CONTENTS

*„The norms themselves are taken as givens,
and no effort is made to examine them. Nor is
there any thought given to the mannes in which
norms might themselves contribute to the development of the problems."*

William Ryan, 1977

PREFACE

Never before in the history of mankind have environmental issues taken on such global importance. Whereas some cultures have always placed distinct emphasis on their environment, unique to their particular relationship to it, today, environmental matters have taken on global importance in their own right, irrespective of the separate and diverse varieties of groups they concern. Thus, in the past, many Native Americans, for example, were typical for true environmental habits, showing a spirit of utmost harmony of the individual with his surroundings in agricultural husbandry, in gaming prey, as well as in all their other activities. European societies, on the other hand, have shown less environmentally sound activity. Not only industrial enterprise in such countries as England and Wales, for example, but over-use in the classical societies of Greece and Rome as well, can be added to the tale of environmental destructiveness, throughout quite a number of centuries. It has mostly been the nature of man to use and utilize, letting nature replenish itself.

However, we find that those societies with an emphasis on nature also behaved naturally. This is still true of such societies today and we should realize, that indigenous peoples all over the world have a vital ecological role to play. Of course, education, advertisement, and a common fear of the consequences, is starting to make its effect felt even beyond scientific circles.

Still, we may find that some cultural and national mentalities find it more difficult to cope meaningfully with their environmental problems than others. Thus, the very potent conviction of the importance of tribal fraternity in Africa is a hindrance not only to peace, but to development in itself and with it to environmental activity and any meaningful progress towards prosperity. Kinship - in itself a valuable bond in life - taken to extremes leads to disagreement, aggression and often war, which leaves poverty and destruction in its wake. These are not only the enemies of meaningful prosperity, but de-organize, damage and even kill any significant societal action, anathema also to environmental stability. What makes this kind of mentality so especially destructive, is its very grounding in the moral and ethical constituents of these societies. For this reason, many essentially prosperous and even wealthy areas become devastated and sometimes even unfit for human habitation. Thus, in India, where social emphasis is put upon a worship of minor gods that, quite often, show more human than divine characteristics - and where there has also been disagreement of diverse religious groups - these realities of their culture often prevent effectual action in socio-economic programs and, together with these, the environment is neglected.

Environmental activity suffers where there is disagreement, corruption, pugnacity, combativeness and militancy. Perhaps the most tragic example of this is the modern-day Palestinian enclaves around Israel, where there is so much incursion on both sides that even very peaceful Palestinians - or Israelis - have little hope of making their voices heard or their actions seen and thus, to derive the impetus to build up any meaningful and lasting societal structures.

Lack of consensus on environmental issues is also rampant in the more industrial, affluent and largely peaceful societies of the West and with them the new - and older - industrial nations in the Far East. Here, different societal parts, such as Industry and Politics can often not agree within themselves, regarding necessary standards of action, let alone with each other. Again, although these societies are proving to guarantee their citizens greater access to material means and affluence, their environmental programs are oftentimes not organized effectively because the emphasis is not put upon the environment itself - actions are often a means to some political or business end - and cultural and moral values needed to support any action are lacking.

And yet, where there is moral concern, it often goes into the wrong direction. Effective environmental effort is not based upon what has often been considered holy and highly moral in Western societies. Poverty, self-abnegation and renunciation are values that, as has largely been shown by more recent studies and been addressed in the world conferences on the environment, are not useful in coping with the many and often very complicated problems that need to be solved.

Ethical and moral values have often only been brought into this context with regard to the individual, but these are perhaps of even more vital relevance to industry and politics. Such moral issues as personal responsibility towards the environment, to one's neighbor, firm and country, is not only pertinent to the individual within his private sphere of influence but to him in his every public action, as Kant once pointed out.

Another issue related to responsibility is knowledge and discernment. Again, this concerns as well the public and the private actions of each individual. Privately, his knowledge is limited largely to his own area of specialty and work and he cannot be held responsible for every minute detail that goes into effective environmental action, since this would be impossible and cannot be managed to this day even by the most modern computers. Indeed, it is irresponsible to ask this of him. However, in his social and public actions, he must be held to task for what he produces and creates, either with his hands, tools or otherwise.

Again, poverty and even simplicity do not guarantee environmental effectiveness. To take a very straightforward example connected to this work: This is apparently not known well enough in the essentially very beautiful country of Poland. Here, nature is often in a very delicate balance where the intrusion of man can only in some cases create fertile soil after much hard labor; in others the soil might never respond to attempts at husbandry at all. Such is the equilibrium - not throughout the whole country, of course, but in areas - that any disturbance of the natural cycles will create havoc for centuries to come and must be stopped now, or problems, very similar to those occuring at this very moment with the cultivation of the rain-forests in South America will take place. Indeed, the more recent floods in the last two years are in part a tribute to this effect. This does not mean however, that all forest areas are to be left to themselves, rather they must be cultivated as a beautiful garden, with even the useage of some woods and other materials allowed for commerce, but only if it is guaranteed, that the strongest trees are to be left to provide for seed - otherwise the quality of the forest deteriorates. Many so-called unspoiled areas of forests are in reality in use all of the time, particularly by those people who live close to them and utilize the wood for their heat and building materials, as, essentially, many poor people still do. Damage done in this respect is sometimes irreversible for centuries. Where wood is sold by the acre and the mentality is rampant that the supply will last, spoilage threatens in a short time, for this becomes the illusion of the majority.

In this context, individuals need to learn to balance their actions, to understand their own needs and to provide for them sensibly, trying always to understand the results of their doings and the outcome of their interaction with their surroundings. This does not contradict what has been said above, it is merely the other side of the same coin, what Kant would have called "enlightened action".

In a way, the insistence that abstinence, self-denial and even rejection of one's needs, of modern conveniences, or of modern society is the answer to the environmental problems that are facing us, is another fallacy of our time. Of much more relevance is a realization of the constant change, expansion and lack of stability that has befallen our modern world. Were the whole of mankind to go back to a simple way of life, for example, it would wreak a greater havoc on the environment than we have at present, largely because simplicity of this kind would not necessarily be ordered. Moreover, the focus on environmental issues in the industry of the developed nations has brought some quite fruitful results and just need to be implemented on a wider scale. It is often a question of utilizing what we know, before we constantly look for new answers.

Conversely, the over-use and degradation of nature is just as imbalanced as its under-use or entire abstinence. The more recent floods in the lower regions of Poland have proven that, as well as the above. Exactly in the area where Poland meets the Czech Republic, more than 300,000 acres of forests have disappeared. Moreover, this region is highly industrialized. Because frequently, produced pollution often disappears in the regions where it is created and appears in others, or in neighboring countries, scientists have called this area the "Bermuda Triangle" of pollution. Poland is a country that prides itself on its clear lakes. Unfortunately, in some cases, this could be the result of a high acidity brought about by pollution, which cleans the water of any living matter and thus produces clarity: actually, clear water is sometimes a sign of very heavy pollution.

Another very important but relatively unknown and understood aspect of environmental integrity is the propensity of man to be stubborn. In fact, we often tend to be most obstinate in the face of opposition, contrary opinion or even fact. Studies in social and most recently environmental psychology have in fact shown, that when a person makes a decision either recently, in the past, or even historically, or when he lives a decision that his parents or society have made for him, he tends to ignore even the most salient arguments or proofs that he is wrong and his actions are erroneous. He will do this even in life-threatening situations, rather creating myths for himself than facing reality and saving his own life. Leon Festinger coined this with the phrase "cognitive dissonance" and it manifests itself largely as a result of our insistence that we are right. It could actually be seen as the other side of tenacity, but taken to an unhealthy extreme. This phenomenon causes people, even in the face of great natural destruction, for example, to perpetuate in keeping with their old habits, ways or habitations and to stubbornly insist that they could not be wrong, have made an error or even be in danger, for so much of their previous action was right. It is perhaps most greatly manifested in the inability to see change and act accordingly. The hardest thing about dealing with change of any kind is perhaps the fact that, in life, some things change and others remain the same. This sounds simple, but the acceptance of this fact is not easy by any means, especially since we are seldom really warned, before change occurs.

Before introducing the following text and its contents, I would now like to take the opportunity to thank all of the colleagues, friends and family who helped me to complete this work.

Warm thanks go especially to colleagues and friends here in Poland, without which this work would never have been concluded. They include Drs. Henryk and Elzbieta Czarniawski, who made all cooperation possible through their kind intervention in all phases of its completion. Next, many thanks go to Dr Leszek Bobrzyk, Mayor of the town of Lublin from 1991-1994, who made contacts to industry easy and convinced several heads of local industry to take part in this study. He gave me hours of his very valuable time and used his position well in order to serve people, putting into effect the very kind of mentality that is necessary if we are to make positive changes in the environment. However, without the encouragement of Prof. Dr. habil. Zofia Kawczynska-Butrym it is possible that this text would never have been published and it is largely due to her friendship and encouragement that last efforts were made to facilitate this. Lastly, I would like to thank Ryszard Brylewicz (who is also translating the text into Polish), for last minute corrections.

In Germany, because of the difficulties I had with getting industry and scientific establishments to cooperate, I was largely helped by my family and friends. In addition though, many thanks also go to Dr Alexander Grob of the University of Bern, Switzerland, for having let me use his questionnaire. As the following text will show, I have found the Polish industry to be much more cooperative than the German one, in fact, there is no comparison. Without the help of my sisters Susanne Souaieh and Claudia Steiner, as well as Rolf Grossjean, no German findings could have been included in this work and I would here like to thank them very warmly. Furthermore, I would like to thank Mrs. Inge Lies-Bohlmann and Mrs. Figge of the IG Metall in Bremen for their help and encouragement. Thanks also go to my sister Mrs. Karen McConathy and her husband, Kevin McConathy, through whom I was better able to cope with the questionnaires, both in original and translation. Mostly though, I would like to thank my mother, Helga Blazkova-Berger, for her continued moral support, her open nature and her love for the truth. They were always an inspiration to me.

„Geist ohne Methode schädigt die Wissenschaft
nicht minder als Methode ohne Geist."

Bernheim, 1908

INTRODUCTION

The following text seeks to make a meaningful contribution to the field of environmental psychology. There are many unsolved questions in this field, perhaps even more in the area of psychology than in those natural sciences that concern themselves with environmental problems: man's dealings with the environment are at least as complicated and many-faceted, as the environmental problems themselves.

As in all research, a meaningful theory must be found to encompass any questions that should arise in a given area. This not only makes the contribution comparable to other research done, it makes the conclusions accessible to others working in the field. Much of environmental study has dealt with the relationship of attitude and behavior, as reiterated more closely in the following Chapter Two. Close to this, but not entirely encompassed by it, is the theory of cognitive dissonance, which seeks to include the aspects and components of cognition in its concept as well.

The underlying assumptions and postulates of this theory will be dealt with in Chapter One and Chapter Two. Before the English reader continues this text, let it be said that the controversy this theory has elicited in the United States has not touched Germany really at all; this is an extremely important point and cannot be overemphasized. In Germany, it has become an accepted theory, especially in the area of ecological psychology and has, in more recent times, provoked a good amount of research with some very interesting results. As shown in Chapter One, the theory of cognitive dissonance, while not entirely encompassed by environmental psychology, was conceived of at the beginnings of the formation of this field and belongs to it, so to speak.

The following - in order to accommodate the controversy, provide some backgro- und information for the development of ecological psychology in Germany and fur- ther furnish the reader with some background information of ecological problem are- as in Germany and in Poland - has been divided into two sections, Theory and Research: accordingly Chapter One - Three and Chapter Four - Eight.

Let it be pointed out clearly here, however. The following is not an apology for the theory of cognitive dissonance. Even presently, the controversy has not been accepted by all American authors, many more recent publications have included it as a viable theory within their texts. It is interesting, however, that a controversy like that should come at a time when the relationship between cognition, attitude and behavior is being discussed in the field of environmental psychology. We have many interesting outcomes in the studies undertaken in this field, as shown further on in Chapter Two. Perhaps the above-mentioned controversy just shows that we must make room for more exact findings that can then find their place in the great puzzle that constitutes the overall picture. Rather than an overreliance on a restrictive hy- pothesis of cognitive dissonance, defined too closely and trying to meaningfully sepa- rate it from other closely related theories, science should now attempt to utilize what has already been translated into real-life findings, which have oftentimes resulted in quite interesting and surprising discoveries and conclusions that mankind, if they were disseminated, could really profit from. To argue that a theory is not true becau- se it is applicable in so many circumstances and that so many findings have gained their place within its wide and generous structure, is to forget that life itself has many manifestations of what, in essence is the same and that, the simpler the truth gets, the more often it seems to be manifested.

In the following, **Chapter One** deals with the controversy of cognitive dissonan- ce to some extent, but of overlying importance is its historical perspective. It both discusses the development of ecological psychology in Germany, reviews Polish issu- es briefly and debates issues of environmental psychology. In the following text, the literature, because of its extent, is always mentioned at the end of each chapter.

Chapter Two seeks to summarize and discuss the findings both in the area of cognitive dissonance as well as in related issues of environmental psychology.

Chapter Three deals primarily with the controversies of ecological issues in Po- land, discussing political issues and some framework for ecological questions and developments. While it puts the more recent European Community developments into quite a positive light, it must be said at this point that not all of the policies from Brussel have been of an ecologically sound nature. The entire controversy dealing with farming is something that must be directly confronted and solved in a more ecological nature, indeed, ecological relationships seem to have been forgotten in the agrarian policies of the EC. Agronomics tends to concentrate more on management and economics than on the needs of the crops!

Chapter Four presents and discusses the hypotheses made within this context and relates them to the controversies of cognitive dissonance. It then presents findings from a questionnaire given out to German and Polish populations in 1990 and 1991 respectively.

Chapter Five further discusses the differences and similarities found in the Polish and German populations studied in the period 1990-1991. The text represents an article that was published in 1994: in it, some minor changes have been made in order to fit the present context. The questionnaire used for this study can be found in Appendix A.

Chapter Six is a copy of an article published in 1995. It discusses further results, some of which could be replicated from the foregoing study. Again, Polish and German populations were involved., this time in the year 1992. The second questionnaire used for these findings can be found in Grob, Alexander (1991): Meinung, Verhalten, Umwelt. Bern: Peter Lang AG.

The content of **Chapter Seven** was used, with some variations, in an oral presentation in Finland in 1996. It shows further results from a German population utilizing the second questionnaire mentioned above. The study was done in 1996.

Chapter Eight seeks to summarize most of the findings found in the above Chapters, particularly in light of a discussion of the hypotheses. One of the findings, a higher belief in technology, found consistently in all of the studies undertaken, could prove to be of meaningful use in the development of ecological psychology in Poland, where these findings will, of course, also be made accessible to the scientific community.

I

FUNDAMENTAL THEORY:
THE BASIS OF COGNITIVE DISSONANCE

1

PSYCHOLOGY AND ECOLOGY

Ecological perspectives in the field of psychology

Issues of ecology can be found in different areas of psychology. Indeed, while it seems to be the last of the social sciences to be influenced by concepts of ecology (Graumann, 1978), these have had effect upon the whole field (Miller, 1984; Rohrmann, 1992), especially in such areas where theory, research and their respective development were limited to individual behavior (Fisch, 1983; Graumann, 1983) and fell short of dealing with contemporary and concrete issues (Miller, 1984). In the following text, these issues will be discussed from many different aspects.

To begin with, more than ever before, the nineteenth century was a time when methods of natural science were applied to questions that more traditionally belonged to the field of philosophy (Bungard, 1988; Graumann, 1978). In these beginnings and within the general development of the social sciences, the problems and issues of the time, such as the conception and subsequent political form of national states, national or cultural heritage and other questions of political and social content, were seen as important issues (Graumann, 1978). These have, of course, since then found their own present content and context, such as economics and political science. It was at this time that specifically the natural sciences - more or less developing alongside the social sciences - some of course, with much longer empirical research traditions - were dealing with methodological research questions as well: one such debate concerned the influence of scientific measurement on the object to be measured. This also influenced the social sciences. However, within this general context of effective measurement, Wundt (1896), the great experimenter, was of the opinion, that experimental research into social phenomenon was not feasible (Fisch, 1983), thus probably hindering the further development of research into issues of social psychology (Lück, 1987) and related subfields for some time (Lück, 1987). Although there were quite a number of publications on the philosophical aspects of these issues in the interim (see Ash, 1984 etc.), there can be no question that Kurt Lewin, from the second to the fourth decade of this century, both in Berlin (de Rivera, 1976) and later in the United States, had great influence upon experimental methods through his research, his writings and his teaching and leaves a legacy of many subsequently well-known students, such as Leon Festinger, Roger G. Barker and many others (Kebeck, 1984). What we fail to remember is that Wundt was partially right in his critique, there are questions of social psychology that cannot be solved by field study or experiments, however, the genius of Kurt Lewin was able to convert theory into workeable problems: it is a shame that they were not able to work together.

Although such authors as Miller, (1984), Lang (1995) and Wundt himself (1913), trace the beginnings of ecological perspectives in psychology to at least the last century and beyond, for purposes of brevity and proper historical reconstruction (Graumann, 1987) the main discussion in the following pages will limit itself to works done in this century, beginning - after this brief introduction - specifically with Jakob Johann v. Uexküll (1864-1944), Willy Hellpach (1877-1955) and Kurt Lewin (1890-1947) and extending on to two of the later's students in the United States: Leon Festinger and Roger G. Barker.

Primarily limiting the discussion to these authors does not seek to ignore the groundwork laid by Wundt (1832-1920). Ernst Haeckel (1834-1919) however, while often having been named within the context of the beginning works of ecology, has perhaps harmed the field more than is generally known today, especially in his later works (Meseke, 1998).

Haeckel - as a Doctor of medicine as well as philosophy - was professor of zoology and director of the Zoological Museum in Jena and had tremendous influence on the thinking of his day. Perhaps his greatest contribution - to zoology as well as ecology - was the publication of his "General Morphology" (1866), in print only six years after Darwin's "Origin of the species" (1859) had been translated into German (1860). Its text shows a profound interest of nature and indeed attempts to classify species with environmental principles in mind.

Beyond his immediate contributions to the field of zoology however, his works need to be carefully scrutinized. While criticizing the methods of the psychology of his day, he assigned psychology to the natural instead of the evolving social sciences. While he did not precisely formulate experimental questions of social psychology, he paved the way for at least some of them to be raised through his descriptions and classifications of human natural and cultural groups and entities (Haeckel, 1924b). Ultimately however, he might have done the field more harm than good, in helping to discredit philosophical psychology, lastly such a necessary part of psychology. Unfortunately, the influence he wielded, especially in his late lifetime, was decidedly negative, if not sinister. Whereby his topics extended to religion, philosophy and ethics, he, on the other hand, advocated the killing of crippled - especially mentally disabled - newborns, because, he argued, as their brain had not developed yet, they could not be called human (1924b). Haeckel maintained that the soul of man was located in his brain and developed along with it, when it did not develop normally, there was no soul to speak of. There are some authors who write that he was influential in creating a climate of intolerance in which Nazism was later to flourish (Gasman, 1971). In this respect, it could be argued that he would have a very negative influence upon the later development of ecological psychology in Germany; to give him a central and founding position in this field as some German writers do to this day, is to explicitly ignore the content of the majority of his writings and to forget the lessons of history. For, instead of only seeking the Nazi developments in the nature of German aggression, we would do well to also look into such past intellectual deficiencies and shortcomings in the German scientific community, take care that they are not repeated in the present day and try to understand their impact on their various audiences, surroundings and societies.

Indeed, time would tell that, within the first half of this century, above all, one series of events comes to mind that brought about many tragic changes: the dramatic events that accompanied the rise of Hitler. Escorting the first waves of destruction within the scientific community, as early as in 1933, more than one-third - that is, of 15 full professors of psychology (Prof. Dr. habil.), six - were discharged for being Jewish. Of those, five emigrated to the United States, leaving only Aloys Fischer behind (Geuter, 1984). Roughly one year later (Geuter, 1984; Rechtien, 1984) Wolfgang Köhler, who had remained in open opposition to the Nazi ideas, followed: he was not willing to accept the structural and contextual changes being made within his institute.

While these events certainly altered the entire course of this scientific field, those professors left at their positions reacted to the changes as a coherent group. By far not all in support of the Nazis and their theories, they generally tended to utilize the new changes for the extension and consolidation of the field (Geuter, 1984). However, Nazi ideology did permeate some methods research and some scientists were openly supportive of racial theories, indeed the research field of racial psychology was even established. As early as 1954, G.W. Allport (Brock, 1992), in trying to interpret the whole phenomenon, maintained that the field of psychology proved to be a fertile ground for Nazi theory. In trying to understand this, it must be pointed out that Ernst Haeckel, mentioned above, was considered to be a respected scientist in his time and many of his ideas, though to us today totally unscientific and racist, were widely read and approved of, at least in Germany. That does not mean that they were necessarily even accepted by the masses, but the intellectual community was certainly interested in them. In order to put this into wider perspective, one must not forget however, that scientific communities all over the world were experimenting with their fellow human beings. Particularly in the field of mental health, patients were often treated more cruelly than prisoners and were subjected to extremely inhuman conditions and treatments. One must however realize, that these ideas did not affect all German scientists. To try to trace this back to Wundt himself is taking the idea too far: As mentioned by Brock, 1992, Wundt's "Völkerpsychologie" was a psychology of culture and of the individual within society (Lück, 1987) moreover, it was criticized by racial psychologists and finally, was used to undermine Nazi theories.

The field itself however, made its greatest gain through the military, (Wehrmacht), not the Nazis (SS, etc.). During the war, differential as well as other areas of psychology were used to appoint soldiers for - and place them into - the right positions, a precursor to human resource management. Perhaps the most important immediate outcome of this was that practical experience in the diagnostic work of "Wehrmachtpsychologie" (Army psychology) was an important criteria for receiving a full professorship (Geuter, 1984). Also, in order to produce students who were efficient at handling the new tests, a new course of studies was formed and made part of the curriculum by 1941. This "Diplomprüfungsordnung" (a Diplom is somewhat equivalent to an M.A.), originally invariably opened a career into the civil service (Geuter, 1984) and was at first kept in its original form after the war ended.

When the war was over, new full professorships were limited to the areas of "Ganzheitspsychologie" and "Gestaltpsychologie". By 1955, out of seventeen full professors, eight represented "Ganzheitspsychologie" and six were "Gestaltpsychologists" (Mattes, 1984). By this time, the literature from such US emigrants as Kurt Lewin was again beginning to be made available.

Even though the influence from the US was immense, three areas could not immediately find a foothold in Germany: Behaviorism, Social Psychology and Methodology (Mattes, 1984). Although changes were being made as scientists went into retirement, psychologists as a group emerged stronger after their common war experience (Mattes, 1984). Beginning in the 1960's however, one could speak of a new generation of scholars, many of whom had gone to the United States as students and had come back with American methods and concepts (Mattes, 1984). The time had come for psychology to become more of an exact science: the "Methodenstreit" (methods dispute) of the 1950's with its attempt to find meaningful standards and to finally depart from and dismiss any Nazi or war ideology had made that possible.

At the present time however, a "Methodenstreit" of another kind seems to keep surfacing in social science literature and is indeed of high relevance: the overemphasis on statistical results and the need for new methods. While there can be no doubt of the importance of statistics in providing answers to a good amount of questions in the fields of the social sciences and indeed in clearly pointing out unknown correlations of high social import, conversely, there are many important questions that cannot be dealt with statistically because numbers, averages and outcomes do not always provide the answers in regard to human conduct.

Important beginning work in ecological and environmental psychology

The more recent emergence, in Germany, of ecological psychology as a distinct discipline a decade after it had been established in the United States, was influenced by two important points: the predominance of environmental damage to an extent noticeable to the lay public and covered in the media, and the acceptance of environmental psychology as a field in the United States. In the following however, the first, fundamental thoughts, will be traced, taking us back, in Germany, into the beginnings of this century.

Johann Jakob v. Uexküll (1864-1944)

Belonging to the first group of scientists that were concerned with environmentalism at an institutional level (v.Uexküll, 1934), von Uexküll wrote books on biological subjects that are more like treatises on the philosophy of life, of being and of the nature of existence. In his works, he pointed to the interactional aspects of nature on a micro- and macroscopic scale, analyzing the structure of bodies and entities and their surroundings.

In his critique of Darwin and Haeckel, (v.Uexküll, 1913), he placed Darwin's theories into the context of materialism, pointing to the fact that not all evolution is a product of chance, but has its place in a more coordinated plan of development and that the very nature of man is to be goal-oriented and to search for the meaning of life and his place in the universe.

Arguing that biology and psychology must needs be regarded as two separate sciences, (v.Uexküll, pg.68), v. Uexküll implied that man has distinct spiritual faculties that cannot otherwise be found in nature. Discussing many topics relevant to psychology, v. Uexküll particularly made some very valuable contributions to the area of perception (v. Uexküll, 1913, 1934, 1936). Underlining the individual aspects of perception, he showed the relationship between experience, expectation and perception and demanded an understanding of each person's stage in life in order to further understand his actions.

This last statement takes on somewhat prophetic aspects for his own actions: Hitler made his influence felt in what was roughly to be the last decade of von Uexküll's life. Even the rise of Nazism was not enough to completely unbalance the equilibrium of a mind such as v.Uexküll's however. In his book, "Staatsbiologie", he, very much in the exploratory tradition of his other writings, analyzed the structure of state and with this such aspects of it as the coherence of work, the goals of the state, and the relationship of the inhabitants to their state. He compared a political entity to a cell, mentioning that this cell is directed by reason (ideas) and trial and error in order to find the most balanced state of being. As an entity, the state can be confronted by things that are not comprehensible to individuals and not accepted by them (v. Uexküll, 1933, 68f.). Although capital and with it industry, as being on a different organizational level than the individual is, seems to be more capable of understanding and addressing itself to the needs of a modern state, they lack the tools that government itself has. To be most effective however, government must have the right political institutions in order to guarantee the health of the state: unfortunately, at this point he mentions the promise that Hitler brings to Germany.

Without condemning Jews directly, he pointed to the fact that members of any race must be classified according to the relationship they have to the state: when they become harmful, they are parasites (v. Uexküll, pg.72), when they are benevolent however, they form a symbiotic tie and can be not only helpful but necessary. Real parasites grow best in a sick state. Although a modern state is indeed dependent upon a mixture of the races, it should protect itself against an intermixture with parasites. Although the above leaves room for interpretation and could be interpreted ironically (in discredit of the Nazi's) von Uexküll seems to have bowed to their pressure, if only to some extent. Such was not the case however, with the following scientist.

Willy Hellpach (1877-1955)

When Willy Hellpach, as Prof. Dr. phil et med., established the Institute of Social Psychology at the Technical University in Karlsruhe, (roughly in 1920, Lück, 1984), and became its chairman, this subject had developed since Wundt - perhaps because of his training in philosophy - would not even accept the term because of the latin-greek mixture of words (Lück, 1984) and his inability to construct problems from ideas. It becomes doubly poignant, if we remember that Hellpach was a student of Wundt's (Lück, 1987).

Hellpach's work: "Psychologie der Umwelt", 1924 (psychology of the environment), has become a standard historical work of psychology. His work "Die geopsychischen Erscheinungen" (1911), being continually in current edition, is even still available today (Miller, 1984).

An important contribution of his was the differentiation of environments into categories: those of a natural, cultural, social and real nature. Hellpach, (1939, see Pawlik, 1992), was primarily influenced by real problems, such as that of a great influx - in his day - of people to the cities.

Hellpach was a scholar who wrote from experience, observation, reasoning and interpretation. His works almost completely lack footnotes and annotations. Thus synthesizing everything he read, observed, and understood, he covered many areas. Calling for a more systematic approach toward using accepted generalizations in explaining psychological phenomena, he criticized several then extant works on the relationship between weather and well-being. Within this context, he made the point that the very cells of the body react to changes in the weather and that this has influence on psychological perception.

Concerning himself with the environment of the work place, he, together with the engineer Richard Lang (who enclosed a work-protocol that takes up half the space of the book: 1922, pg. 93ff.), analyzed work in the factory with its lack of proper recompensation and recognition and demanded that workers be offered a more stable life-style, especially in view of their excruciating, demeaning and dehumanizing work (Hellpach & Lang, 34f.). Pointing to the fact that bureaucracies as well as many other forms of work also deny their employees knowledge of the entire work-process, he mentioned that they are guaranteed something else instead: security and prestige. Whereas, of course, group tasks are much better than assembly line work (Hellpach & Lang, pg.50), above all, workers must be given such benefits as are common to other citizens. Because modern life demands factories, they must be optimized in order to guarantee normal and healthy working conditions, something of benefit to all concerned.

In a more human approach, of important social impact to the concept of individual and environment, Hellpach, in his 1928 edition of "Politische Prognose für Deutschland" (political prognosis for Germany) explicitly supported the Jewish race. Notice that this was before Hitler came into power! Countering the ideas of Arianism and pointing to the fact that typical Arian characteristics are mostly found in the northern parts of Germany (Hellpach, 1928, pg.9), he mentioned that Germans are the most heterogenous of all of the larger nations of Europe (Hellpach, 1928, pg.12) pointing out that the Jews themselves are not a distinct and homogenous group (Hellpach, 1928, pg.20). Considering how the development of psychology was negatively influenced and stifled in its development by Hitler and his political machinery, one can really conclude, that, in this brilliant call for reason to govern behavior, Hellpach can truly be considered among the most important beginning figures (Miller, 1984), of ecological psychology.

Hellpach, while still publishing during the war (see above), is said to have lost influence after 1923 (Schneider, 1993). One must consider however, that this exactly coincides with the time when he became politically active - he was Minister for culture and education in Baden from 1922-1925 and in 1925 candidate for the office of president of parliament (Reichstagsprasident). At the beginning of his political career he, of course, resigned from his office as Head of the Institute of Social Psychology (Lück, 1984). Nevertheless, his work did not stop him from writing and analyzing the political situation correctly.

In one of his last publications, Hellpach, (1955), wrote about the history of social psychology. While his influence - in the area of environmental psychology - must of course not be overrated, (Pawlik, 1992), his chief contribution (Lück, 1984), is his orientation to research and the value of observation; this is reflected even in his accomplishments as a human being caught in what was - historically - a great time of adversity.

Kurt Lewin (1890-1947)

Lewin can be seen as one of the central personalities of American and later also of European social psychology (Lück, 1984, pg.165), and one who had important influence on the development of ecological psychology - even to the point of being considered its founder (Miller, 1984). In his phenomenological orientation to descriptions of environment (1917 etc., see Pawlik, 1992), he, in general, greatly influenced methods of psychology; more specifically, he had a tremendous directing effect upon his many students. Lewin, in retrospect historically one of the most influential German psychologists in America - since Hugo Münsterberg went to Harvard University (Ash, 1984) - was able to adapt himself to the research community in the United States (Ash, 1992) quite well. Upon his arrival there in 1933, Lewin first went to Cornell and then, in 1935, to the University of Iowa. After the end of the war, he became Director of the Research Center for Group Dynamics of the Massachusetts Institute of Technology. In the United States, his impact and influence seemed to have been greatest during his lifetime, later, his writings played a more ambivalent role in American psychology (Ash, 1992).

Himself influenced by the Berlin school of "Gestalttheorie" (Lück, 1984) - Lewin was made a "Dozent" in Berlin in 1922 and became Professor of Psychology there in 1927. He proved to have a driving effect upon the American origins of group dynamics, ironically enough providing for its re-acceptance in Europe (Rechtien, 1990) after the war. In his theoretical approach, Lewin depicted an interrelatedness of person and environment, representing a relational and systems approach to his theory and analysis (Deutsch, 1992). In his notion of life spaces, he assigned focus and direction to every living being. Attributing psychological being only to humanity, he was convinced of a distinct personal perception, due to experiences (Westgaard, 1989); this also makes his findings applicable to such areas as learning, needs assessment and task analysis (Westgaard, 1989).

Similarly to von Uexküll, Hitler influenced the life of this great scientist in what was to be only a little more than the last dozen years of Lewin's life. When, in 1933, Kurt Lewin, as a Jew, was discharged from his position, he was able to emigrate to the United States, taking much of his work with him. Who is to say what ecological psychology would be today in Germany, had Hitler not intervened in the course of history.

When Lewin left Germany, he carried some material with him in the form of a completed book. The content of "Grundzüge der topologischen Psychologie" (Characteristics of topological psychology), had been ready to be published in Germany and Lewin, in fact, needed to be released from his contract in Germany before the book was published - in English in 1935 - (Lewin 1969, Foreword). When the English version was finished and published, Lewin, in 1936, sent one of the first copies to Wolfgang Köhler (1887-1967), who was already in the United States by then. After the war, because not all of the original German manuscript could be found, some material needed to be re-translated into German (Lewin, 1969, pg.16), a task which was only undertaken in the 1950's, almost 20 years after the appearance of the published English version and some years after Lewin's untimely death. A later version (in 1969), while providing still more of the original manuscript - which had been uncovered meanwhile - still needed to rely on some retranslation however (Lewin, 1969).

Perhaps most noteworthy is, that content and style of Lewin's writings are more in the nature of works on natural science. Although his formula $V = f(P, U)$, (Lewin, 1969 pg. 86) - "Verhalten ist eine Funktion von Person und Umwelt" - (behavior is a function of person and environment), has since gone into the annals of psychology and has, of itself, prompted much research (Miller, 1984), more often than not, many of Lewin's original conceptions have been misunderstood and the richness of his data, research and methodology have often been ignored.

Remembering that Lewin also added $V = f(S)$ (Lewin, 1969, pg. 84) - "Verhalten ist eine Funktion von Situation" - (behavior is a function of the situation), and that $V = f(S)$ is related to $V = f(P, U)$ somewhat widens the hypothetical premises. Furthermore, Lewin endowed U (environment) not only with the characteristics of room and time, but also with more exact properties such as closeness or propensity of movement or occupation of area, of one or more objects and their relations to and influence on one another (Lewin, 1969, pg.86). Environment was not only a cognitive field for him (Kruse, 1978), as he mentioned that many events and situations took place precisely outside of cognitive recognition and thus that individuals, and indeed nations, often let themselves be formed by a series of unrecognized events in their immediate environment - something he certainly experienced in Germany. However, it is precisely this lack of awareness that he criticizes, having himself seen and lived through its adverse effects!

Although primarily with his work "Psychologische Ökologie" (1943; psychological ecology), Lewin has greatly influenced ecological psychology in Germany and its subsequent orientation (Miller, 1984), what is perhaps just as important, he has left - still even now - a living legacy in his many students and they in their students after them.

Roger G. Barker

R.G. Barker, building on the research and observations that Lewin had developed (Lück, 1984), studied processes and their development in their real environment (Pawlik & Buse, 1992, pg. 10), himself coining the phrase "behavior setting" (Pawlik et al., pg. 11). Barker's theories have had influence on the subfields of ecological psychology, environmental psychology and eco-behavioral science (Wallenius, 1990).

Barker, working with Lewin in studying varied primary psychological vectors in different contexts, published his findings in a manner typical for results presented in today's psychology journals (Barker, Dembo & Lewin, 1943) - something that was very unusual for his time.

Barker (1964a), in studying the variations of characteristic human behavior of children in various settings, differentiated between a psychological and an ecological environment (Barker et al., 1943, pg.5). He saw the various components of society to be parts of a complex, interdependent system. To Barker, the "naturally occurring life space" (Barker et al., 1943, pg.6), is not the ecological environment, which in itself is not easily understood because of its natural complexity. Both settings for a persons' behavior: his immediate life-space; as well as his ecological environment must be understood if his actions are to be interpreted. In order to distinguish between the two, it is important to differentiate between physical attributes and "extra-individual patterns of behavior" (Barker et al., 1943, pg.10).

Barker (pg.10), setting behavior patterns into their surrounding ecological units and requiring an analysis of the "synomorphic" structural congruency between a situation and the action it calls forth (see also Bosch, 1978, pg.17; Kruse, 1990, pg.5), argues - in this respect - similar to another Lewin student (Lück, 1984) - Leon Festinger - in his theory of "cognitive dissonance".

Finally of relevance in this context is his characterization of the complete structure encompassing behavior-setting, or life-space within an ecological environment. An individual located at any point within this system is a "component part", his behavior being "anonymous and replaceable, subject to nonpsychological laws" (Barker, 1964b, pg.17). At the same time, he is "a unique person subject to the laws of individual psychology, where his own private motives, capacities and perception are the causal variables" (Barker, 1964b); Barker called this type of relative value of a person within a given context, relationship or task the "inside-outside question" (Barker, 1964b). It is just such aspects of the dynamic flow of life that Lewin talked about (Matthaei, 1963, pg. 15).

Barker, in conveying the results of his phenomena-oriented field and experimental work, surely made descriptive statistics his submissive agent: his results are clear and clean. This must not lead to the assumption, however, that this is his only contribution, for he addresses himself to the very problem that has been of such interest to ecological psychology ever since it has dealt with environmental problems: the need of a plurality of methodology (Kruse, 1978, pg.183) in order to solve urgent problems of mankind.

Leon Festinger

Shortly after Kurt Lewin died, Leon Festinger, who had been his student and later colleague, left MIT, taking a study on student housing at MIT with him to be published at Stanford. Although the empirical context was a simple one, Festinger and his co-authors succeeded in discussing such diverse questions as the spatial ecology of group formations (Festinger, et al., 1950, pg.33ff.), physical and functional space and distance, group standards and communication processes (Festinger et al., 1950, see also Kruse, 1978). These various items still provide material to the area of social psychology today and have also become important within the context of ecological and environmental psychology.

With his first publication of what was probably to be his most important work, Festinger, in 1957, in his book on cognitive dissonance, laid the groundwork to an area of psychology that has since seen a great number of publications and been verified in many different circumstances, cultures and theoretical questions. His genius was perhaps not so much in the formulation of entirely new ideas, but of putting them succintly and expressing them within an empirical context. With his attempt to further explain human behavior, he has contributed a theory that has become relevant to ecological psychology (Festinger, 1962), as will be shown later and further on in Chapter Two.

When, after spending forty years of research in the field of psychology and para-doxically, when publications on the theory of cognitive dissonance were coming in from all corners of the globe, (see Appendix by Irle & Möntmann in Festinger, 1978), Festinger retired, he turned his genius to the field of archeology and more specifically to such topics as: man in his environment; tool use and production and the formation of groups and social organizations within various environments. Surely one can say that his contributions have been immeasurable and have certainly continued the research traditions that Lewin himself represented and which have proven to be such a valuable base for the entire field of psychology.

More recent beginnings of theoretical and empirical work in Germany

Similar to the development in the United States, and, as happens with many other areas of psychology, both ecological and environmental psychology were created in context with the need to find real answers (Graumann, 1978), as was mentioned above. Whereas the public awareness of a forthcoming environmental crisis and the subsequent urgent call to the social sciences, began, as a process, in the 1960's in the United States (Kruse, 1990) and finally allowed research to look into systematic answers (Engermann, 1990), this development did not extend to Germany until the early 1970's.

Particularly the year 1974 was significant for the unfoldment of ecological psy-chology in the German scientific community (Kaminski, 1978; Lück, 1984). It was in this year - at a congress of the German Society for Psychology in Salzburg, Austria - that a symposium under the heading of "environmental psychology" (Umweltpsy-chologie; Graumann, 1978) - was organized by Kaminski. The same year also saw the completion of a dissertation by Kruse (1974) under the same heading and super-vised also by Kaminski (Kruse, 1990, pg.7).

The title of the symposium seems to have been influenced by such books as Stokols, 1974 and others (Ittelson, 1977), and their use of the term "environmental psychology", as well as the general consensus that this was the most popular term in use in the United States at the time (see also Kruse, 1990 and Pawlik et al., 1992 for similar discussions).

Perhaps it is a characteristic of the German scientific community, or perhaps it was in devotion to the works of that great man and scientist Lewin (Miller, 1984), that subsequently and somewhat in differentiation of American developments, in 1978, the German Research Society (Deutsche Forschungsgesellschaft = DFG) created a program under the heading of "ecological psychology" (Ökologische Psy-chologie), which has since been responsible for funding research projects and some of the more important publications in this field. It was also in the 1970's that the first psychology journals made their appearance in this field (Lück, 1984).

Leaving a differentiation between environmental and ecological psychology etc. to the discussion in the next two sections below, it seems important to present a contextual definition of this area at this point. Since there seems to be no complete consensus over the content of the terms environmental or ecological psychology (Pawlik et al.,1992), perhaps it is wise to talk about the perspective that scientific findings in the field of eco-psychology (Lück, 1984) present.

Methodologically speaking, present deficiencies seem to point to a lack of unified procedural standards (Sichler et al., 1993). Furthermore, since, at least at present, scientific progress in this field must always be tested by its applicability to real problems, there seem to be, contextually speaking, some inadequacies in customary procedural techniques (Engermann, 1990; Kruse, 1978; Kruse, 1990; see also Pawlik et al., 1992), especially where they seek to comply with the demand of interdisciplinary and intercultural (Kruse, 1990; Pawlik et al., 1992) applications of its results. It is at this point that we must remember that Lewin as well as Barker, although quite successful in their quantitative presentation of concrete results, both went beyond defining environmental ecology in terms of limited equational conceptions.

To this belongs the question of synomorphic congruency (Barker, 1964b) where - for example - Bosch (1978) demands the necessity of interpreting the status of the correspondence of cognitive processes with the problem structures they issue from, that is, that cause their development. The instrumental and constellative meaning and content of this correspondence can then be supplied with a vector-direction and its point of object-valence determined (Bosch, 1978, see also Lewin, 1969), always remembering that a single action is only a part of an entirety, making it important to consider its direction as well as its superior action-regulators on higher levels. An evaluation of the cognitive judgement or assessment that human actors make in reacting to eco-psychological or eco-behavioral systems, which - in addition to being hard to comprehend because of their intricacy, are open and dynamic - would also take into consideration that human reactions often lead to contrain-tuitive results (Engermann, 1990, pg.106).

Considering its content, ecological psychology, reflecting the establishment of a field that has, since the writings of Lewin etc. seen a more firm scientific institutionali-zation, concentrates upon the influences of the environment on human experience and behavior and the corresponding refracted effects of this (Pawlik et al., 1992). In this connection, it is important to remember that human projection of environ-mental content and context into an objectified system that can be comprehended, that can be put to discussion or projected into action programs, is mostly structured by social connotation (Bosch, 1978). This brings to mind that a problem - albeit its solution be of foremost necessity, even of highest scientific concern - can only be treated as such when society as a whole accepts its nature as a problem and can, however, only be acted upon when relevant and restorative remedies have been found and have subsequently been acknowledged by all.

When, as Engermann (1990) suggests, one considers that in addition to their content and context complexity, ecopsychological or ecobehavioral systems are open and dynamic, one begins to comprehend why their solution is so difficult, especially when one remembers the world-encompassing nature of even the minutest aspects of many environmental dilemmas, which, it must be remembered, in addition almost always demand their own individual scientific, technical, societal or organizational interpretation and solutions. That the area of ecological psychology has been examined and commented upon by psychologists of so many theoretical orientations and empirical specializations (Graumann, 1978), both reflects this complexity and promises to proffer more sustainable answers to urgent problems in the future.

Thematic contents: definitions and differences

Although, in Germany, some differentiation has been made between environmental and ecological psychology (Günther, 1989; MIller, 1984), assigning concrete issues of a man-environmental nature, to the environmental, and basic research problems of ecological psychology, (Miller, 1984), more recent German publications have tended to prefer the terms ecopsychology or ecological psychology as the concept encompassing both meanings (Miller, 1984, pg. 183).

Although the general popularization of the term ecological psychology seems to go back to Lewin, the use of environmental psychology can be traced, not primarily to Hellpach, but to the influence American psychology has had on the development of this field in Germany, as mentioned above.

Perusing the writings of Lewin and Hellpach, it is difficult to substantiate an implication sometimes made, that concrete problems of man-nature relationships should be assigned to environmental psychology and hence date back to the writings of Hellpach. Hellpach also philosophized about basic research problems, albeit in a less mathematical and quantitative way than Lewin did. Moreover, Lewin, on the other hand, did not only concentrate on basic research problems, as the joint article Barker, Lewin et al. (1943) proves. Thankfully, such arguments and differentiations mainly no longer seem to be valid (Führer, 1983 and Kaminski & Bellows, 1982: cited in Miller, 1984 pg.183). Indeed, according to Hoyos (1983), there no longer seems to be any real differentiation made between basic and applied research; albeit the methodology might be somewhat different, results may be equally relevant to both types of scientific findings and many studies will contain aspects of both.

Neither term however, has been exclusively assigned to topics concerned with the global ecological crisis that mankind is now facing (Sichler & Seel., 1993), but articles dealing with problems of this nature can be found under both headings. Although some authors (Sichler, et al., 1993, etc.) demand the establishment of a psychology of human nature, it should be relatively difficult to combine the present diversity of research under one singular subject, as the following section will attempt to show.

Ecological contents in different subfields of psychology

As shown above, the field of environmental or ecological psychology is very complex. Moreover, the very nature of the real-life problems often confronting psychology demand an interdisciplinary approach, as these problems are of an a-disciplinary kind (Hoyos, 1983). Unfortunately, although there has been a rapid increase in the amount of publications, by and large, psychology has found but few solutions to these dilemmas of human nature, that in character also have a social, political and economical constitution (Hoyos, 1983, pg. 29) and that are an extension of the relationship that man - on a societal level (Boehme, 1993; Kruse, 1978) - has to nature.

Discussion of the issues involved

Social Psychology: while beginning publications in this area were of a more general nature (McDougall, 1926; Müller-Freienfels, 1930) and might rightfully be considered inaugural works on cultural psychology or other areas, such areas as man in his life-space, the relationship between group and environment, man as designer of his environment and life-span conflicts are also important topics in this field (Müller-Freienfels, 1930).

More recently there have been efforts to consolidate some relevant subjects into what has been called, more specifically, environmental social psychology, in which such things as community problems (Granada, 1991), perception (Dennis, 1990) and work environment (Canter, 1990) have received special attention. A perusal of some standard works in social psychology however, will show a broad range of subjects (Frey, Stahlberg & Wortmann, 1983; Frey, Heise, Stahlberg & Wortman, 1987) related generally or specifically to environmental psychology, albeit such works as Tajfel, 1984, for example, in his discussion of morality view the relevant questions in a broader manner.

Indeed, the broad range of topics has prompted Graumann (1983) to contend that too many incompatible techniques, practices and interpretations are gathered within the area of social psychology to be able to confer upon it an identity of any kind (Graumann, 1983, pg.32). In the same edition, Fisch & Daniel (1983), in their summary of 1059 articles from two English and one German journal of social psychology (throughout the period 1971-1980), found - of the subjects relating to environment - diverse articles on such themes as closeness and proximity, noise, life-quality, leisure and recreation and disposal of waste (Graumann, 1983, pg. 20), all showing topics of more or less relevance to environmental or ecological psychology. Interestingly enough, Fisch et al. (1983) also found some basic topics to be specifically Anglo-American, others to have a particularly European tradition (Graumann, 1983, pg. 26f.).

To summarize the above: As far as Germany is concerned, we have the phenomenon that, at the same time that the scope of ecological psychology was being defined, articles were also appearing in the domain of social psychology. The scientific upsurge, as mentioned above, of course also coincided with public interest in this range of topics and necessarily, practical methods of measurement were needed in order to define problematic areas more clearly (Kley & Fietkau, 1979).

Finally, while the field of ecological psychology is still seeking new methods in order to cope with the diversity of difficulties it is asked to solve, social psychology, in defining itself as the scientific study of the experience and behavior of the individual in relation to social stimulus situations (Kruse, 1978, pg.177), is still capable of making a meaningful contribution to this area of human concern.

Cultural Psychology: while a number of subjects, such as "Völkerpsychologie" (psychology of races, again, really not to be confused with Nazi ideology, see above), "Ethologie" (behavior of organisms), "Ethnologie" (social or cultural anthropology) and others similar in scope have contributions to make to the environmental problems facing mankind (Schneider & Müller, 1993), they cannot be dealt with in this context. Briefly, the topics of cultural psychology, viewed according to their content, have often overlapped with social (McDougal, 1926 etc., see above) and also environmental psychology (Boesch, 1971; Lang & Führer, 1993; and Preuss, 1991). Also, social environment is frequently used interchangeably with cultural environment (Boesch, 1980 and Graumann, 1976). Cultural psychology is, of course, a distinct subfield of psychology, with its own methodology (Boesch, 1978) and specific contexts, which treats, among other subjects, frequently also those of an environmental nature - under various aspects.

Ecological Psychology: whereas ecological psychology seems to have more of the characteristics of a particular school of psychology in the US, (Kruse, 1978), having its origin in the research and works of Lewin and Barker, it has a somewhat different connotation in Germany, as has been shown above. Although, as already mentioned, a specific differentiation between the two is not preferred (Führer, 1983; Kaminski and Bellows, 1982 and Miller, 1984) the term ecological psychology seems to be used in preferance (Führer, 1983 and Miller, 1986 etc.) in Germany, but is used in a different context in the United States. More recent titles both in Germany and in the United States however, oftentimes use both concepts i.e. environment and ecology or some form thereof.

Paradoxically, the following two areas pertaining to ecology though, seem to have found greater use in the United States than in Germany, especially in terms of institutionalized research.

Human Ecology: whereas in Germany, the term social ecology is often interchanged with human ecology, formally, the latter, dating back to the writings of Park, Burgess and McKenzie (1925 etc.) who initiated research into urban planning, is a distinct field of research in the United States where there are several colleges of Human Ecology as will be shown below. Distinct from the term social ecology (Kruse, 1978, pg.171) - if alone from an organizational context - the research done in human ecology also overlaps with the other subfields mentioned here. The research, undertaken by such schools as the Kansas State University College of Human Ecology; the College of Human Ecology, Michigan; Cornell College of Human Ecology; Howard University School of Human Ecology; Antioch College, Human Ecology Center and the Human Ecology Research Foundation in California etc. and published in diverse Psychology journals (i.e. Psychology - A Quarterly Journal of Human Behavior; Psychiatria Quarterly; Environment and Behavior etc), has been in many different areas of psychology and does not only pertain to the area of environmental psychology, even were the term to be defined in a very wide sense.

Of the 59 articles reviewed in the 1990-'95 period, only one was on methods of ecology and one on office environment but fully 19 were on the subject of children and families. Interestingly enough, of the 88 articles reviewed in the 1974-'79 period, nine were on some aspect of the environment (such as "work environment"; "environmental sociology"; "ecological construct validation" etc.), perhaps suggesting a research trend, at least in the areas reviewed.

Social Ecology: although, as mentioned above, it is differentiated from human ecology, social ecology is primarily organizationally distinct from human ecology, the contents of their research seem to be the same. Social ecology also goes back to the work of Park et al. (1925, cited in Sommer, 1991). Several institutes, such as the Institute of

Social Ecology in California and the Institute of Social Ecology in Israel, carry this name, differentiating it formally from Human Ecology, however the content of their research is much the same and they often publish in the same Psychology journals.

In Germany however, social ecology goes back to the work of Moos and Insel (Kruse, 1978, pg.175), who put their research emphasis on the measurement of objective characteristics of environments, temperature, rainfall etc. and on short-term evolutionary and adaptive consequences of these environments.

Environmental Psychology: although the term ecological psychology is still preferred in many German publications when referring to the general field, a perusal of the literature given at the end of this book shows that both the terms ecological and environmental psychology are equally prevalent. Out of a total of 31 publications in German which mention either term, 14 use the term ecological, 12 use the term environmental and 5 have both in their title (including the title of the edition where relevant). The themes do not vastly differ in any of the publications. English publications, on the other hand, seem to be more consequential in preferring the term environmental psychology (Cone, 1980; Heimstra, 1974; Holahan, 1978; Ittelson, Proshansky, Rivlin & Winkel, 1974; Kates, 1976; Little, 1976; Schoggen, 1989 and Wicker, 1979) in differentiation from the term ecological psychology.

Applied Psychology: appears - at least in Germany - to be a subfield or area of psychology that is mostly limited to university research (Hoyos, Frey & Stahlberg, 1988, pg. 34). Although it has been called upon to solve practical problems, (Hoyos et al., 1988, pg.21) and some interesting research has been done in this field, it is still often seen to have less prestige than basic research (Hoyos, et al., 1988, pg. 25), albeit its contents and research questions are often dealt with under scientific and methodological rules that are seen to be quite singular to this area (Bungard, 1988). Perhaps most interesting within this context have been the efforts to encourage a more economical use of energy (Bergius, 1984; Frey et al., 1987 and Wortmann, Stahlberg & Frey, 1988). It is seen to have made a significant contribution to the area of Ecological Psychology, (Pawlik, 1992).

An Overview of the Polish Literature

Ecological themes were discussed in Poland even before the fall of communism: jurisdictional, political and institutional beginnings go back to the 1970's and the industrial balance of this was that every larger company had its own environmental commissioner. It was at this time, that, in cooperation with the entire Soviet Block, new laws were made and international regulation was initiated (Hohmann,

Seidenstecher & Vajna, 1973; Hudson, 1980 and Wanless, 1980). On a local level, several beginning efforts were made: for instance, school children were encouraged to separate and collect certain kinds of trash, bringing cans and containers to school and were even remunerated for this, bottles and paper were collected in front of homes, etc. When, with the end of the Girek era money ran out, many programs were stopped, only receiving new impetus with the advent of the Solidarity movement.

Sponsored by such associations as the United Workers Party (Pastusiak, 1988), the Polish Academy of Sciences (Holubowicz, Owskinski & Straszak, 1987), or by the Minister of Health, who published a whole series on health standards concerning such emissions as sulfur oxides (Wronska-Nofer, 1987) and carbon monoxide (Majka, 1987) etc., new attempts were made to ascertain, define and describe environmental requirements (Haigh, Bora & Zentain, 1987).

While some of this came from the area of psychology, (Biela, 1983, 1989; Drzewiecki & Kostrzewska-Kijik, 1986; Gustowski, 1987; Izyk, 1989; Karney, 1988; Osinska, 1987; Wolanski & Szemile, 1984 and Zaremba, 1986), other impulses came from the ecological and peace movements or related international themes (Cichy, 1988; Czajkowska, 1989; Lawniczak & Hladkiewicz, 1986; Nadzieja, 1987 and Szalek, 1988) and some were written to present the latest available information to academia (Michalec, 1987; Solowiej, 1987 and Stanislaw & Krawczyk, 1987).

In the 1990's, after the fall of communism, various ecological causes have received momentum from many sides. The media - there are several television programs on ecological themes - has done its best to put environmental and ecological themes to popular discussion and there is a great amount of action by concerned citizens. Waste sites have been modernized, new criteria set for filtering water and air and many old standards have been newly discussed.

Of the publications on the subject of ecology, the vast majority are, of course, in areas other than psychology. Thus, many are written from an economic, international relations, or sociological viewpoint (Budnikowski, 1992; Czerwinski, 1991; Dolega, 1993; Glinski, 1990; Haber, 1993; Honkisz, 1993; Piantek, 1992; Pietras, 1990; Stacewicz, 1993; and Spiewakowski, 1995), others contain more philosophical views (Bonenberg, 1992; Brozi, 1992; Dabrowski, 1992; Gorka, Poskrobko & Radecki, 1991; Laslowski & Rafinski, 1992; Napiorkowska, 1992; Skolimowski, 1993; Skrzynska, 1990 and Zawada, 1993) and still others are more health (Lewinska, Bascik & Bulat, 1995; Zakrewski, 1995 and Zukowski, 1994), education (Brown, Flavin & Postel, 1994), architecture (Krol-Bac, 1992) or natural science oriented (Janikowski, 1993; Jopkiewicz, 1993; Kalinowska, 1992 and Kostrowicki, 1992).

Of the publications that belong to the area of psychology, Eliasz (1993), is perhaps most suited to give an overview of the development of Ecological Psychology in Poland. Interestingly enough, while he takes many of his themes from the English literature available in the field of Environmental Psychology, the title of his book is Ecological Psychology. While Eliasz briefly refers to Polish authors, much of the book is based on English literature, as the Bibliography at the end of the book readily shows. He covers various issues ranging from such themes as crowding, noise and architecture, to stress and the environment in larger cities. Comparable to this - as far as the level of information is concerned - is a volume issued by the Polish Psychological Society. The 1993 publication focuses on local action potential and its importance for societal changes. Other important works include such topics as work environment (Engel & Sadowski, 1992; Niezabitowski, 1991 and others), analysis of workplaces (Biela, 1992), migration of workers (Zaleski, 1991) due to environmental factors; architectural psychology (Lenartowicz, 1992 and Ostrowska, 1991 and others) and coping (Biela, 1991).

While ecology has quite a long tradition in Poland, especially in the area of biology and agriculture (Kowalik, 1974; Trojan, 1984), it seems that ecological psychology is a field with a tradition of at least ten years in Poland, one that is defining its own position within international literature and shaping itself according to the problems that it is confronted with in its own country.

Conclusion

Issues of ecology were an established part of psychological thinking long before they managed to form into a separate field either in the United States or in Germany. There are several items in these early writings, that, while not specifically belonging to the field of ecological psychology as it is defined today, are of particular importance to ecological problems. According, for example, to von Uexküll - who, while not specifically writing on such ecological issues as are discussed and popular today, did manifest an ecological way of thinking in his writings - man has spiritual faculties not common to nature, is goal-oriented and looking for the meaning of life and his place in the universe. While the nature of experience, perception and expectation is common to man, each human being has his own closely related cycle, where the actions of a single person are not always accessible to others: they become comprehensible only once the cycle is understood.

It it precisely this goal-orientedness and singularity of experience, that would, for example, logically place the greatest burden for the environment on capital, industry and the state, rather than the individual. In a political entity, where ecological well-being is not a goal of the state and industry, it is nearly impossible for an individual to be oriented in this way. As von Uexküll points out, there are different spheres of action and those that political and industrial structures are confronted with, are not necessarily comprehensible to the individual. Furthermore, individuals lack a great amount of the tools that state, capital and industry have.

Lastly, an individual must be goal-oriented in achieving a place for himself in society. His goals can overlap with those of higher entities as himself and he can, to a certain extent influence the higher goals that he is confronted with, but he can only determine them to a certain extent. How much easier is it for those entities with more means, influence and power, to define his relationship to such a complex question as that of ecology, providing, of course, that the right political, democratic institutions are in place.

It is precisely the complexity of the context mentioned above, that speaks for the necessity of the institutionalization of the concepts, research and methods of ecology. In this, the individual certainly plays a part, but neither can he be required to take the brunt of the responsibility for his actions, nor to make the all but impossible choice that a fully conscious ecological performance on his part would necessitate. Such performance, possible in higher spheres of action, simply overtax the individual and his possibilities.

Moreover, there is an even higher degree of complexity in the interaction of the above factors, as has been mentioned above. Because of this, simple methods must be found to co-ordinate these levels of action to a much higher degree than is common today. For example: whereas much of environmental policy is decided on the national level and is often dependent upon political periods of activity - a very difficult problem in Poland, for example, where governments have not stayed in place more than one year to date, although the present one seems to be more stable, and much of bureaucracy is not given a chance to form, let alone gain experience - local activity is much easier to follow and is often, as grass-roots movements have shown, much more effective in forcing changes to come about. This has even recently been re-discovered by the United Nations in their definition of Habitat as places where social development and economic growth take place.

To date, in Poland, as well as in Germany, there is much activity going on in the field of environment. Unfortunately, very little of it is co-ordinated, whether locally, nationally, or internationally. However, especially in the field of environmental protection, which cannot allow itself to be static, but must change as the conditions of mankind change, whether in politics, industry, or human awareness - co-ordination, communication and exchange of information is vital. Were activities to be co-ordinated on a local level and, where national control and inspection is necessary, to provide local information in a more condensed, classified and interrelated form, communication to the national level would be much more succinct and allow better and easier interpretation. From a national level, communication could then be sent to an international level and more easily be used for those necessary changes that need to be made as new demands arise. This would be really utilizing political entities for specific goals, especially in such cases - as in environmental protection - which quite possibly need to be defined as new requirements show themselves.

Communication and cooperation could be used as a tool in this context, with funds - for example - being made available only to those whose local activity is co-ordinated. This would certainly help trim down the bureaucracy that is proving to be such a tax-burden in many states and free money that could be used to encourage private enterprise in such areas where it is really needed. Such co-operation need not harm democracy or capitalism, indeed, it only frees its forces, so that freedom and competition can take place in a more human context.

REFERENCES

Selected Bibliography:

Ash, Mitchell (1984): Psychologie in Deutschland bis 1933. In H.E. Lück, R. Miller & W. Rechtien (Eds.): Geschichte der Psychologie. München: Urban & Schwarzenberg, 17-22.

Ash, Mitchell, G. (1992): Cultural contexts and scientific change in psychology: Kurt Lewin in Iowa. *American psychologist*. Feb., 47(3), 198-207.

Barker, Roger, G.; Dembo, Tamara & Lewin, Kurt (1943): Frustration and Regression. In R.G. Barker, J.S. Kounin & H.F. Wright (Eds.): Child Behavior and Development. New York: McGraw-Hill, 441-458.

Barker, Roger, G. (1964a): The Ecological Environment. In R.G. Barker & P.V. Gump (Eds.): Big School, Small School Stanford: Stanford University Press, 3-10.

Barker, Roger, G. (1964b): Ecological Units. In R.G. Barker & P.V.Gump (Eds.): Big School, Small School. Stanford: Stanford University Press, 11-28.

Bergius, R.(1984): Forschungen zum Energieproblem der Wirtschaft. *Psychologische Rundschau*, 35, 185-197.

Biela, Adam (1983): Świadomość sytuacji ekologicznej mieszkańców regionu nieuprzemysłowionego. *Roczniki-Filozoficzne-Psychologia*, 31(4), 267-294.

Biela, Adam (1989): Współczesne tendencjie w psychologii poznawczej. *Przegląd Psychologiczny*, 32(1), 27-43.

Biela, Adam (1991): Initiating of the local ecological activity (Sejmik) at heavily polluted areas. Lublin: Catholic University of Lublin.

Boehme, Gernot (1993): Natur - ein Thema für die Psychologie? In H.-J. Seel, R. Sichler & B. Fischerlehner (Eds.): Mensch - Natur. Zur Psychologie einer problematischen Beziehung. Westdeutscher Verlag, 27-39.

Boesch, Ernst, E. (1971): Zwischen zwei Wirklichkeiten. Prolegomena zu einer ökologischen Psychologie. Wien:Hans Huber.

Boesch, Ernst, E. (1978): Kultur und Biotop. In: C.F. Graumann (Ed.): Ökologische Perspektiven in der Psychologie. Bern: Hans Huber, 11-32.

Brock, Adrian (1992): Was Wundt a "Nazi"? Volkerpsychologie, racism and antisemitism. *Theory and Psychology*. May 2(2), 205-223.

Bungard, Walter, Schultz-Gambard, Jürgen & Antoni, Conny (1988): Zur Methodik der Angewandten Psychologie. In D.Frey, C.G. Hoyos & D. Stahlberg (Eds.): Angewandte Psychologie. München:Psychologie Verlags Union, 588-606.

Canter, David (1990): In search of objectives. *Human Behavior and Environment Advances in Theory and Research*, 11, 315-338.

Cone, John, D. & Hayes, Steven, C. (1980): Environmental Problems/ Behavioral Solutions. Monterey: Brooks/Cole Publishing Company.

deRivera, Joseph (1976): Field Theory as Human-Science. New York: Gardner Press.

Dennis, Michael, L.; Soderstrom, E. Jonathan; Kocinski, Walter S.; Cavanaugh, Betty (1990): Effective dissemination of energy-related information: Applying social psychology and evaluation research. *American Psychologist*, Oct., 45(10), 1109-1117.

Deutsch, Morton (1992): Kurt Lewin: The tough-minded and tender-hearted scientist. *Journal of Social Issues*, 48(2), 31-43.

Diekmann, Andreas & Preisendorfer, Peter (1992): Persönliches Umweltverhalten: Diskrepanzen zwischen Anspruch und Wirklichkeit. *Kölner Zeitschrift für Soziologie und Sozialpsychologie*, Jun, 44,(2), 226-251.

Diekmann, Andreas & Preisendörfer, Peter (1993): Erwiderung auf kritische Anmerkungen von Lüdermann. *Kölner Zeitschrift für Soziologie und Sozialpsychologie*, 45,(1), 125-134.

Dierkes,Meinolf & Fietkau, Hans-Joachim (1988): Umweltbewusstsein - Umweltverhalten. Kohlhammer.

Eliasz, Andrzej (1993): Psychologia ekologiczna. Warszawa: Wydawnictwo Instytutu Psychologii PAN.

Engel, Zbigniew & Sadowski, Jerzy (1992): Hałas i wibracje w środowisku. Warszawa: Liga Ochrony Przyrody.

Engermann, Alwin (1990): Systemtheorie. In L. Kruse, C.-F. Graumann, E.-D. Latermann (Eds.): Ökologische Psychologie. München: Psychologie Verlags-Union, 107-111.

Ernst, Andreas, M. & Spada, Hans (1991): Bis zum bitteren Ende? *Psychologie heute*, 18(11), 62-70.

Ernst, Andreas, M., Bayen, Ute, J. & Spada, Hans (1992): Informationssuche und -verarbeitung zur Entscheidungsfindung bei einem ökologischen Problem. In K. Pawlik & K.H. Stapf (Eds.): Umwelt und Verhalten. Göttingen: Verlag Hans Huber, 107-127.

Festinger, Leon; Schachter, Stanley & Back, Kurt (1950): Social Pressures in Informal Groups. Stanford: Stanford University Press.

Festinger, Leon (1957): A Theory of Cognitive Dissonance. Stanford: Stanford University Press.

Festinger, Leon (1978): Theorie der Kognitiven Dissonanz. Translated by Martin Irle and Volker Montmann (Eds.). Stuttgart: Hans Huber.

Festinger, Leon (1983): The Human Legacy. New York: Columbia University.

Fisch, Rudolf & Daniel, Hans, Dieter (1983): Forschungsthemen der Sozialpsychologie. In D. Frey & S. Greif (Eds.): Sozialpsychologie. München:Urban & Schwarzenberg, 17-31.

Frey, Dieter (1981): Reversible and irreversible decisions. Preference for consonant information as a function of attractiveness of decision alternatives. Per-Breitenbach.

Haeckel, Ernst (1924a): Die Welträtsel. Leipzig: Alfred Kröner Verlag.

Haeckel, Ernst (1924b): Die Lebenswunder. Leipzig: Alfred Kröner Verlag.

Haigh, Nigel; Bora, Gyula; Zentain, Violetta (1987): The Background to Environmental Protection in Market and Planned Economy Countries. In G. Enyedi, A.J. Gijswijt & B. Rhode (Eds.): Environmental Policies in East and West. London: Taylor Graham, 2, 2-29.

Heimstra, Norman, W. & McFarling, Leslie, H. (1974): Environmental Psychology. Monterey: Brooks/Cole Publishing Company.

Hellpach, Willy (1921): Psychologie der Umwelt. Berlin:Urban & Schwarzenberg.

Hellpach, Willy (1922): Gruppenfabrikation. In W. Hellpach (Ed.): Sozial-psychologische Forschungen. Berlin:Julius Springer

Hellpach, Willy (1928): Politische Prognose fur Deutschland. Berlin: S. Fischer

Hohmann, Hans-Hermann; Seidenstecher, Getraud & Vajna, Thomas (1973): Umweltschutz und okonomisches System in Osteuropea. Stuttgart:Verlag W. Kohlhammer.

Holahan, Charles, J.(1978): Environment and Behavior. New York: Plenum Press.

Holubowicz, K.; Owskinski, J.W. & Straszak, A.(1987): Polish Case Study: Regional Impact of large-scale mining and energy development. In L. Kairiukstis, A. Buracas & A. Straszak (Eds.): Ecological sustainability of regional development. Warszawa: Polish Academy of Sciences, 157-172.

Hoyos, Carl, Graf, Frey, Dieter & Stahlberg, Dagmar (1988): Angewandte Psychologie: Zur Eingrenzung und Beschreibung einer psychologischen Disziplin. In: D. Frey, C.G. Hoyos & D. Stahlberg (Eds.): Angewandte Psychologie. München: Psychologie Verlags Union, 21-35.

Hudson, Cameron (1980): Economic Reforms and the Consumer in Eastern Europe. In: Economics Directorate. Economic Reforms in Eastern Europe and Prospects for the 1980's. Frankfurt:Pergamon Press, 121-137.

Ittelson, William H.; Proshansky, Harold, M.; Rivlin, Leanne, G. & Winkel, Gary, H. (1974): An Introduction to environmental psychology. New York: Holt, Rinehart & Winston, Inc.

Ittelson, W.H. (1977): Einführung in die Umweltpsychologie. Stuttgart: Klett-Cotta, eine Übersetzung von *An introduction to environmental psychology*.

Janikowski, Ryszard (1993): Wielokryterialny model decyzyjny jako narzędzie oceny oddziaływania projektowanej działalnosci człowieka na środowisko. Katowice: Instytut Ekologii Terenów Uprzemysłowionych.

Kafel, Krzysztof & Szymaniak, Iwona (1995): Wartość środowiska. Metody wyceny ekonomicznej. Translated from the English: James T. Winpenny (1993): Values for the Environment: A Guide to Economic Appraisal. Warszawa: Państwowe Wydawnictwo Ekonomiczne.

Kalinowska, Anna (1992): Ekologia - wybór przyszłości. Warszawa: Editions Spotkania.

Kaminski, Gerhard (1989): The relevance of ecologically oriented conceptualization to theory building in environment and behavior research. In E.H. Zube & G.T. Moore (Eds.): Advances in environment, behavior & design. Volume 2. New York: Plenum Press, 3-36.

Kaminski, Gerhard (1993): Einige Charakteristika und Leitgesichtspunkte einer ökopsychologischen Praxeologie. In H.J. Harloff (Ed.): Psychologie des Wohungs- und Siedlungsbaus. Psychologie im Dienste von Architektur und Stadtplanung. Verlag für Angewandte Psychologie, 17-27.

Kates, Robert, W. (1976): Experiencing the environment as hazard. In S. Wapner, S.B. Cohen & B. Kaplan (Eds.): Experiencing the environment. New York: Plenum Press, 133-156.

Kebeck, Günther (1984): Feldtheorie. In H.E. Lück, R. Miller & W. Rechtien (Eds.): Geschichte der Psychologie. München: Urban & Schwarzenberg, 96-102.

Kley, J. & Fietkau, H.J. (1979): Verhaltenswirksame Variablen des Umweltbewußtseins. *Psychologie und Praxis*, 23(1), 13-22.

Kowalik, Piotr (1974): Some Cybernetic Ideas in the Theory of Control of Land Ecosystems. In R.M. Dmowski (Ed.): Systems Analysis and Modelling Approaches in environment systems. Warszawa: Institute of Applied Cybernetics, Polish Academy of Sciences, 165-179.

Kruse, Lenelis (1978): Ökologische Fragestellungen in der Sozialpsychologie. In C.F. Graumann (Ed.): Ökologische Perspektiven in der Psychologie. Bern:Hans Huber, 171-190.

Kruse, Lenelis; Graumann, Carl-Friedrich & Lantermann, Ernst-Dieter (1990): Ökologische Psychologie. München: Psychologie Verlags Union.

Lang, Alfred & Fuhrer, Urs (1993): What Place for Culture in Psychology? *Schweizerische Zeitschrift für Psychologie*, 52, (2), 65-69.

Lang, Alfred (1995): Dritte Tagung der Gesellschaft für Kulturpsychologie. *Informationen zur Umweltpsychologie*, 1,1, 3-4.

Lawrence, Douglas, H. & Festinger, Leon (1962): Deterrents and Reinforcement. Stanford:Stanford University Press.

Lewin, Kurt (1943): Psychologische Okologie. In: Feldtheorie in den Sozialwissenschaften (1963). Bern: Huber, 98-101.

Lewin, Kurt (1969): Grundzüge der topologischen Psychologie. Stuttgart: Hans Huber

Lewin, Kurt (1974): Die Psychologische Situation bei Lohn und Strafe. Stuttgart: S. Hirzel Verlag.

Lewińska, Janina; Baścik, Jerzy & Bułat, Anna (1995): Warunki klimatyczne a kształtowanie zespołów mieszkaniowych Radomia. *Człowiek i Środowisko*, 19(1), 197-212.

Little, Brian, R. (1976): Specialization and the varieties of environmental experience. In S. Wapner, S.B. Cohen & B. Kaplan (Eds.): Experiencing the environment. New York: Plenum Press, 81-116.

Lück, Helmut E., (1984): Sozialpsychologie. In H.E. Lück, R. Miller & W. Rechtien (Eds.): Geschichte der Psychologie. München: Urban & Schwarzenberg, 161-170.

Luedemann, Christian (1993): Diskrepanzen zwischen theoretischem Anspruch und forschungspraktischer Wirklichkeit. *Kölner Zeitschrift für Soziologie und Sozialpsychologie*, 45, (1), 116-124.

Matthaei, Friedrich, Karl (1963): Untersuchungen zum Problem kausal-dynamischer Ansätze in der empirischen Psychologie seit Narziss Ach und Kurt Lewin. Marburg: G.g. Nolte.

Mattes, Peter (1984): Psychologie im westlichen Nachkriegsdeutschland und in der Bundesrepublik. In H.E. Lück, R. Miller & W. Rechtien (Eds.): Geschichte der Psychologie. München:Urban & Schwarzenberg, 28-34.

Matthies, Ellen (1994): Bedroht durch Luft, Wasser und Nahrung? Bericht, Nr.43, Sondersammelgebiet Psychologie an der Universitätsbibliothek Saarbrücken.

McDougall, William (1926): An Introduction to Social Psychology. Boston: John W. Luce & Co.

Meseke, Cornelia (1995): Predicting attitudes to the environment from behavior: The differences between Polish and German industrial workers. *Polish Psychological Bulletin*, 26(1), 43/56.

Meseke, Cornelia (1998): Religion and science: a common border between two frontiers. In P. Bytniewski & J. Mizińska (Eds.): Dialog Kultur: O granicach pluralizmu. Lublin: Uniwersytet Marii Curie-Skłodowski, 143-153.

Michnowski, Lesław (1995): Jak żyć? Ekorozwój albo... Białystok: Wydawnictwo Ekonomia i Środowisko.

Miller, Rudolf (1984): Ökologische Psychologie. In H.E. Lück, R. Miller & W. Rechtien (Eds.): Geschichte der Psychologie. München:Urban & Schwarzenberg, 178-184.

Miller, Rudolf (1986): Einführung in die Ökologische Psychologie. Leske & Budrich.

Mosler, Hans-Joachim (1990): Selbstorganisation von umweltgerechtem Handeln: Der Einfluss von Vertrauensbildung auf die Ressourcennutzung in einem Umweltspiel. Universität Zürich, Philosophische Fakultät I.

Mosler, Hans-Joachim (1993): Selbstverbreitung von umweltgerechtem Handeln: Der Einfluss von Vertrauen in einem ökologisch-sozialen Dilemmaspiel. *Journal of Environmental Psychology*, 13,(2), 111-123.

Müller-Freienfels (1930): Allgemeine Sozial- und Kulturpsychologie. Leipzig:Johann Ambrosius Barth.

Pawlik, Kurt (1991): Management Summary. In K. Pawlik (Ed.): Perceptions and Assessment of Global Environmental Conditions and Change. (PAGEC): Report 1. Barcelona: HDP Secretariat.

Pawlik, Kurt & Stapf, Kurt H. (1992): Ökologische Psychologie:Entwicklung, Perspektive und Aufbau eines Forschungsprogramms. In K. Pawlik & K.H. Stapf (Eds.): Umwelt und Verhalten. Bern: Verlag Hans Huber, 9-24.

Pawlik, Kurt & Buse, Lothar (1992): Felduntersuchungen zur transsituativen Konsistenz individueller Unterschiede im Erleben und Verhalten. In K. Pawlik & K.H. Stapf (Eds.): Umwelt und Verhalten. Bern:Verlag Hans Huber, 25-69.

Preuss, Sigrun (1991): Umweltkatastrophe Mensch. Heidelberg: Roland Ansanger Verlag.

Rechtien, Wolfgang (1984): Gestalttheorie. In H.E. Lück, R. Miller & W. Rechtien (Eds.): Geschichte der Psychologie. München: Urban & Schwarzenberg, 88-95.

Rechtien, Wolfgang (1990): Zur Geschichte der Angewandten Gruppendynamik. Gruppendynamik, Feb., 21(1), 103-120.

Rohrmann, Bernd (1992): Gestaltung von Umwelt. In D. Frey, C.G. Hoyos & D. Stahlberg (Eds.): Angewandte Psychologie. Weinheim: Psychologie Verlags Union, 265-282.

Schneider, Christa M. & Müller, Martin (1993): Die Völkerpsychologie - Entstehung und Weiterentwicklung unter kulturpsychologischen Aspekten. *Schweizerische Zeitschrift für Psychologie*, 52,(2), 93-102.

Schoggen, Phil (1989): Behavior Settings. A Revision and Extension of Roger G. Barker's Ecological Psychology. Stanford: Stanford University Press.

Schübel, Hubert, R. (1993): Gemeinsame Grundlagen und Perspektiven in der Vielfalt umweltpsychologischer Anwendungsfelder. *Umweltpsychologische Mitteilungen*, 1, 1-8.

Scott, David & Willits, Fern K. (1994): Environmental Attitudes and Behavior. A Pennsylvania Survey. *Environment and Behavior*, (26), 2, 239-260.

Seel, Hans-Jürgen & Sichler, Ralph (1993): Perspektiven einer Psychologie der menschlichen Naturbeziehung. In H.-J. Seel, R. Sichler & B. Fischlehner (Eds.): Mensch-Natur. Zur Psychologie einer problematischen Beziehung. Westdeutscher Verlag, 14-26.

Sichler, Raph & Seel, Hans-Jürgen (1993): Von der Umweltkrise zum menschlichen Naturverhältnis. Zur konzeptionellen Neuorientierung in der ökologischen Psychologie. *Journal für Psychologie*, 1, (4), 5-17.

Sommer, Robert; Wicker, Allan, W. (1991): Gas station psychology: The case for specialization in ecological psychology. *Environment and Behavior*, March, 23(2), 131-149.

Spada,Hans & Opwis,Klaus (1985): Die Allmende-Klemme: Eine umweltpsychologische Konfliktsituation mit ökologichen und sozialen Komponenten. In: A. Dietrich (Ed.): Bericht über den 34. Kongress der Deutschen Gesellschaft für Psychologie in Wien 1984. Band II: Anwendungsbezogene Forschung. Hogrefe, 840-843.

Spada, Hans & Ernst, Andreas, M. (1992): Wissen, Ziele und Verhalten in einem ökologisch-sozialen Dilemma. In K. Pawlik & K.H. Stapf (Eds.): Umwelt und Verhalten. Göttingen:Verlag Hans Huber, 83-106.

Spiewakowski, Eugeniusz (1995): Koncepcja długofalowej polityki ekologicznej dla miasta Bydgoszczy. *Ekologia i Technika*, 1(13), 4-8.

Stäudel, Thea (1990): Ökologisches Denken und Problemlösen. In L. Kruse, C.F. Graumann & E.-D. Lantermann (Eds.): Ökologische Psychologie. München:Psychologie Verlags Union, 288-292.

Stapf, Kurt, H. (1978): Ökopsychologie und Systemwissenschaft. In C.F. Graumann (Ed.): Ökologische Perspektiven in der Psychologie. Bern: Hans Huber, 251-273.

Stokols, Daniel (1974): Readings in Environmental Psychology. New York: MSS Information Corporation.

Tajfel, Henri (Ed., 1984): The Social Dimension. Vol. 2. Cambridge: Cambridge University Press.

Trojan, Przemysław (1984): Ecosystem Homeostasis. Warszawa: PWN - Polish Scientific Publishers.

Üexkull, Jakob, J. von (1913): Bausteine zu einer biologischen Weltanschauung. München: F. Bruchmann.

Üexkull, Jakob, J. von (1933): Staatsbiologie. Hamburg:Hanseatische Verlagsanstalt.

Üexkull, Jakob, J. von (1934): Streifzüge durch die Umwelten von Tieren und Menschen. Berlin: Julius Springer

Üexküll, Jakob, J. von (1936): Niegeschaute Welten. Berlin:S.Fischer Verlag.

van Leeuwen, Cees; Stins, Joku (1994): Perceivable information or: The happy marriage between ecological psychology and Gestalt. *Philosophical Psychology*, 7(2), 267-285.

Wall, Helmut, Oelkers, Martin (1993): Psychologen und Mediziner gemeinsam pro Umwelt. In: A. Gebert & U. Winterfeld (Eds.): Arbeits-, Betriebs- und Organisationspsychologie vor Ort. Bericht über die 34. Fachtagung der

Sektion Arbeits-, Betriebs- und Organisationspychologie im Berufsverband Deutscher Psychologen. Bad Lauterberg:Deutscher Psychologen Verlag, 493-499.

Wallenius, Margit (1980): Roger Barker's ecological psychology: Present situation and future developments. *Psykologia*, 25(3), 188-195.

Wanless, P.T. (1980): Reform of the System of Economic Management in Poland 1973-1979. In: Economics Directorate. Economic Reforms in Eastern Europe and Prospects for the 1980's. Frankfurt: Pergamon Press, 105-118.

Westgaard, Odin (1989): Allow me to introduce...Kurt Lewin. *Performance Improvement Quarterly*, 2(4), 67-75.

Wicker, Allan, W. (1979): An Introduction to Ecological Psychology. Monterey: Brooks/Cole Publishing Company.

Wolanski, Napoleon & Szemile, Małgorzata (1984): Studies in Human Ecology. Warszawa: Polish Scientific Publishers.

Wundt, Wilhelm (1983): Ausgewählte psychologische Schriften, Abhandlungen, Aufsätze, Reden. Band II. (1858-1888) Leipzig: Zentralantiquariat der Deutschen Demokratischen Republik.

Wundt, Wilhelm (1911): Einführung in die Psychologie. Leipzig: R.Voigtländer Verlag.

Wundt, Wilhelm (1913): Reden und Aufsätze. Leipzig:Alfred Kröner Verlag.

Zawada, Piotr (1993): III Forum Ekologniczne. Lublin: Katolicki Uniwersytet Lubelski, Lubelska Fundacja Ochrony Środowiska Naturalnego.

Zarembia, Piotr (1986): Urban Ecology in Planning. Warszawa: Ossolineum.

Żukowski, Paweł (1994): Zdrowa żywność a degradacja środowiska. Rzeszow: FOSZE

References from Polish data bases:

Biela, Adam (1984): Stres psychiczny w sytuacji kryzysu ekologicznego. Badania z zakresu sozopsychologii. Lublin: Wydawn. Tow. Nauk. KUL.

Biela, Adam (1992): Kwestionariusz Lubelski Analizy Stanowiska Pracy. Lublin: Redakcja Wydawnictw KUL.

Bonenberg, Marek, M. (1992): Etyka środowiskowa: założenia i kierunki. Kraków: Uniwersytet Jagielloński.

Brown, Lester, L.; Flavin, Christopher & Postel, Sandra (1994): Na ratunek ziemi jak budować gospodarkę światową w duchu ekorozwoju. Warszawa: Wydawn. Szkolne i Pedagogiczne.

Brozi, Krzysztof, J. (1992): Ludzie i kryzys cywilizacji: szkice antropologiczne. Lublin: Norbertinum.

Budnikowski, Adam (1992): The Ecological dimension of the Polish-EC relations. Warsaw: Foreign Trade Research Institute.

Cichy, Danuta (1988): Kształtowanie świadomości ekologicznej młodego pokolenia Polaków. I Seminarium Młodzieżowego Ruchu Ekologicznego. Warszawa: Biuro Wydawnictw i Reklamy Zarządu Głównego Towarzystwa.

Czajkowska, Przemysława (1989): Ruchy i organizacje ekologiczne w Europie. Warszawa: PAX.

Czerwinski, Andrzej i Czaja, Leszek (1991): Wstęp do sozologii. Białystok: Wydawnictwo PB.

Dąbrowski, Kazimierz (1991): Moralność w polityce. Warszawa: BIS.

Dołęga, Józef, M. (1993): Człowiek w zagrożonym środowisku: Z podstawowych zagadnień sozologii. Warszawa: Wydawn. Akademii Teologii Katolickiej.

Drzewiecki, Lech; Kostrzewska-Kijik, Stanislawa (1986): Dyrektor przedsiębiorstwa przemysłu spożywczego w warunkach reformy gospodarczej. Warszawa: IERiGZ

Engel, Zbigniew & Sadowski, Jerzy (1992): Hałas i wibracje w środowisku. Warszawa: Liga Ochrony Przyrody.

Glinski, Piotr; Sicinski, Andrzej & Wyka, Anna (1990): Społeczne aspekty ochrony i kształtowania środowiska w Polsce.

Gustowski, Alexander (1987): Społeczno-ekonomiczne warunki życia w określonym środowisku jako czynniki wpływające na schorzenia układu płciowego kobiet pracujących. Bydgoszcz: Wydaw. Uczelniane AM.

Haber, Josef, A. (1993): Globalny problem ekologiczny a procesy transformacji.

Honkisz, Małgorzata (1993): Polska polityka ekologiczna. Rzeszow: UMCS.

Izyk, Wanda (1989): Socjologia pracy z elementami psychologii pracy. Vol.2. Więź społeczna i środowisko pracy. Wrocław: Wydaw. Uczelniane AE.

Jopkiewicz, Krystyna (1993): Kto jest kim w inżynierii ekologicznej. Warszawa: Zakład Inżynierii Ekologicznej.

Karney, Janina, E. (1988): Człowiek w środowisku pracy. Warszawa: Instytut Wydawniczy Związków Zawodowych.

Kostrowicki, Andrzej, S. (1992): System "Człowiek-Środowisko" w świetle teorii ocen. Wrocław: Zakład Narodowy im. Ossolinskich.

Krol-Bac, Elżbieta (1992): Wpływ uwarunkowań fizjofizycznych na kształtowanie najbliższego otoczenia człowieka. Wrocław: Wydaw. PW.

Laslowski, Krzysztof & Rafinski, Marek (1992): Idee ekologii w świadomości społecznej. Poznań - Daszewicz: Sorus.

Lawniczak, Ryszard, Hładkiewicz, Wiesław (1986): Ruchy pokojowe i ekologiczne w Europie: materiały z konferencji naukowej, Raculka 5-12 Maja, 1985. Zielona Gora: Wydaw. Wyższej Szkoły Pedagogicznej.

Lenartowicz, J. Krzysztof (1992): O psychologii architektury. Kraków: PK.

Majka, Jerzy (1987): Kryteria zdrowotne środowiska. Warszawa: Państ. Zakład Wydawnictw Lekarskich.

Michalec, Tadeusz (1987): Ochrona środowiska. Radom: WSI.

Nadzieja, Cybulska & Sarosiek, Jerzy (1987): Problemy związane z postępem cywilizacji. Szczecin: ODN.

Napiorkowska, Celestyna & Koca, Wiesława (1992): Chronić, by przetrwać: materiały z sympozjum ekologicznego w Łodzi-Lagiewnikach 19-20 Listopada, 1988. Niepokalanów:Wydaw. Ojców Franciszkanów.

Niezabitowski, Andrzej (1991): Wybrane problemy teoretyczne relacji między człowiekiem a sztucznym środowiskiem przestrzennym w aglomeracjach przemysłowych. Gliwice: Wydaw. PS.

Osinska, Wanda (1987): Wartości w świecie techniki. Warszawa: Instytut Wydawniczy Związków Zawodowych.

Ostrowska, Maria (1991): Czlowiek a rzeczywistość przestrzenna. Szczecin: Autorska Oficyna Wydawnicza "Nauka i Życie".

Pastusiak, Longin (1988): Globalne zagrożenia współczesnego świata. Warszawa: Książka & Wiedza.

Pietras, Marek (1990): East European countries facing ecological cooperation in Europe. Lublin: UMCS

Piontek, Franciszek (1992): O współzależnosciach między ekonomią i ekologią. Katowice: Wydział Ekologii Urzędu Wojewódzkiego.

PTP (1993): Raj globalny:działania lokalne. Warszawa: Polskie Towarzystwo Psychologiczne. Mlodzieżowy Ośrodek Psychologiczny.

Skolimowski, Henryk (1993): Filozofia życia: eco-filozofia jako drzewo życia. Warszawa: Wydaw. Pusty Obłok.

Skrzynska, Wiesława (1990): Być czy mieć? Siedlce: Wydawnictwa Uczelniane WSR-P.

Solowiej, Daniela (1987): Podstawy metodyki oceny środowiska przyrodniczego człowieka. Poznań: Wydaw. Naukowe UAM.

Stacewicz, Janusz (1993): Pomiędzy spoleczeństwem ekonomicznym i ekologicznym. Warszawa: PAN.

Stanislaw, Janik; Krawczyk, Zygmunt (1987): Ochrona środowiska naturalnego. Poznań: Wydaw. PP.

Szalek, Jerzy (1988): Psychologia obrony cywilnej. Warszawa: Wydaw. Min. Obrony Narodowej.

Wronska-Nofer, Teresa (1987): Kryteria zdrowotne środowiska. Warszawa: Państ. Zakład Wydawnictw Lekarskich.

Zakrzewski, Sigmunt, F. (1995): Podstawy toksykologii środowiska. Warszawa: Wydawn. Nauk. PWN

Zaleski, Zbigniew (1991): Psychologia ekologicznego exodusu. Wrocław: Zakład Narodowy im. Ossolinskich.

2

COGNITION, ATTITUDE AND BEHAVIOR

The inexorable correlation: attitude and behavior

The relationship between attitude and behavior is, of course, not necessarily a direct one (Triandis, 1971). There are many reasons for consciously concealing, disguising or suppressing our attitudes, among others these include: the nature of the attitude, the social context within which it is to be manifested or veiled, the actor(s) and receiver(s) more immediately involved and their various personalities, the time factor and various cultural and regional considerations. For instance, people often hide their real attitudes and evince a certain behavior because it is the only one that is socially accepted. So, whether attitudes are manifested in behavior depends upon context and setting and has also, in many cases, been programmed by family and society. Indeed, whether we are termed normal or not and accepted by those around us, often depends, not so much upon the attitudes we have, but rather on the extent to which our behavior reflects accepted norms.

As was indicated in the first chapter, the measurement of social phenomena is very difficult, has always been of some concern to social scientists and quantifying attitude - behavior relationships is no exception to this. Even in the natural sciences, the process of mensuration itself often changes properties, extent and content of what is to be plotted, but within the realm of the social sciences, where external factors are so hard to control, this activity is often error-ridden and subject to personal interpretation. This, of course, would be particularly true of attitude - behavior studies, because they are of such a subjective nature and embedded in a context that makes their interpretation so difficult. This in no way reduces their importance, nor negates any effort to construe real incidence. Although their relationship seems to be as delicate and elusive as a spider's web, science and especially medicine has found the products of some arachnids to be of practical and healing use and has found ways, not only for their storage but also for their distribution and of course, subsequent application. It is to be hoped that, as research continues, the many attributes of the attitude - behavior relationship will become equally well-known and their management well employed.

Attitudinal aspects of behavior in relation to environmental questions

As will be shown in the following pages, there are quite a number of studies on the correlation between attitudes and behavior (Preuss, 1991; Scott & Willits, 1994). One subject - first embedded within the field of cognitive social psychology - that, primarily because of the theories involved, concerns itself with this relationship is that of cognitive dissonance, the findings of which will be discussed below, both in terms of German and English authors. Another area where this contingency has become important is that of more immediate concern within this context: that of environmental and ecological psychology.

The measurement of attitude and behavior depends, not only upon the above-mentioned items, but also upon the comparability of the two to one another (Pawlik, 1991) where the relationship can be an extremely complex one (Dierkes & Fietkau, 1988). Quantification in terms of environmental ecology thus depends upon many contiguous factors: and the relationship must be in a state of "closure" or commensurability in order to allow any statements or hypotheses and eventual predictions to be made.

In addition to the above, many other elements play an important part in the correlation of attitude and behavior; among others, the following authors have made studies in the areas of commitment (Mosler, 1993); behavior setting (Schoggen, 1989); transsetting consistence (Pawlik & Buse, 1992); example-setting (Spada, 1992); information (Ernst, Bayen & Spada, 1992) and cognitive dissonance (Frey, 1990). All of these areas will be discussed further, but, because of its complexity and the specifities of the theories involved, the cognitive components of information processing and cognitive dissonance will be examined more particularly below.

The relationship of information processing to attitude and behavior

Cognitive dissonance, embedded within the field of cognitive social psychology is - as a theory - of considerable import within environmental, ecological research, because it considers important aspects of the behavior - attitude relationship. Belonging to the consistency theories (see Stahlberg & Frey, 1983 for further information), Leon Festinger's theory of cognitive dissonance, tracing its origins as far back as

1877, when Charles S. Pierre first investigated man's motivation to ascertain certainties and to avoid doubt, (Frey & Benning, 1983, pg.147), explores the relationship between consonant and dissonant aspects that confront people within the pattern of daily life. As already discussed in Chapter One, however, Leon Festinger did not merely copy already existing theories but sought to explain phenomena and herein lies the brilliance of his contribution, one that, we must remember, is partly a legacy of his mentor, Kurt Lewin. In the best scientific tradition, Festinger combined his experience, learning and knowledge to bring us closer to what psychology should really attempt to understand: what makes humans function under certain circumstances and in different settings.

In contrast to the self-awareness theory (Bem, see Frey et al., 1983), which also belongs within the realm of cognitive social psychology, (Frey, 1983), when cognitive dissonance delves into the mechanisms of information classification or organization, it considers motivational aspects (IBID, pg. 58). Bem, as a Skinner-Behaviorist (IBID, pg.58, Aronson, 1980, pg.150), in contrast concentrates on information-processing itself.

Although some of the original laboratory and experimental research was not able to substantiate some of the hypotheses made within the context of this theory, and indeed, upon closer examination of the results proved not even to be significant (Osnabrügge & Frey, 1983, pg.462), there are many aspects that deserve the closer examination given it in following. As Abele, (1980), however, points out, many of the moderating variables of the experimental situation itself can lead to methodological errors. Although she concedes that the activation of behavior can in many cases really lead to significant attitude changes and vice-versa (Abele, 1980, pg.57) - this being one of the main subjects of dissonance research - (and of course of subsequent interest in the following pages), and that behavior which is dissonant to personal cognitive structure can, under certain circumstances change cognition, she points out the errors that can arise within the research variables themselves, the confounding or limiting factors of the experiment and the manipulated variables (Millon & Diesenhaus, 1972, pg.72), according to the nature and structure of the experiment (Abele, 1980, pg.37f.) itself. Use of the theory of cognitive dissonance however, has been made in field study, where other limits must be considered. Indeed, this is one area where Festinger proved to be particularly brilliant, again in the tradition of Lewin.

Perhaps one of the most cogent arguments in favor of a theory is the brilliance of its defenders and the fact that intense research of a qualitatitve and quantitative nature is coupled with its use to explain natural phenomena. Beyond that, already within the experimental situation itself, there are certain indications of its veracity, perhaps not at first transferable into real-life situations, at least not until the full picture is gotten. Sometimes, findings are not easily understood outside of their laboratory conditions. For example, Frey (1983, pg.63f.) mentions a phenomenon that has been observed within the course of the experimental situation itself: where attitudes have been manipulated and questionnaires clearly point to significant before and after differences, subjects maintained however, that their attitudes did not change, this pointing to the fact that much of this process is not rational and conscious (Frey, 1983) and that, further, we are not always able to articulate what we really feel, depending upon the mitigating circumstances of the setting. Whereas critical voices (Frey, 1983, pg.65f.) have maintained that man, as a rational being cannot be subject to controlling forces that keep him from actively changing the world around him, history shows us that man is not so logical and deductive as we would like to see him and that his sagacity leaves room for improvement. Aronson, (1980, pg.104) maintains that cognitive dissonance conceives people to be - not rational, but *"rationalizing beings, motivated to believe that they are right"* - and supports this argument with discussions of real-life situations. Taking his inspiration from the environment that Lewin fled from in 1933 (remembering that Leon Festinger, as a student of Lewin embedded his theory within the constructions of his teacher - Frey, 1983, pg.62), he points to the rationalizing the Jews did in the face of clear, unmistakable, immediate and life-threatening information (Aronson, 1980, pp.109, 114 and 138). Citing several other historical examples, he points out that information by itself is of limited use in changing behavior and attempts to delineate several aspects of the theory of cognitive dissonance, again proving his point with several real-life cases. Furthermore, we find arguments of this nature in literature. George Eliot, in **Silas Marner**, (pg. 35), for example, points out that what is familiar to us as a safe environment remains so in our subjective appraisal and assessment of the situation even when the objective fact changes and the environment becomes dangerous - to the point of life-threatening. Rather than ignoring this association, psychology should attempt to explore and explain it in theory and fact.

Allowing, nay even making theoretical postulation necessary therefore, cognitive dissonance almost always appears following a decision, especially when one's commitment to the decision is tested by alternative possibilities. For this reason, the process of information seeking is one where, above all, reassurance is sought (Aronson, 1980, pg.112). This has been experimentally demonstrated when, given arguments in agreement or disagreement to existing opinions, *"subjects did not remember in a rational-functional manner. They tended to remember the plausible arguments that were in agreement with their own position and the implausible arguments that were in agreement with the opposing position"* (Aronson, 1980, pg. 110).

One of the indications of the presence of dissonance was an indirect measurement, again performed in an experimental situation. Postulating that the existence of dissonance would likely produce discomfort, subjects were measured according to degree of dissonance and difficulty of the task performed. Outcomes revealed that *"the low-dissonance subjects performed better than the high-dissonance subjects in a complex task, whereas the high-dissonance subjects performed better than the lows in a simple task"* (Aronson, 1980, pg.153).

In considering the merit of this discussion, one must remember that the occurence of dissonance is not necessarily based upon formal, logical criteria and that *"inconsistencies that produce dissonance are psychological inconsistencies"* and that it is *"sometimes difficult to be certain what will be psychologically inconsistent for any one person"* (Aronson, 1980, pg.147-8).

Cognitive Dissonance in Polish Psychology

The few studies that have been done in Poland (Garai, 1979; Grzelak et al., 1965; Lukaszewski, 1970; Malewski, 1962, 1964) - who provided alternative, political meanings much in accordance with the times - and Falkowski, (1990) will not be further discussed here.

Cognitive Dissonance in German Psychology

When Leon Festinger published his **Theory of Cognitive Dissonance** in 1957, Germany was just pulling out of a post-war period in the field of psychology (see Chapter One). While some articles were already published in the late 1960's (Cohen et al., 1968; Irle, 1966; Luhr, 1966; Schönbach, 1966 and von Cranach, et al., 1965) most were written in the 1970's, many of them before the official translation was made available (Irle et al., 1978), some of these even only as internal work papers (Graff, 1979; Hintermüller, 1973; Lippert, 1976 and Mufti, 1971), never to be published.

Relying on the data provided by the PSYNDEX base (1979-1995) and the compilation made by Möntmann and Irle, provided at the end of the Festinger translation, the distribution of the articles was five from the period 1960-69; thirty-three from 1970-79; twenty-four from 1980-89 and seven from 1990 to the present. Some authors, such as Peters, 1971; Frey et al., 1972 and Kupf et al., 1973 also published on this topic in English circulations. Those authors with the most frequent publications on the subject were Dieter Frey and Martin Irle (see also bibliographies at the end of this chapter). In order to compare this to the available English literature, the above mentioned compilation, while counting 856 publications (from 1956-1977), mentioned only a total of 28 German titles.

Especially interesting within this context, is that research tended to replicate the findings mentioned above regarding information processing (Beckmann et al., 1982a, 1982b, 1984; Dönsback, 1989, 1992 - a study of 1397 newspaper readers - Ernst et al., 1992; Feger et al., 1983; Frey, 1993; Frey et al. 1984a, 1984b; Grabitz et al., 1982; Hager et al., 1991; Rosch, 1982; Tazelaar et al., 1982 and Spada et al., 1992). Other findings also discussed within this design were social support or social aspects (Frey, 1993; Frey et al., 1993 and Spada et al., 1992), discrepancy between attitude and behavior (Diekmann et al., 1992), stability of decisions (Ernst et al., 1992), the relationship of cognitive dissonance to information-processing theories (Möntmann, 1985), the unimportance of reality (Frey et al., 1982) and ecological aspects (Diekman et al., 1992; Ernst et al., 1992 and Spada et al., 1992). Although not the subject of research per se, information processing results have also been mentioned in, or connected to, some ecological studies, (Ernst et al., 1992; Schütze, 1986; Frey et al.,1987, 1990; Grob, 1991; Nöldner, 1990; Schaible-Rapp, 1988 and Wortmann, 1988) also linking cognitive dissonance research to that in the field of ecological psychology.

Cognitive Dissonance in the English Literature

When Leon Festinger retired from his research in the field of psychology to devote his time to the study of archeology and ancient history (an outcome of which was the book "**The human legacy**" (1983), see also chapter One), research on the theory of cognitive dissonance had culminated in some of its most brilliant results. However, it is important to realize that it has, also in the United States, continued in the meantime and produced some very valuable further conclusions. Some of these will be mentioned in the following, in order to give an overview of the most important findings appropriate to this work. The careful reader will find some German (and other English-speaking) authors among the following. These have been included because the articles were printed in English, in an English-speaking journal, and were included in the PSYCHLIT computer data base: all of these points seem to indicate that they have had some influence upon the English-speaking scientific community.

The following does not attempt to claim that it makes all of the literature on cognitive dissonance available, it merely presents a collection and compilation of those authors found to be of relevance. No doubt, many important ones were over-looked, but those here mentioned, do tend to give an overview of the field.

All of the work here mentioned, only one-seventh of all of the work reviewed, could easily be said to have an implication for research in the field of environmental psychology. In the period 1970-79, work was done on information-processing - indicating that information was not taken up in a logical manner, but tended to strengthen hypotheses already existing - (Bear et al., 1975; Cummings et al., 1976; Frey et al., 1978; Jastrebske, 1974 and Olshavsky et al., 1974), on the effects of self-monitoring on the acceptance of discrepant overt behavior (Snyder et al., 1976), on re-organization of conceptions in order to establish consistency (DeChenne,1980), on attitude change (Widgery et al., 1973; Ross et al., 1973; Woodyard et al., 1974; Shaffer, 1974; Green, 1974; Shaffer, 1975a & b; Nemeth et al., 1976 and Higgins et al., 1979), on attitude-behavior consistency (Liska, 1974), on the effect of possible unwanted consequences on attitude change after discrepant behavior (Goethals et al., 1975), on equity and dissonance (Van-Avermaet et al., 1978), responsibility (Insko et al., 1975), and on confidence when seeking discrepant information (Schultz, 1974).

Interestingly enough, even at that time a link was provided between cognitive dissonance research and environmental psychology such as those of Menasco et al., 1978, who studied consumer behavior and by Pallak et al., 1976, who measured the question of stricter controls on water pollution.

There were also those studies that challenged some of the alleged principles of cognitive dissonance. Frey et al. (1979), for example, found that, where manifested behavior was congruent to already existing attitudes, attitude change toward that performed behavior was stronger with a decreasing amount of reward. Further, where attitude-discrepant behavior was tested, there was a dissonance effect if the Ss were insufficiently rewarded. This finding provides some added information to one of the experiments done by Festinger & Carlsmith (1959) and seeks to differentiate findings that according to Frey, (1983), were not found to be valid in the experiment in the first place. This does not mean that Frey disagreed with the entire findings of cognitive dissonance, for he has, indeed, proven to be one of the most prolific writers on the subject, especially when one considers the German literature (see above).

Where others were able to replicate cognitive dissonance results, (Himmelfarb et al., 1974), according to Khokhlov et al. (1973), evidence suggests that the assumption of a universally operative model of cognitive consistency needs to be rethought. Results from Krause (1973), claim to show that substantive opinion changes are not attributable to either dissonance or deviance or many other items associated with initial dissonance.

For a review of the 1971-73 literature on methodological issues in attitude research, dissonance, attribution theory, learning and conditioning of attitudes and the decline in popularity of the dissonance theory, see Kiesler et al. (1975). In retrospect, we can argue against this last point and say that dissonance theory has experienced many low and high tides, seeming to want, especially, to confound those researchers that pronounced its death-sentence, or even those that merely sought to place it on some convenient back-shelf.

Further, in the spirit of critique, Fazio et al., 1979 pronounced neither dissonance nor self-perception theory to be able to explain the data they had obtained. Contrary to their explanations, Ronis and Greenwald, 1979 found new analyses based on the results of Fazio et al., to indicate that their data provided an insufficient basis for preferring their own theory to earlier versions of dissonance and self-perception theories and that Fazio et al. integrated the dissonance and self-perception processes. Prior to this, Greenwald and Ronis, (1978), had found the cognitive dissonance theory to have changed, no longer encompassing some of the examples, data and hypotheses that were part of Festinger's original statement - especially those pertaining to consistency among cognitions. Weiner, (1974) maintains that the theory of self-perception is a viable alternative to cognitive dissonance. These contentions will not be further discussed here.

While the general critical point made by Truzzi, (1973) that the balance theories (among them cognitive dissonance) in referring to attitude change did not address the problem of relevance has been challenged by cognitive dissonance literature, his particular problem of providing relevance between attitudes within a logical, cultural and instrumental context seems never to have been particularly approached.

To end on a more positive note: Kahle, 1978, found dissonance and impression management theories to be complementary in their view of attitude change and dissonance. Cummings et al., (1976) mentioned that the evidence in favor of the applicability of dissonance theory is more voluminous and more substantial than the evidence against it. He refers also to two categories - of especial importance within this context - where the theory has proven especially fruitful: to the measurement of the effects that dissonance arousal has on attitude change and the tendency to repurchase, and to the effects of dissonance arousal on selective information-seeking by customers.

In the period 1980-89, there was no particular change in the choice of topics, (essentially, they are an inherent part of the theory), although there was more specification of the theory itself. Again, of especial interest within this context is the work that was done in the following areas. These include: behavioral influences on attitudes (Heberlein et al., 1981; Steele et al., 1981; Eiser et al., 1988), attitude change and behavior (Cotton et al., 1980; Cooper et al., 1984; Baron et al., 1987), information seeking (Frey, 1981; Frey, 1982), commonalities between psychoanalytic theory and cognitive dissonance theory (Hishinuma, 1987), collective action (Cooper et al., 1983; Zanna et al., 1987), a compilation of cognitive-dissonance theories (Hoyos, 1987), ecological dissonance (Miller et al., 1989), incongruity between beliefs and behaviors (Quattrone), evaluation of alternatives (Frey et al., 1984), dissonance and attribution (Stroebe et al., 1981) and re-establishment of consistency through reorganization of self-conceptions (DeChenne, 1980).

Critique did not abate at this time, but, if anything, became sharper and found more contributors in addition to some of the ones already mentioned. Interestingly enough, much of it was not on the specific merits of cognitive dissonance and/or the replicability of its findings, but upon its relative importance to the field of social psychology. The discussion between Berkowitz and Devine vs. Cooper and Fazio exemplifies this (Lord, 1989), where an analytic vs. synthetic approach to studying human social behavior becomes the crux of the matter. In reply to this (Cooper et al., 1989), Cooper and Fazio doubt that research can be divided into analytic or synthetic strategies and questions. Berkowitz and Devine's portrayal of contemporary social psychology as too heavily analytic and too lightly synthetic, mentioning that synthesis is not at all incompatible with the fields present cognitive orientation. Then again, Berkowitz et al., 1989, believe that social psychology favors an analytic over a synthetic approach.

Some of the critique is based on misconceptions, as when Berkowitz et al., 1989, see the influence of dissonance theory to wane in the same year that a book of selected works of Leon Festinger made its appearance. Berkowitz et al.,1989, however, go on to mention that cognitive dissonance theory finds itself on the outside of the core assumptions in the research tradition of dominant cognitive orientation.

As ever, cognitive dissonance finds its champion in Aronson, 1989, who responds to Berkowitz et al., 1989, mentioning that he himself favors a "circus tent" approach to theory building and testing. On the other hand, analysis and synthesis are both of great importance in the development of theory. However, it is the research process itself that hinders synthesis, much of this itself being dependent upon a slavish fascination with fashion instead of a search for truth and a recognition of the importance of independent investigation.

In the period 1991-94, themes have remained largely the same, with the following subjects represented: attitude and behavior change (Wright et al., 1992; Cooper et al., 1994); timing and suitability of rewards (Gerard, 1992); self-consistency (Greenwald, 1992; Goethals, 1992); moral reasoning (Mwamwenda, 1992); speech assessment (Axsom, 1992); public commitment (Dickerson et al., 1992); environmental research (Burger et al., 1991); consumer attitudes (Geva et al., 1991) and attitude change (Losch et al., 1990). Of especial interest is the fact, that the field of economics has shown interest in cognitive dissonance (Davis, 1993). Of no less importance are the books that have been published in this period, all with reference to, and containing at least one chapter specifically on, the theory of cognitive dissonance (Rajecki, 1990; Zimbardo et al., 1991; Plous, 1993; Perloff, 1993; Aronson et al., 1994 and Gerard, 1994).

Of course, of no less importance within this context is the controversy that is contained in one of the 1992 editions of **Psychological Inquiry**. Within this editiion, Aronson (1992a), mentions the fact that while, by the mid-1970's, the theory of cognitive dissonance had not been considered to be as important as it was in the first two decades after 1957, it had stimulated much research. Especially recently, social psychology seems to have rediscovered motivation and several minitheories have emerged blending cognition with motivation. Within this context, the theory of cognitive dissonance is seen to provide a synthesis to cover relevant research findings (Aronson, 1992b)

While Wilder (1992) and Kruglanski (1992), for example, support Aronson's call for a change in emphasis within the discipline from multiple, tenuously connected minitheories to a greater integration across those theories, Vallacher (1992), maintains that Aronsons concern over the minitheories should consider the evolutionary nature of scientific progress. The main question he addresses is whether dissonance theory is capable of summarizing the theoretical developments of the last three decades. On the other hand, Swann (1992), supporting Aronson's call for a synthesis of social psychology research, wants the field not to forget what researchers have productively addressed in recent years. Schlenker (1992), while endorsing Aronson's synthesis of research in social psychology, mentions that dissonance theory should not be revitalized because it suffers from the weakness of assuming whatever form its devotees want it to take.

Lord (1992) criticizes more forcefully. Doubting that, as Aronson mentioned, the theory of cognitive dissonance has only been repressed during the past decade of social cognition but is making a comeback, he contends that the theory of cognitive dissonance may have been a mistake in the first place in terms of blinding researchers to more useful concepts. Kunda (1992), albeit seemingly in a milder manner, agrees that dissonance is not capable of serving as a unified theory to account for the "plethora of classical and novel motivational phenomena".

Yet while Jussim (1992) maintains that cognitive dissonance could illuminate confusing areas in social psychology and that many findings could be interpreted in the light of dissonance, Berkowitz (1992) agrees to the synthesis proposed by Aronson but does not find cognitive dissonance to be the proper label for it. Cooper (1992) of course, champions the new look position (see Cooper and Fazio) with Thibodeau et al. (1992) seeming to want to mediate between the two.

Regional differences in the interpretation of the theory

As a perusal of the last two above sections will show, the theory of cognitive dissonance has contributed a large amount of interesting research in the last two decades, despite the fact that a number of researchers, especially in America, (Gerard, 1994), have negated its importance, written off its findings, or relegated it to the shelf as a "minitheory" (Gerard, 1994). Whether or not this is due to the "counterintuitive inverse effect of reward on attitude change", or to the fact that the term is no longer fashionable, it would seem to be a sad end (in America) for a theory with such a promising start, were it not for the fact that a small but influential amount of researchers include it in their publications.

Comparison between the last two sections will show that there are some regional differences in the direction the research has taken, at least according to that available in this context. By far the most important contribution in dissonance theory in Germany has been in the area of information-processing, also making it of particular value to ecological psychology. While German literature does not attempt to explain all motivational behavior with the theory of cognitive dissonance, indeed, as Frey (1983) mentions, mainly individual behavior is sought to be explained within this context, the discussion on the relevance of dissonance within the field of social psychology has never been questioned to the extent that it has been in the United States.

Indeed, there are several arguments for the veracity of this theory. Paradoxically, if a theory proves to be counterintuitive, there are good reasons to assume that its main assumptions are true. Natural science is full of theories of this kind that have been well-proven in modern-day physics, engineering and technology. Anyone who has seen almost any experiment in a physics laboratory (at university level), will testify to the fact that intuition must be schooled in order to cope with the various factors dealt with in this context. It is a simple fact of life: whereas simple processes are intuitively predicted because we have learned about them, taking factors into consideration that we do not deal with on a daily level, are no longer predictable if experience does not make them so. Anyone driving a car for example, must either consider this or learn the hard way that he can no longer rely only on his five senses in order to insure accident-free driving but must rely on his experience (on relative distance and movement, for example) in addition, of course to receiving the normal sensual information.

Whereas, because of the amount of information it contains, any field of natural science must be diligently studied in order to be mastered, social science is just beginning to develop to the stage where it can be of real value to mankind. A theory predicting human behavior, whatever its name and whoever its author, can only be of human value if it serves mankind. If it is at least of interest and begets research, it has served some purpose, but if it succeeds in explaining difficult areas of human interaction, interpreting unnecessary behavior and alleviating even some small form of human misery, can it not be said to have optimally fulfilled its objective?

As one of the least matured sciences, the field of psychology could take an example from the development of the natural sciences. Even to the last century, Geologists (for example), argued about the available evidence suggesting the earth's creation and evolution (sedimentary vs. volcanic). Now we know that - to some extent - both were right.

When we are in a position to look at the development of the field of psychology from a more historical perspective, we might find this kind of development too. We will also assuredly find that this entire area of scientific effort is one of the most complex components of human endeavour, necessitating, for its advancement, the finest, most creative and determined intellectual involvement. It is then that we might consider those origins in a more positive light.

Attitude-behavior studies and the affiliation of their research

Studies concerned with the formation of attitudes have long been an important part of social psychology and indeed, have sometimes been considered to be its central theme (Rosch et al., 1983). Fisch et al., 1983, see attitude-behavior studies as belonging to the entire area of research on attitudes which also includes social attitudes, acquisition and change of attitudes and their structure (Fisch et al., 1983).

As will be seen in the next two sections however, attitude-behavior studies have also permeated the fields of ecological and environmental psychology, that is, the research and literature both of Germany and the United States. This body of research will be referred to in the following. Due to the large amount of information and results available in the English literature, only the most recent studies are presented in this context.

Attitude-behavior studies in Germany

Although many of the most recent studies within the area of ecological psychology pertain more explicitly to environmental pollution, some are more generally oriented or concern themselves with more traditional findings. In some works of Kaminski (1987), for example, he finds that cognitive processes conform to behavior setting as postulated by Barker and that definition and integration of concepts are important within the context of social representation (Kaminski, 1992).

Although Schreiber (1989) finds a discrepancy between attitudes and behavior, Pawlik (1992), finds a consistency in individual differences, that is, that significant person-situation changes are more seldom than coincidence would predict. Guenther (1989) deals with the regulation of action and Cramer (1989) with the different aspects of behavior and experience and how this influences expectations in the future and planing of future actions. Lang (1988), more in the tradition of cultural psychology, researched on the ecological orientation in the storage of information.

Of those more directly involved in research regarding environmental pollution, Schahn et al. (1994), has done work on the excuses and justifications that people find for their polluting behavior and has found that evoking personal concern, especially concerning local and regional environmental damage lessens the gap between attitude and behavior outcomes (Schahn, 1993). Especially in this context however, rationalizations and neutralization can negate feelings of shame and embarassment in regards to personal behavior. As in the cognitive dissonance research mentioned above, Mosler (1993), has found commitment to have a positive effect on attitude and behavior change. Finally, Hillenbrand (1993), worked on interindividual differences in the perception of nature.

Attitude-behavior research in English publications

In the following pages, it will become clear that a great amount of research is done within the context of the attitude-behavior relationship, usually, of course, including other moderators such as information, knowledge, status of the person, technology etc. Of all of the available studies, only those with relevance to environmental psychology and thus to the material to be presented in the next chapters, were chosen for the following discussion. European authors have been included because, as they made their findings available in the English language, they were considered to have some influence on the area. Some reviews have been made to cover a part of the vast amount of material available, (see Leeming et al., 1993, for a review of 34 environmental education studies published since 1974) but these will not be covered here.

As mentioned above, most studies included research on some aspects of the attitude-behavior relationship. Thus, Verplanken (1989) examined n = 2,439 in the Netherlands and found moderating effects of involvement and need for cognition in the relationships between beliefs, attitudes, and behavioral intentions towards large-scale use of nuclear energy and large-scale use of coal in the production of electricity, finding involvement to have a moderating role in the beliefs-attitude relationship. Heberlein (1989), discussing cases that describe how attitude studies can play a role in environmental management, predicts that the demand for attitude studies as part of environmental management will increase.

Where behavior encompassed sports and outdoor activities, Jackson (1986), studying n = 662, found that participants in appreciative activities (sports), hold stronger pro-environmental attitudes than participants in consumptive activities (hunting) or mechanized activities (trail biking etc.) and that outdoor recreation participation is more strongly related to attitudes reflecting those activities than to those regarding the general environment. In the same line, Shepard et al., (1985-86), n = 613, and Westphal et al., (1985-86), n = 51, found activities in outdoor sports to produce more positive attitudes and greater awareness.

Within the same context and also supporting the findings mentioned in the last two sections above, commitment has been found to have an interesting effect. Thus, Mosler (1993), reviewing n = 100, found that public commitment had its greatest effect on persons whose environmental consciousness was low. Dickerson (1992) even found significant behavior changes after commitment had taken place. The complexities of this can be demonstrated by the finding that Hooper et al., (1991) made with n = 122, where a block leader program in which Ss encouraged their neighbors to recycle, influenced altruistic norms and increased recycling. However, prompting and information strategies increased recycling but did not affect norms and attitudes. Katzev et al., (1994), also found commitment to change behaviors, especially in the case of resource conservation.

As pointed out above, especially in the discussion on cognitive dissonance, the proffering of information does not always have the desired effect upon attitude-behavior outcomes. Associations of this type were confirmed by Vining (1987), who, in studying n = 544, mentioned that environmental decisions may be sensitive to relatively subtle differences in the way information is presented. However, de Young, (1993) n = 103, reported that distributed pamphlets with information on how to reduce waste led to significant increase in reported behavior, and Austin et al., (1993), with n = 217 found that information increased recycling behavior (dependent upon how it was offered). This may reflect previous commitment, as mentioned above, or other moderators such as Hackett (1992) found when he mentioned that in environmental action, specific personal variables are important in structuring evaluations. In this light: in a study done by Ostman (1986-87), n = 336, newspapers and television were found to be the most frequently used media, however, when subjects wanted to inform themselves, other media were preferred for believable information.

However, access - for example - has greater effects, as Kallgren et al., (1986) found with n = 49, where Ss with relatively high levels of access were likely to act in a manner consistent with their opinion. Derksen et al, (1993), n = 448 and n = 797, found that people with access to a program (in Canada), had much higher levels of recycling behavior and that attitudes correlated with behavior. Findings in projected behavior were also similar: Williams (1991), with n = 237, found that nearly three-quarters of Ss reported that they would be at least somewhat likely to recycle their non-returnable containers if drop-off facilities were available on campus.

Knowledge, as a modifying variable - representing something that is already part of the personal attitude frame, and hence has been subject to information-processing - has totally different implications than information alone. Ostman, (1987), with n = 336, found a connection between environmental knowledge, concerns and behaviors. Rutte, (1987), found the environmental knowledge of an entire group to be more important than mere group elements. Hines, (1986-87), n = 315, defines the variables associated with responsible environmental behavior to be knowledge of issues, knowledge of action strategies, locus of control, attitudes, verbal commitment and an individual!s sense of responsibility. Where information is coupled with additional elements of behavioral strategies, results are more favorable: Jordan et al., (1986), n = 62, for example, found that students receiving instruction in both environmental's issues and action strategies demonstrated an increased level of knowledge and changed their behavior, whereby issue awareness instruction to another group of students did not show this effect.

More specifically, Pearson, et al., (1986), studying n = 353, found that a spatial ability factor accounted for 13.69% of variance in the environmental knowledge factor and Bright et al., 1993 also mentions the moderating power of reasoned action in influencing attitude and behavior change. Powers, (1985-86), n = 120, found that simulation teaches environmental thinking. He then created a game which provided an additional understanding of the social dilemma involved and motivated discussion of possible solutions to it. Mio et al., 1993, n = 346, also had similar results with dilemma playing. For Maule, 1985, n = 72, sampling done by participants was dependent on a constant updating of the internal representation of the environment. In the study done by Ellen, 1994, n = 307, objective knowledge was significantly related to committed recycling behaviors, whereas perceived knowledge was positively associated with committed recycling behaviors, source reduction and political action behaviors. For Syme et al.,1993, n = 73, knowledge of issues led to problem assessment and arousal and influenced reported conservation behavior, positive association between degree of arousal and reported behavior. Yount et al., 1992, found no significant differences between n=68 non-science compared to a control group of n = 68 science students, but that rather those who had higher cognitive reasoning scores were more prone to increase defensibility. For Fortner et al., 1991, 1979 = 3,637, 1983 = 3,523, 1987 = 1,732 over the years of study, knowledge scores increased slightly except for humanities items and classrooms were the most important source of student information. Gigliotti, (1992), found that with 1,500 students in 1990 results suggest, that students are more materialistic today than students were 20 years ago. For Gamba, 1994, relevant recycling knowledge was the most significant predictor of observed behavior and Bagozzi et al., 1994, n = 133, found that attitudes and past behvior intervened between goals and intentions in decision making.

For Newhouse, 1990, however, internal locus of control, a strong sense of responsibility, a solid understanding of issues and action strategies and a positive attitude are contributing factors for more responsible behavior. Arcury, 1990, n = 680, sees a direct relationship between environmental knowledge and attitude. Schahn, 1990, n = 167, found that knowledge and gender moderated the relationship between attitudes and behavior. Similar to this, Arcury, (1987), n = 516, in a multi-item survey, found that men tended to be more concerned and knowledgeable about acid rain than women, whereas other single-research done by other authors, had showed that women were more concerned and knowledgeable. Satow (1987), on the other hand, found that 214 female undergraduates had the same attributes as 316 male undergraduates.

Status has also played a part in many surveys and field observations. Balderjahn, (1988), n = 1,945 found West German behavioral patterns to have their own cluster of predictions and that ecologically concerned consumers belong to the upper social classes. For Samdahl, (1989), however, n = 2,131 analysis indicated that sociodemographic variables were ineffective in explaining any of the environmental concerns measured, but that proregulatory liberal ideology was a strong predictor of support for environmental regulation and underlying belief structures were most important.

Thompson, (1985), n = 3,414 (1971) and n = 3,867 (1981), in measuring changes in attitude, found significant differences between the two surveys he made, with most of the differences associated with political leanings, income, gender and geographical background. The changes were in the direction of a more materialistic lifestyle with less consideration for environmental energy issues and concerns. Pierce, (1987), studying 1,208 citizens and 575 elites (elected and appointed officials, technical experts on environmental issues), in the US and Japan, found elite and public belief systems in Japan to be more closely related than in the US. Ray, (1981), surveying 11 meetings of environmentalist groups, found that 88 individuals were in non-manual occupations and 37 in manual occupations. Connerly, (1986), n = 983, found partial support for a hypothesis that social status is a significant determinant of attitudes toward limited growth when costs of growth control are made explicit and anti-growth proposals are discussed. Grieve et al., (1985), in studying n = 535 female youth, 523 male youth and 541 female adults and 532 male adults in South Africa, found that scores differed with age, sex, and language groups, with English-speaking women showing the greatest degree of environmental concern. Scores also correlated with educational qualifications, membership of youth organizations and participation in nature-oriented activities. McGuire, (1984), n = 73, in interviewing different socio-economic levels and making an analysis of household refuse, showed similar patterns of disposal of recyclable materials by households of differing socioeconomic characteristics. Scott, (1994), n = 3,632 found that support for environmental action was predictive of environmental behavior, but not strongly and that social characteristics were more predictive of environmentally oriented behaviors. Vining (1992), in studying n = 74, an environmental group; n=75 forest service managers and n = 77 the general public, found decisions and emotions of the environmental group and the public sample to be similar but that both differed from those of the managers.

For Oskamp, (1991), n = 221 predictors of curbside recycling were: living in a single-family home, owning their own house, recycling by friends and neighbors and acknowledging environmental problems and motives to recycle. For Baldassare, (1992), n = 640, personal environmental threat was a better predictor of overall environmental practices than were demographic variables or political factors. Results from Lansana, (1992), show that recyclers, compared to nonrecyclers, were more likely to be homeowners, aged 40-64 years, aware of the recycling program, preferring mandatory recycling and perceiving a greater need for recycling.

Sherkat et al., (1993), in working with n = 1,699 high school students and n = 1,562 parents found that efficacy, religious affiliation, race and region distinguished environmental activists from other protesters. Kanagy et al., (1993), n = 3,632 found - interestingly enough - that religious affiliation and church attendance had an impact on environmental behaviors, however that it was negatively related to attitudes. When attitudes were controlled for however, there was a net positive relationship between church attendance and environmental behaviors. Greeley, (1993), n = 300, found a correlation between religion and environmental concern. For him, low levels of environmental concern correlate with bibilical literalism. Confidence in the existence of God and being Christian correlated positively with support for environmental spending.

Prester et al., (1987), in studying n = 229 West Germans, found exposure level, environmental-related attitudes and personal characteristics to be initial determinants for active participation in a situation of environmental deterioration but that general interest in politics was also important. Dresner (1989-90), n = 201, also perceived political activity to be related to the likelihood of taking action.

Further measures of personal characteristics were made by Jackson, (1985), n=446, who found preferences for specific options, that is, for soft vs. hard energy paths, were strongly associated with environmental attitudes. Whereas "ecocentrists" favored a soft path, "technocentrists", favored a hard path - especially nuclear power. For Smith et al., (1992), n = 120, cooperation and competition were more important than environmental concern in predicting behavior in a commons dilemma simulation game. For Iwata, (1992), n = 124, social evaluation, noise sensitivity and emotional sensitity had positive and significant partial correlations with environmental evaluations. Herrera, (1992), studying n = 86 activists and n = 410 nonactivists, found that nonactivists were more likely to value technology, material well-being, social competitiveness and pursuit of social change. O'Connor, (1990), n = 93, found that Ss generally considered both themselves and others to be quite cooperative, when in fact they were not.

Further attitude-behavior studies were done by McCarthy et. al., 1994, n = 134, who found that attitudes about the inconvenience of recycling had a negative relationship to recycling behaviors. Aitken et al., 1994, n = 264, found that attitudes, habits and values were very poor predictors of water consumption. Mielke, (1985), n = 102, found attitude-behavior correlation to be .49, with littering behavior being inferred from interviews; the attitude-behavior relationship was closer in Ss with higher attitude accessibility. AA influenced the relationship between social norms and behavior, when AA was low, norms were better predictors of behavior than attitudes. Van der Pligt, (1985), n = 219, however, found general environmental concern to be a poor predictor of energy-conservation behaviors, yet non-conservationists evaluated their own behavior only marginally favorable and in some cases clearly unfavorable. Kinsey et al., (1984), n = 82, n = 52, n = 199, found that while value judgements showed no change, there were significant scores supporting the notion of connective vectors between the cognitive and affective domains of attitudes. For Ungar, (1994), however, attitudes do not predict behaviors very well. Smith et al., (1994), n = 198, mentions that attitude strength might moderate the extent to which affective reactions account for additional variance in behavior. For Shrum,

(1994), n = 134, values did not have a direct relationship with behavior. Values did, however, have direct influences on attitudes about the inconvenience of recycling and attitudes about the importance of recycling. Attitudes about the inconvenience of recycling had a negative relationship with recycling behaviors. Perkins et al., (1992), n = 244, found that attitudes and subjective norms influenced behavior intentions. Krause, (1993), n = 300, found a willingness for change in lifestyles dependent upon perception of how difficult those adjustments were going to be. Vining et al., (1992), n = 1028, found that over a period of three years, environmental concern and specific attitudes regarding recycling became more favorable over time, with recyclers clearly showing stronger pro-environmental attitudes than nonrecyclers. Ryan, (1991), studying n = 504, within the context of a conservation education program, found that Ss attitudes were affected by parental behavior and participation in outdoor activities. Iwata, (1990), n = 138, also found that stronger pro-environmental attitudes have stronger pro-preservation attitudes. For McCarthy et al., (1994), n = 134 attitudes about the inconvenience of recycling had a negative relationship with recycling behaviors. Aitken et al., 1994, n = 264 found attitudes, habits and values were very poor predictors of water consumption. For Pettus, (1987), n = 74, the relationship of attitudes towards environmental issues and personality characteristics - that is, measured in terms of locus of control, openness of belief system and perceptions about self gave the results that self-controlled, well-organized and goal oriented Ss, were more likely to display favorable environmental behaviors, but that Ss who viewed themselves as having more control over events in their environment were less likely to favor laws or restrictive measures designed to preserve or improve environmental quality. For Diamond et al., (1991), n = 74, n = 254, attitude change was not affected by type of reward.

Where issues of technology were concerned, Van der Pligt, (1987), n = 184, in the UK, found that results showed that the more technologies Ss had to rate, the smaller were the percentage ratings they gave to any single technology. Sia, et al., (1985-86), found that among 105 Sierrra Club members and 66 Elderhostel members belief in technology was nonsignificant, but that knowledge and attitude correlated significantly.

For Simmons, et al., (1990), n = 500, recyclers were more likely to hold to a conservation ethic or to feel a sense of responsible action. Samuelson et al., (1991), n = 1000, found consumer concerns about comfort and health to be important. Axelrod et al., (1993), studying n = 259 undergraduates, n = 105 adults, found that behavior depended on threat perception, issue importance and efficacy constructs. For Messick, (1984), results suggest that harvest decisions are influenced by the Ss self-interest, a desire to protect and maintain the resource pool, and pressures to conform to the norms established by the behavior of fictitious others. Milliken (1987), found environmental uncertainty to be the perceived inability to predict something accurately because of external factors. For Kempton, 1985, n = 400 consumer perceptions led to an overemphasis on curtailment and management methods and to a neglect of efficiency investments. De Young, 1986, studying n = 107, found that Ss derived a series of separate and distinct satisfactions from recycling and re-using materials. Where Howard, 1993 argues that counseling psychologists, as having experience in human attitudes and behaviors, should take more of an active part in environmental counseling, Ford, 1993, mentions that counseling psychology is not the answer because of the many complex factors involved.

Conclusion

The relationship of attitude-behavior and information-processing research to environmental action is central to the field of ecological psychology. For this reason, both attitude-behavior and cognitive dissonance research have been listed in the above, for they naturally contain the aspects of this relationship.

It is important to remember, that, while cognitive dissonance is treated differently in English and German-speaking publications, both in the content and the extent of the studies, attitude-behavior studies in English-speaking literature differ - to a large extent - only in scope and extent.

Whereas German researchers, especially in the last decade, have replicated results found in the area of information-processing that tended to support cognitive dissonance theory, popular American investigation has - albeit the theory has been included in some important publications - tried to negate its content and effect in recent years. In the German studies, especially Grob (1991), Ernst (1992) and Frey (1993 etc.) have pointed out, that attitude has an influence on behavior and, furthermore, that attitude/behavior even influences information processing.

Although this has also been supported by some American findings it, unfortunately, does not seem to belong to popular American theory at the moment because there has been some discreditation of cognitive dissonance. When research becomes the subject of fashion however, there is always a possiblity that its main objective - a search for the' truth - is somewhat or completely obscured. Particularly where a certain fashion is only accepted by one country, international communication can be somewhat limited by this. However, in the case of cognitive dissonance, a deeper inquiry into the publications of the last decade even reveal a lack of consonance as far as the theory is concerned. Perhaps it is time for a more thorough exposition - far beyond the scope of this work unfortunately.

Within attitude-behavior research, we find no such break. In the much smaller amount of German research, we again find cognition has an influence on attitude/

behavior and vice-versa and that influencing cognition is by no means simple or easily done, but the most effective way of changing attitudes/behaviors.

The much greater amount of English literature is somewhat more complicated to summarize. Briefly, the effects of involvement, sports, commitment, proffering of information, making alternatives more accessible and issue awareness all contributed to changed attitude-behavior modes. Such individual traits as spatial ability factor (also trainable), knowledge instruction and cognitive reasoning could also have effect. Personal values such as responsibility, sense of control and positive attitude also had an influence. Male/female differences however, where found, could not be replicated, that is, there were no clear differences. Status, and material well-being, on the other hand, were found to have an influence, as did political leaning and geographical background and religious affiliation. Belief in technology, while under some circumstances of favorable influence, also contributed to a wait and see attitude (they will fix it with time).

To summarize: Pro-environmental behavior (and of course the preliminary attitudes responsible for this and the subsequent ones resulting from a change in behavior) is significantly influenced by material means and knowledge. Of course, this does not place environmental behavior only at the disposal of the well-to-do, on the contrary, it underlines the importance of municipal, regional and national organization. Pro-environmental action must be institutionalized, as well on an individual, industrial and state-oriented basis - remembering that industry, capital and the state - as pointed out in Chapter One, (see especially the conclusion) - have special possibilities and responsibilities that the individual does not have. Special rewards on the other hand, or concentration on specific groups does not seem to bring overall relief. The evidence seems to point fairly clearly to the fact that pro-environmental behavior seems to have become a part of responsible living and that people have only to be shown how to do it and to be required to be personally accountable, in order for meaningful action to take place. Perhaps this is another positive trend of 1990's, that, a decade ago, generally found only apathetic response.

In the following chapter however, it will be shown that the development in Poland has been somewhat different from this.

REFERENCES

Selected Bibliography:

Abele, Andrea (1980): Einstellungsänderung durch einstellungskonträres Verhalten - Methodische Probleme dissonanztheoretisch orientierter Forschung. In: W.Bungard (Ed.): Die gute Versuchsperson denkt nicht. München: Urban & Schwarzenberg, 31-60.

Aronson, Elliot (1980): The Social Animal. San Francisco: W.H. Freeman.

Beckmann, Jürgen; Rosch, Marita; Erber, R.; Möntmann, Volker & Irle, Martin (1982a): Der Einfluss von subjektiven Hypothesen auf die Informationsverarbeitung bei Entscheidungsprozessen. Mannheim: Universität, Sonderforschungsbereich 24.

Beckmann, Jürgen & Kuhl, Julius (1982b): Umbewertung von Entscheidungsalternativen als Mittel zur Erlangung von Handlungskontrolle. Mannheim: Universität, Sonderforschungsbereich 24.

Beckmann, Jürgen (1984): Kognitive Dissonanz. Eine handlungstheoretische Perspektive. Mannheim: Universität

Beckmann, Jürgen & Kuhl, Julius (1984): Altering information to gain action control: Functional aspects of human information processing in decision making. *Journal of Research in Personality*, 18,(2), 224-237.

Beckmann, Jürgen (1985): Absichtskontrolle als primäre Funktion von Dissonanzreduktion. In: D. Albert (Ed.): Bericht uber den 34. Kongress der Deutschen Gesellschaft für Psychologie in Wien, 1984. Vol. I, Grundlagenforschung. Hogrefe, 55-59.

Beckmann, Jürgen & Irle, Martin (1985): Dissonance and action control. In: J. Kuhl & J. Beckmann (Eds.): Action control. From cognition to behavior. Springer: 129-150.

Cramer, Manfred (1989): Umweltkrise und der psychosoziale Bereich. In: W. Stark (Ed.): Lebensweltbezogene Prävention und Gesundheitsforderung. Konzepte und Strategien für die psychosoziale Praxis. Lambertus.

Diekmann, Andreas & Preisendorfer, Peter (1992): Persönliches Umweltverhalten. Diskrepanzen zwischen Anspruch und Wirklichkeit. *Kölner Zeitschrift für Soziologie und Sozialpsychologie*, 44,(2), 226-251.

Diekmann, Andreas & Preisendorfer, Peter (1993): Erwiderung auf kritische Anmerkungen von Lüdermann. *Kölner Zeitschrift für Soziologie und Sozialpsychologie*, 45,(1), 125-134.

Dierkes, Meinolf & Fietkau, Hans-Joachim (1988): Umweltbewusstsein - Umweltverhalten. Kohlhammer.

Donsbach, Wolfgang (1989): Selektive Zuwendung zu Medieninhalten. Einflussfaktoren auf die Auswahlentscheidungen der Rezipienten. In: M. Kaase & W. Schulz (Eds.): Massenkommunikation, Theorien, Methoden, Befunde. Westdeutscher Verlag, 392-405.

Donsbach, Wolfgang (1992): Die Selektivität der Rezipienten. Faktoren, die die Zuwendung zu Zeitungsinhalten beeinflussen. DFG Forschungsbericht, VCH Verlagsgesellschaft, 25-70.

Ernst, Andreas, M. & Spada, Hans (1991): Bis zum bitteren Ende? *Psychologie heute*, 18(11), 62-70.

Ernst, Andreas, M.; Bayen, Ute,J. & Spada, Hans (1992): Informationssuche und - verarbeitung zur Entscheidungsfindung bei einem ökologischen Problem. In K. Pawlik & K.H. Staph (Eds.): Umwelt und Verhalten. Göttingen: Verlag Hans Huber, 107-127.

Feger, Hubert & Sorembe, Volker (1983): Konflikt und Entscheidung. In: H. Thomae (Ed.): Theorien und Formen der Motivation. Hogrefe, 536-711.

Fisch, Rudolf & Daniel, Hans-Dieter (1983): Forschungsthemen der Sozialpsychologie. In: D. Frey & S. Greif (Eds.): Sozialpsychologie. München: Urban & Schwarzenberg, 17-31.

Frey, Dieter (1981a): Informationssuche und Informationsbewertung bei Entscheidungen. Göttingen:Hans Huber.

Frey, Dieter (1981b): The effect of negative feedback about oneself and cost of information on preferences for information about the source of this feedback. *Journal of Experimental Social Psychology*, 17, (1), 42-50.

Frey, Dieter (1982): Different levels of cognitive dissonance, information seeking, and information avoidance. *Journal of Personality and Social Psychology*, 43(6), 1175-1183.

Frey, Dieter (1983): Kognitive Theorien. In: D. Frey & S. Greif (Eds.): Sozialpsychologie. München: Urban & Schwarzenberg, 50-67.

Frey, Dieter; Irle, Martin; Montmann, Volker, Kumpf, Martin; Ochsmann, Randolph & Sauer, Claudius (1982): Cognitive dissonance:experiments and theory. In: M. Irle (Ed.): Studies in decision making. Social psychological and socio-economic analyses. Berlin: de Gruyter, 281-310.

Frey, Dieter & Benning, Elke (1983): Dissonanz. In D. Frey & S. Greif (Eds.): Sozialpsychologie. München:Urban & Schwarzenberg,147-153.

Frey, Dieter; Kumpf, Martin; Irle, Martin & Gniech, Gisla (1984a): Re-evaluation of decision alternatives dependent upon the reversibility of a decision and the passage of time. *European Journal of Social Psychology*, 14(4), 447-450.

Frey, Dieter & Rosch, Marita (1984a): Information seeking after decisions. Personality and Social Psychology Bulletin, 10,(1), 91-98.

Frey, Dieter & Benning, Elke (1984b): Informationssuche von Konsumenten nach Entscheidungen. Einige Spekulationen. *Marketing*, 6,(2), 107-113.

Frey, Dieter; Heise, Christian; Stahlberg, Dagmar & Wortmann, Klaus (1987): Psychologische Forschung zum Energiesparen. In: Jürgen Schultz-Gambard (Ed.): Angewandte Sozialpsychologie. München: Psychologie Verlags Union, 275-289.

Frey, Dieter; Stahlberg, Dagmar & Wortmann, Klaus (1990): Energieverbrauch und Energiesparen. In: L. Kruse, C.-F. Graumann & E.-D. Lantermann (Eds.): Ökologische Psychologie. München: Psychologie Verlags Union, 680-690.

Frey, Dieter & Gaska, Anne (1993): Die Theorie der kognitiven Dissonanz. In: D. Frey & M. Irle (Eds.): Theorien der Sozialpsychologie. Vol. I. Huber, 275-324.

Frey, Dieter (1993): Experimentelle Untersuchungen zur selektiven Informationssuche und einige Spekulationen zur Übertragung auf politische Sachverhalte. *Zeitschrift für Politische Psychologie*, 1,(2), 109-137.

Gerard, Harold, B. (1994): A retrospective review of Festinger's. A Theory of Cognitive Dissonance. *Contemporary Psychology*, 39, (11), 1013-1018.

Grabitz, Hans-Joachim & Haisch, Jochen (1982): Subjective hypotheses in diagnosis problems. In: M. Irle (Ed.): Studies in decision making. Social psychological and socio-economic analyses. de Gruyter, 235-279.

Graff, Jörg (1979): Ein Modell der Theorie der kognitiven Dissonanz. Mannheim: Fakultät für Sozialwissenschaften.

Grob, Alexander (1991): Meinung - Verhalten - Umwelt. Frankfurt: Peter Lang

Günther, Rudolf (1989): Ökologische Psychologie und Umweltpsychologie. Fachentwicklung und Forschungsperspektiven unter Berücksichtigung der Schnittstellengestaltung zwischen Natur- und Sozialwissenschaften. Verlag für Interkulturelle Kommunikation.

Hager, Willi & Weissmann, Sabine (1991): Bestätigungstendenzen in der Urteilsbildung. Hogrefe

Hammann, Peter & Schuchard-Ficher, Christiane (1980): Messung von Nachkauf-Dissonanz im Automobilmarkt. *Marketing*, 2,(3), 155-161.

Hillenbrand, Martin (1993): Der Mensch als Faktor im Naturschutzgeschehen. In: J. Schahn & T. Giesinger (Eds.): Psychologie für den Umweltschutz. München:Psychologie Verlags Union, 163-171.

Hintermüller, Alfred (1973): Der Systemcharakter der Kaufentscheidung. Universität Salzburg: Philosophische Fakultät.

Kaminski, Gerhard (1987): Cognitive bases of situation processing and behavior-setting participation. In G.R. Semin & B. Krahe (Eds.): Issues in contemporary German social psychology. History, theories and application. Sage, 218-240.

Kaminski, Gerhard (1992): Probleme der ökologischen Psychologie mit dem Wissen:Ein schreckliches Beispiel. In M. von Cranach, W. Doise & G. Mugny (Eds): Social representations and the social bases of knowledge. Hogrefe, 96-103.

Kaminski, Gerhard (1993): Einige Charakteristika und Leitgesichtspunkte einer ökopsychologischen Praxeologie. In: H.J. Harloff (Ed.): Psychologie des Wohnungs- und Siedlungsbaus. Psychologie im Dienste von Architektur und Stadtplanung. Verlag für Angewandte Psychologie, 17-27.

Lang, Alfred (1988): Die kopernikanische Wende steht in der Psychologie noch aus! Hinweise auf eine ökologische Entwicklungspsychologie. *Schweizerische Zeitschrift für Psychologie*, 47,(2-3), 93-188.

Lippert, Ilse (1976): Entscheidung und Dissonanz. Universität Wien:Grund- und Integrativwissenschaftliche Fakultät.

Loinger, Wolfgang (1988): Ein attributionstheoretischer Beitrag zum Postulat der aversiven Zuständigkeit kognitiver Dissonanz. Innsbruck:Naturwissenschaftliche Fakultät.

Lück,Helmut E. (1984): Sozialpsychologie. In: H.E. Lück, R. Miller & W. Rechtien (Eds.): Geschichte der Psychologie. München:Urban & Schwarzenberg, 161-170

Lüdermann, Christian (1993): Diskrepanzen zwischen theoretischem Anspruch und forschungspraktischer Wirklichkeit. Kölner Zeitschrift für Soziologie und Sozialpsychologie, 45,(1), 116-124.

Mielke, Rosemarie (1985): Eine Untersuchung zum Umweltschutz-Verhalten (Wegwerf-Verhalten): Einstellung, Einstellungs-Verfügbarkeit und soziale Normen als Verhaltensprädikatoren. *Zeitschrift für Sozialpsychologie*, 16,(3), 196-205.

Möntmann, Volker & Irle, Eva (1978): Bibliographie der wichtigen seit 1956 erschienenen Arbeiten zur Theorie der kognitiven Dissonanz. In M. Irle & V. Möntmann (Eds.): Theorie der kognitiven Dissonanz, 366-413.

Möntmann, Volker (1985): Kognitive Dissonanz und Gewinn von Information als Konsequenzen eines kognitiven Hypothesentests. Centaurus.

Mosler, Hans-Joachim (1990): Selbstorganisation von umweltgerechtem Handeln:Der Einfluss von Vertrauensbildung auf die Ressourcennutzung in einem Umweltspiel. Universität Zürich, Philosophische Fakultät I.

Mosler, Hans-Joachim (1993): Selbstverbreitung von umweltgerechtem Handeln:Der Einfluss von Vertrauen in einem ökologisch-sozialen Dilemmaspiel. *Journal of Environmental Psychology*, 13(2), 111-123.

Mufti, Heitham, M. (1971): Entscheidung, Risiko und Verantwortung. Universität Innsbruck:Philosophische Fakultät.

Nöldner, Wolfgang (1990): Abfall. In: L. Kruse; C.-F. Graumann & E.-D. Lantermann (Eds.): Ökologische Psychologie. München: Psychologie Verlags Union, 673-679.

Ochsmann, Randolph (1981): Veränderung der Sicherheit in der Bewertung von Alternativen als alternativer Weg der Dissonanzreduktion bei Entscheidungen. *Zeitschrift für Sozialpsychologie*, 12,(3), 217-232.

Osnabrügge, Gabriele & Frey, Dieter (1983): Kognitive Folgen forcierter Zustimmung:das klassische Experiment von Festinger und Carlsmith. In: D. Frey & S. Greif (Eds.): Sozialpsychologie. München:Urban & Schwarzenberg, 459-464.

Pawlik, Kurt & Buse, Lothar (1992): Felduntersuchungen zur transsituativen Konsistenz individueller Unterschiede im Erleben und Verhalten. In K. Pawlik & K.H. Stapf (Eds.): Umwelt und Verhalten. Bern:Verlag Hans Huber, 25-69.

Pogoda, Georg (1981): Aspekte einer kognitiven Theorie der Verdrängung. *Psychoanalyse*, 2,(2), 194-209.

Preuss,Sigrun (1991): Umweltkatastrophe Mensch. Heidelberg:Roland Ansanger Verlag.

Rosch, Marita (1982): Das Verarbeiten diskrepanter Information durch Personen mit unterschiedlicher Vorerfahrung. Mannheim: Sonderforschungsbereich 24.

Rosch, Marita & Frey, Dieter (1983): Soziale Einstellungen. In: D. Frey & S. Greif (Eds.): Sozialpsychologie. München:Urban & Schwarzenberg, 296-305.

Schahn, Joachim (1990): Umweltpsychologie und Umweltschutz - eine anwendungsorientierte Perspektive. *Report Psychologie*, 15,(10), 10-17.

Schahn, Joachim (1993a): Die Kluft zwischen Einstellung und Verhalten beim individuellen Umweltschutz. In J. Schahn & T. Giesinger (Eds.): Psychologie für den Umweltschutz. München:Psychologie Verlags Union, 29-49.

Schahn, Joachim (1993b): Die Rolle von Entschuldigungen und Rechtfertigungen für umweltschädigendes Verhalten. In J. Schahn & T. Giesinger (Eds.): Psychologie für den Umweltschutz. München: Psychologie Verlags Union, 51-61.

Schahn, Joachim; Dinger, Johanna & Bohner, Gerd (1994): Die Rolle von Rationalisierungen und Neutralisation für die Rechtfertigung umweltschädigenden Verhaltens. Bericht aus dem Psychologischen Institut, Diskussionpapier Nr. 80.

Schaible-Rapp, Agnes (1988): Das Entsorgungsproblem. In: D. Frey; C.G. Hoyos & D. Stahlberg (Eds.): Angewandte Psychologie. München: Psychologie Verlags Union, 283-297.

Schoggen, Phil (1989): Behavior Settings. A Revision and Extension of Roger G. Barker's Ecological Psychology. Stanford: Stanford University Press.

Schreiber, Klaus (1989): Wertewandel - Einstellungswandel ohne Konsequenzen? Planung und Analyse,16,(6), 187-192.

Schütze, Monika (1986): Die Entwicklung und Anwendung neuer Techniken zur Erfassung subjektiver Umweltwahrnehmung. Bonn: Rheinische-Friedrich-Wilhelms-Universität. Dissertation.

Scott, David & Willits, Fern, K. (1994): Environmental Attitudes and Behavior. A Pennsylvania Survey. *Enivronment and Behavior*, (26),2, 239-260.

Silberer, G. (1979): Dissonanztheoretische Forschungsarbeiten im Marketing-Bereich. *Psychologie und Praxis*, 23,(4), 145-153.

Spada, Hans & Opwis, Klaus (1985): Die Allmende-Klemme:Eine umweltpsychologische Konfliktsituation mit ökologischen und sozialen Komponenten. In: A. Dietrich (Ed.): Bericht über den 34. Kongress der Deutschen Gesellschaft für Psychologie in Wien 1984. Band II:Anwendungsbezogene Forschung. Hogrefe, 840-843.

Spada, Hans & Ernst, Andreas, M. (1992): Wissen, Ziele und Verhalten in einem ökologisch-sozialen Dilemma. In K. Pawlik & K.H. Stapf (Eds.): Umwelt und Verhalten. Göttingen:Verlag Hans Huber, 83-106.

Stahlberg, Dagmar & Frey, Dieter (1983): Konsistenztheorien. In: D. Frey & S. Greif (Eds.): Sozialpsychologie. München: Urban & Schwarzenberg, 214-221.

Tazelaar, Frits & Wippler, Reinhard (1982): Die Theorie mentaler Inkongruenzen und ihre Anwendung in der empirischen Sozialforschung. *Angewandte Sozialforschung*, 10, (3), 237-275.

Triandis, Harry, C. (1971): Attitude and Attitude Change. London: John Wiley.

Vogt, Roland (1981): Individuelle, innovative Problemlösungsprozesse - Erklärungsmodelle individueller, innovativer Problemlösungsprozesse im theoretischen Bezugsrahmen des Informations-Verarbeitungs-Ansatzes und ihre wissenschaftstheoretische Einordnung. Haag und Herchen.

Westermann, Rainer (1988): Strukturalistische Rekonstruktion psychologischer Forschung: Kognitive Dissonanz. *The German Journal of Psychology*,12,(3), 218-231.

Wortmann, Klaus; Stahlberg, Dagmar & Frey, Dieter (1988):Energiesparen. In D. Frey; C.G. Hoyos & D. Stahlberg (Eds.): Angewandte Psychologie. München: Psychologie Verlags Union, 289-316.

Bibliography from PSYCLIT data base on cognitive dissonance:

Aksom, Danny & Lawless, William, F. (1992): Subsequent behavior can erase evidence of dissonance-induced attitude change. *Journal of Experimental Social Psychology*, 28,(4), 387-400.

Aronson, Elliot (1989): Analysis, synthesis, and the treasuring of the old. *Personality and Social Psychology Bulletin*, 15,(4), 508-512.

Aronson, Elliot (1992a): The return of the repressed: Dissonance theory makes a comeback. *Psychological Inquiry*, 3,(4), 303-311.

Aronson, Elliot (1992b): Totally provocative and perhaps partly right. *Psychological Inquiry*, 3,(4), 353-356.

Aronson, Elliot; Wilson, Timothy, D. & Akert, Robin, M. (1994): Social psychology: The heart and the mind. New York: Harper Collins College Publishers

Bagby, R. Michael; Parker, James, D. & Bury, Alison, S. (1990): A comparative citation analysis of attribution theory and the theory of cognitive dissonance. *Personality and Social Psychology Bulletin*, 16,(2), 274-283.

Baron, Robert, A. & Byrne, Donn (1987): Social psychology: Understanding human interaction. Boston: Allyn & Bacon.

Bear, Gordon & Hodun, Alexandra (1975): Implicational principles and the cognition of confirmatory, contradictory, incomplete, and irrelevant information. *Journal of Personality and Social Psychology*, 32, (4), 594-604.

Berkowitz, Leonard & Devine, Patricia, G. (1989): Research traditions, analysis, and synthesis in social psychological theories: The case of dissonance theory. *Personality and Social Psychology Bulletin*, 15,(4), 493-507.

Berkowitz, Leonard (1992): Even more synthesis. *Psychological Inquiry*, 3,(4), 312-314.

Burger, Joanna & Gochfeld, Michael (1991): Fishing a Superfund site: Dissonance and risk perception of environmental hazards by fishermen in Puerto Rico. *Risk Analysis*, 11,(2), 269-277.

Collins, Barry, E. (1992): Texts and subtexts. *Psychological Inquiry*, 3, (4), 315-320.

Cooper, Joel (1992): Dissonance and the return of the self-concept. *Psychological Inquiry*, 3,(4), 320-323.

Cooper, Joel & Mackie, Diane (1983): Cognitive dissonance in an intergroup context. *Journal of Personality and Social Psychology*, 44,(3), 536-544.

Cooper, Joel & Croyle, Robert, T. (1984): Attitudes and attitude change. *Annual Review of Psychology*, 35, 395-426.

Cooper, Joel & Fazio, Russel, H. (1989): Research traditions, analysis, and synthesis: Building a faulty case around misinterpreted theory. *Personality and Social Psychology Bulletin*, 15,(4), 519-529.

Cooper, Joel & Scher, Steven, J. (1994): When do our actions affect our attitudes? In S. Shavitt & T.C. Brock (Eds.): Persuasion: Psychological insights and perspectives. Boston: Allyn & Bacon, 95-111.

Cotton, John, L. & Hieser, Rex, A. (1980): Selective exposure to information and cognitive dissonance. *Journal of Research in Personality*, 14,(4), 518-527.

Cummings, William, H. & Venkatesan, M. (1976): Cognitive dissonance and consumer behavior: A review of the evidence. *Journal of Marketing Research*, 13,(3), 303-308.

Davis, William, L. (1993): Economists' uses for cognitive dissonance: An interdisciplinary note. *Psychological Reports*, 73,(3, Pt 2), 1179-1183.

DeChenne, Timothy, K. (1980): Affective-cognitive consistency and self-conceptual structure. *Psychological Reports*, 46,(1), 163-170.

Dickerson, Chris, A.; Thibodeau, Ruth; Aronson, Elliot & Miller, Dayna (1992): Using cognitive dissonance to encourage water conservation. *Journal of Applied Social Psychology*, 22,(11), 841-854.

Eiser, John, Richard & van der Pligt, Joop (1988): Attitudes and decisions. London:Routledge

Falkowski, Andrzej (1990): Podobienstwo poznawcze w kategoryzacji percepcyjnej: Badania empiryczne w egzemplarzowym modelu kategoryzacji. *Przeglad Psychologiczny*, 33,(2), 293-312.

Fazio, Russel, H.; Zanna, Mark, P. & Cooper, Joel (1979): On the relationship of data to theory: A reply to Ronis and Greenwald. *Journal of Experimental Social Psychology*, 15,(1), 70-76.

Festinger, Leon; Schachter, Stanley & Gazzaniga, Michael (1989): Extending psychological frontiers: Selected works of Leon Festinger. New York:Russell Sage.

Frey, Dieter (1979): The effects of discrepant or congruent behavior and reward upon attitude and task attractiveness. *Journal of Social Psychology*, 108,(1), 63-73.

Frey, Dieter (1981): Reversible and irreversible decisions: Preference for consonant information as a function of attractiveness of decision alternatives. *Personality and Social Psychology Bulletin*, 7,(4), 621-626.

Frey, Dieter (1982): Different levels of cognitive dissonance, information seeking, and information avoidance. *Journal of Personality and Social Psychology*, 43,(6), 1175-1183.

Frey, Dieter & Wicklund, Robert, A. (1978): A clarification of selective exposure: The impact of choice. *Journal of Experimental Social Psychology*, 14,(1), 132-139.

Frey, Dieter; Kumpf, Martin; Irle, Martin & Gniech, Gisla (1984): Re-evaluation of decision alternatives dependent upon the reversibility of a decision and the passage of time. *European Journal of Social Psychology*, 14,(4), 447-450.

Garai, Laszlo (1979): Limits of social influence. *Przeglad Psychologiczny*, 22,(1), 3-16.

Gerard, Harold, B. (1992): Dissonance theory: A cognitive psychology with an engine. *Psychological Inquiry*, 3,(4), 323-327.

Geva, Aviva & Goldman, Arieh (1991): Duality in consumer post-purchase attitude. *Journal of Economic Psychology*, 12,(1), 141-164.

Goethals, George, R. (1992): Dissonance and self-justification. *Psychological Inquiry*, 3,(4), 327-329.

Goethals, George, R. & Cooper, Joel (1975): When dissonance is reduced: The timing of self-justificatory attitude change. *Journal of Personality and Social Psychology*, 32,(2), 361-367.

Green, Duane (1974): Dissonance and self-perception analysis of "forced compliance": When two theories make competing predictions. *Journal of Personality and Social Psychology*, 29,(6), 819-828.

Greenwald, Anthony, G. (1992): Dissonance theory and self theory: Fifteen more years. *Psychological Inquiry*, 3,(4), 329-331.

Greenwald, Anthony, G. & Ronis, David, L. (1978): Twenty years of cognitive dissonance: Case study of the evolution of a theory. *Psychological Review*, 85,(1), 53-57.

Heberlein, Thomas, A. & Black, J. Stanley (1981): Cognitive consistency and environmental action. *Environment and Behavior*, 13,(6), 717-734.

Higgins, E., Tory; Rhodewalt, Frederick & Zanna, Mark, P. (1979): Dissonance motivation: Its nature, persistence, and reinstatement. *Journal of Experimental Social Psychology*, 15,(1), 16-34.

Himmelfarb, Samuel & Arzai, Daniella (1974): Choice and source attractiveness in exposure to discrepant messages. *Journal of Experimental Social Psychology*, 10,(6), 516-527.

Himmelfarb, Samuel & Anderson, Norman, H. (1975): Integration theory applied to opinion attribution. *Journal of Personality and Social Psychology*, 31,(6), 1064-1072.

Hishinuma, Earl, S. (1987): Psychoanalytic and cognitive dissonance theories: Producing unification through the unifying theory review. In A.W. Staats & L.P. Mos (Eds.): Annals of theoretical psychology. New York:Plenum Press, 157-178.

Hoyos, Carl, Graf (1987):Motivation. In: G.Salvendy (Ed.): Handbook of human factors. New York: John Wiley & Sons, 108-123.

Insko, Chester, A.; Worchel, Stephen; Folger, Robert & Kutkus, Arunas (1975): A balance theory interpretation of dissonance. PSYCHOLOGICAL REVIEW, 82,(3),169-183.

Jastrebske, Ellen, M. (1974): Dissonance, knowledge about consequences, and task experience. *Psychological Reports*, 34,(2), 471-477.

Jussim, Lee (1992): Dissonance: A second coming? *Psychological Inquiry*, 3,(4), 332-333.

Kahle, Lynn, R. (1978): Dissonance and impression management as theories of attitude change. *Journal of Social Psychology*, 05,(1), 53-64.

Khokhlov, Nikolai, E. & Gonzalez, Arthur, E. (1973): Cross-cultural comparison of cognitive consistency. *International Journal of Psychology*, 8,(2), 137-145.

Kiesler, Charles, A. & Munson, Paul, A. (1975): Attitudes and opinions. *Annual Review of Psychology*, 26, 415-456.

Krause, Merton, S. (1973): Opinion change associated with dissonance and deviance. *Educational and Psychological Measurement*, 33, (4), 823-835.

Kruglanski, Arie, W. (1992): To carry the synthesis a little further. *Psychological Inquiry*, 3,(4), 334-336.

Kunda, Ziva (1992): Can dissonance theory do it all? *Psychological Inquiry*, 3,(4), 337-339.

Liska, Allen, E. (1974): Attitude-behavior consistency as a function of generality equivalence between attitude and behavior objects. *Journal of Psychology*, 86,(2), 217-228.

Lord, Charles, G. (1989): The "disappearance" of dissonance in an age of relativism. *Personality and Social Psychology Bulletin*, 15,(4), 513-518.

Lord, Charles, G. (1992): Was cognitive dissonance theory a mistake? *Psychological Inquiry*, 3,(4), 339-342.

Losch, Mary, E. & Cacioppo, John, T. (1990): Cognitive dissonance may enhance sympathetic tonus, but attitudes are changed to reduce negative affect rather than arousal. *Journal of Experimental Social Psychology*, 26, (4), 289-304.

Menasco, Michael, B. & Hawkins, Del.-I. (1978): A field test of the relationship between cognitive dissonance and state anxiety. *Journal of Marketing Research*, 15,(4), 650-655.

Miller, Duane, I.; Topping, Jeff, S. & Wells-Parker, Elisabeth, N. (1989): Ecological dissonance and organizational climate. *Psychological Reports*, 64,(1), 163-166.

Mwamwenda, Tuntufye, S. (1992): Studies on attainment of higher moral reasoning. *Psychological Reports*, 71,(1), 287-290.

Nemeth, Charlan & Endicott, Jeffrey (1976): The midpoint as an anchor: Another look at discrepancy of position and attitude change. *Sociometry*, 39,(1), 11-18.

Olshavsky, Richard, W. & Summers, John, O. (1974): A study of the role of beliefs and intentions in consistency restoration. *Journal of Consumer Research*, 1,(1), 63-70.

Pallak, Michael, S. & Kleinhesselink, Randall, R. (1976): Polarization of attitudes: Belief inference from consonant behavior. *Personality and Social Psychology Bulletin*, 2,(1), 55-58.

Perloff, Richard, M. (1993): The dynamics of persuasion. Hillsdale: Lawrence Erlbaum Associates.

Plous, Scott (1993): The psychology of judgement and decision making. New York: McGraw-Hill Book Company.

Quattrone, George, A. (1985): On the congruity between internal states and action. *Psychological Bulletin*, 98,(1), 3-40.

Rajecki, D., W. (1990): Attitudes. Sunderland:Sinauer Associates, Inc.

Ronis, David, L. & Greenwald, Anthony, G. (1979): Dissonance theory revised again: Comment on the paper by Fazio, Zanna, and Cooper. *Journal of Experimental Social Psychology*, 15,(1), 62-69.

Ross, Michael & Shulman, Ronald, F. (1973): Increasing the salience of initial attitudes: Dissonance versus self-perception theory. *Journal of Personality and Social Psychology*, 28,(1), 138-144.

Scheier, Michael, F. & Carver, Charles, S. (1980): Private and public self-attention, resistance to change, and dissonance reduction. *Journal of Personality and Social Psychology*,39,(3), 390-405.

Schlenker, Barry, R. (1992): Of shape shifters and theories. *Psychological Inquiry*, 3, (4), 342-344.

Schultz, Charles, B. (1974): The effect of confidence on selective exposure: An unresolved dilemma. *Journal of Social Psychology*, 94,(1), 64-69.

Shaffer, David, R. (1974): Attitude extremity as determinant of attitude change in the forced-compliance experiment. *Bulletin of the Psychonomic Society*, 3,(1B), 51-53.

Shaffer, David, R. (1975a): Some effects of initial attitude importance on attitude change. *Journal of Social Psychology*, 97,(2), 279-288.

Shaffer, David, R. (1975b): Some effects of consonant and dissonant attitudinal advocacy on initial attitude salience and attitude change. *Journal of Personality and Social Psychology*, 32,(1), 160-168.

Snyder, Mark & Tanke, Elizabeth, D. (1976): Behavior and attitude: Some people are more consistent than others. *Journal of Personality*, 44,(3), 501-517.

Steele, Claude, M. & Liu, Thomas, J. (1981): Making the dissonant act unreflective of self: Dissonance avoidance and the expectancy of a value-affirming response. *Personality and Social Psychology Bulletin*, 7,(3), 393-397.

Stroebe, Wolfgang & Diehl, Michael (1981): Conformity and counterattitudinal behavior: The effect of social support on attitude change. *Journal of Personality and Social Psychology*, 41,(5), 876-889.

Swann, William, B. (1992): Dance with the one who brung ya? *Psychological Inquiry*, 3,(4), 346-347.

Thibodeau, Ruth & Aronson, Elliot (1992): Taking a closer look: Reasserting the role of the self-concept in dissonance theory. *Personality and Social Psychology Bulletin*, 18,(5), 591-602.

Truzzi, Marcello (1973): The problem of relevance between orientations for cognitive dissonance theory. *Journal for the Theory of Social Behavior*, 3,(2), 239-247.

Vallacher, Robin, R.(1992): Come back to the future. *Psychological Inquiry*, 3,(4), 348-350.

Van-Avermaet, Eddy; McClintock, Charles, G. & Moskowitz, Joel (1978): Alternative approaches to equity: Dissonance reduction, pro-social motivation and strategic accomodation. *European Journal of Social Psychology*, 8,(4), 419-437.

Weiner, Michael, J. (1974): Cognitive dissonance or self perception, 1965-1974. *Personality and Social Psychology Bulletin*, 1,(1), 144-146.

Widgery, Robin, N. & Miller, Gerald, R. (1973): Attitude change following counterattitudinal advocacy: Support for the adversive consequences - interpretation of dissonance theory. *Journal of Communication*, 23,(3), 306-314.

Wilder, David, A.(1992): Yes, Elliot, there is dissonance. *Psychological Inquiry*, 3,(4), 351-352.

Williams, Robert, H. (1980): Attitude change and simulation games: The ability of a simulation to change attitudes when structured in accordance with either the cognitive dissonance or incentive models of attitude change. *Simulation and Games*, 11,(2), 177-196.

Woodyard, Howard, D. & Chris, Stephen, A. (1974): Self-perception and commitment to attitudes existing prior to manipulation. *Psychological Reports*, 35,(1, Pt 1), 217-218.

Wright, Edward, F.; Rule, Brendan, G.; Ferguson, Tamara, J. & McGuire, Gregory, R. (1992): Misattribution of dissonance and behaviour consistent attitude change. *Canadian Journal of Behavioural Science*, 24,(4), 456-464.

Zanna, Mark, P. & Sande, Gerald, N. (1987): The effects of collective actions on the attitudes of individual group members: A dissonance analysis. In: M.P. Zanna; J.M. Olson & C.P. Herman (Eds.): Social influence: The Ontario symposium. Hillsdale:Lawrence Earlbaum, 151-163.

Zimbardo, Philip, G. & Leippe, Michael, R. (1991): The psychology of attitude change and social influence. New York: McGraw-Hill.

Bibliography from PSYCLIT data base on environmental and ecological psychology:

Aitken, Campbell, K.; McMahon, Thomas, A.; Wearing, Alexander, J. & Finlayson, Brian, L. (1994): Residential water use: Predicting and reducing consumption. *Journal of Applied Social Psychology*, 24,(2), 136-158.

Arbuthnot, Jack & Lingg, Sandra (1975): A comparison of French and American environmental behaviors, knowledge, and attitudes. *International Journal of Psychology*, 10,(4), 275-281.

Arbuthnot, Jack (1977): The roles of attitudinal and personality variables in the prediction of environmental behavior and knowledge. *Environment and Behavior*, 9,(2), 217-232.

Arcury, Thomas, A.; Scollay, Susan, J. & Johnson, Timothy, P. (1987): Sex differences in environmental concern and knowledge: The case of acid rain. Sex-Roles, 16,(9-10), 463-472.

Arcury, Thomas, A. (1990): Environmental attitude and environmental knowledge. *Human Organization*, 49,(4), 300-304.

Arcury, Thomas, A. & Christianson, Eric, H. (1990): Environmental worldview in response to environmental problems: Kentucky 1984 and 1988 compared. *Environment and Behavior*, 22,(3), 387-407.

Austin, John; Hatfield, David, B.; Grindle, Angelica,C. & Bailey, Jon, S. (1993): Increasing recycling in office environments: The effects of specific, informative cues. *Journal of Applied Behavior Analysis*, 26,(2), 247-253.

Axelrod, Lawrence, J. & Lehman, Darrin, R. (1993): Responding to environmental concern: What factors guide individual action? *Journal of Environmental Psychology*, 13,(2), 149-159.

Bagozzi, Richard, P. & Dabholkar, Pratibha, A. (1994): Consumer recycling goals and their effect on decisions to recycle: A means-end chain analysis. *Psychology and Marketing*, 11,(4), 313-340.

Baldassare, Mark & Katz, Cheryl (1992): The personal threat of environmental problems as predictor of environmental practices. *Environment and Behavior*, 24,(5), 602-616.

Balderjahn, Ingo (1988): Personality variables and environmental attitudes as predictors of ecologically responsible consumption patterns. *Journal of Business Research*, 17,(1), 51-56.

Becker, Lawrence, J.; Seligman, Clive; Fazio, Russel, H. & Darley, John, M. (1981): Relating attitudes to residential energy use. *Environment and Behavior*, 13,(5), 590-609.

Boerschig, Sally & de Young, Raymond (1993): Evaluation of selected recycling curricula: Educating the green citizen. *Journal of Environmental Education*, 24,(3), 17-22.

Bright, Alan, D.; Manfredo, Michael, J.; Fischbein, Martin & Bath, Alistair (1993): Application of the theory of reasoned action to the National Park Service's controlled burn policy. *Journal of Leisure Research*, 25,(3), 263-280.

Bruvold, William, H. (1973): Belief and behavior as determinants of environmental attitudes. *Environment and Behavior*, 5,(2), 202-218.

Chaiken, Shelly & Baldwin, Mark, W. (1981): Affective-cognitive consistency and the effect of salient behavioral information on the self-perception of attitudes. *Journal of Personality and Social Psychology*, 41,(1), 1-12.

Connerly, Charles, E. (1986): Growth management concern: The impact of its definition on support for local growth controls. *Environment and Behavior*, 18,(6), 707-732.

Crabb, Peter, B. (1992): Effective control of energy-depleting behavior. *American Psychologist*, 47,(6), 815-816.

Dennis, Michael, L. & Soderstrom, E. Jonathan (1992): Effective dissemination of energy-related information: Applying social psychology and evaluation research. *American Psychologist*, 47,(6), 816-817.

Derksen, Linda & Gartrell, John (1993): The social context of recycling. *American Sociological Review*, 58,(3), 434-442.

de Young, Raymond (1986): Some psychological aspects of recycling: The structure of conservation satisfactions. *Environment and Behavior*, 18,(4), 435-449.

de Young, Raymond (1993): Changing behavior and making it stick: The conceptualization and management of conservation behavior. *Environment and Behavior*, 25,(4), 485-505.

de Young, Raymond; Duncan, Andrew; Frank, Jeffrey & Gill, Nancy (1993): Promoting source reduction behavior: The role of motivational information. *Environment and Behavior*, 25,(1), 70-85.

Diamond, William, D. & Loewy, Ben, Z. (1991): Effects of probabilistic rewards on recycling attitudes and behavior. *Journal of Applied Social Psychology*, 21,(19), 1590-1607.

Dickerson, Chris, A.; Thibodeau, Ruth; Aronson, Elliot & Miller, Dayna (1992): Using cognitive dissonance to encourage water conservation. *Journal of Applied Social Psychology*, 22,(11), 841-854.

Dresdner, Marion (1989-90): Changing energy end-use patterns as a means of reducing global-warming trends. *Journal of Environmental Education*, 21,(2), 41-46.

Dunlap, Riley, E. (1975): The impact of political orientation on environmental attitudes and actions. *Environment and Behavior*, 7,(4), 428-454.

Ellen, Pam (1994): Do we know what we need to know? Objective and subjective knowledge effects on pro-ecological behaviors. *Journal of Business Research*, 30,(1), 43-52.

Ford, Donald, H. (1993):The end does not justify the means. *Counseling Psychologist*, 21,(4), 618-623.

Fortner, Rosanne, W. & Mayer, Victor, J. (1991): Repeated measures of students marine and Great Lakes awareness. *Journal of Environmental Education*, 23,(1), 30-35.

Gamba, Raymond, J. (1994): Factors influencing community residents' participation in commingled curbside recycling programs. *Environment and Behavior*, 26,(5), 587-612.

Geller, E. Scott (1992): It takes more than information to save energy. *American Psychologist*, 47,(6), 814-815.

Gigliotti, Larry, M. (1992): Environmental attitudes: 20 years of change? *Journal of Environmental Education*, 24,(1), 15-26.

Greeley, Andrew (1993):Religion and attitudes toward the environment. *Journal for the Scientific Study of Religion*, 32,(1), 19-28.

Grieve, Katharine, W. & Van Staden, Frederik, J. (1985): Environmental concern in South Africa: An attitudinal study. *South African Journal of Psychology*, 15,(4), 135-136.

Griffin, Robert, J. (1989): Communication and the adoption of energy conservation measures by the elderly. *Journal of Environmental Education*, 20,(4), 19-28.

Hackett, Paul, M. (1992): The understanding of environmental concern. *Social Behavior and Personality*, 20,(3), 143-148.

Heberlein, Thomas, A. & Black, J. Stanley (1981): Cognitive consistency and environmental action. *Environment and Behavior*, 13,(6), 717-734.

Heberlein, Thomas, A. (1989): Attitudes and environmental management. *Journal of Social Issues*, 45,(1), 37-57.

Heckler, Susan, E. (1994): The role of memory in understanding and encouraging recycling behavior. *Psychology and Marketing*, 11,(4), 375-392.

Herrera, Marina (1992): Environmentalism and political participation: Toward a new system of social beliefs and values? *Journal of Applied Social Psychology*, 22,(8), 657-676.

Hines, Jody, M.; Hungerford, Harold, R. & Tomera, Audrey, N. (1986-87): Analysis and synthesis of research on responsible environmental behavior: A meta-analysis. *Journal of Environmental Education*, 18,(2), 1-8.

Hopper, Joseph, R. & Nielsen, Joyce, M. (1991): Recycling as altruistic behavior: Normative and behavioral strategies to expand participation in a community recycling program. *Environment and Behavior*, 23,(2), 195-220.

Horsley, A. Doyne (1977): The effects of a social learning experiment on attitudes and behavior toward environmental conservation. *Environment and Behavior* 9,(3), 349-384.

Howard, George, S. (1993): Ecocounseling psychology: An introduction and overview. *Counseling Psychologist*, 21,(4), 550-559.

Iwata, Osamu (1990): Relationships of proenvironmental attitudes to wildernism-urbanism and pro-preservation attitudes toward historical heritages. *Psychologia:An International Journal of Psychology in the Orient*, 33,(4), 203-211.

Iwata, Osamu (1992): The relationship of social evaluation and subjective sensitivity to environmental evaluation. 24th International Congress of Applied Psychology. *Psychologia: An International Journal of Psychology in the Orient*, 35,(2), 69-75.

Jackson, Edgar, L. (1985): Environmental attitudes and preferences for energy resource options. *Journal of Environmental Education*, 17,(1), 23-30.

Jackson, Edgar, L. (1986): Outdoor recreation participation and attitudes to the environment. *Leisure Studies*, 5,(1), 1-23.

Jordan, James, R.; Hungerford, Harold, R. & Tomera, Audrey, N. (1986): Effects of two residential environmental workshops on high school students. *Journal of Environmental Education*, 18,(1), 15-22.

Kallgren, Carl, A. & Wood, Wendy (1986): Access to attitude-relevant information in memory as a determinant of attitude-behavior consistency. *Journal of Environmental Social Psychology*, 22, (4), 328-338.

Kanagy, Conrad, L. & Willits, Fern, K. (1993): A "greening" of religion? Some evidence from a Pennsylvania sample. *Social Science Quarterly*, 74,(3), 674-683.

Katzev, Richard & Wang, Theodore (1994): Can commitment change behavior? A case study of environmental actions. *Journal of Social Behavior and Personality*, 9,(1), 13-26.

Kempton, Willett; Harris, Craig, K.; Keith, Joanne, G. & Weihl, Jeffrey, S. (1985): Do consumers know "what works" in energy conservation? *Marriage and Family Review*, 9,(1-2), 115-133.

Kinsey, Thomas, G. & Wheatley, Jack, H. (1984): The effects of an environmental studies course on the defensibility of environmental attitudes. Journal of Research in Science Teaching, 21,(7), 675-683.

Klein, Hans, J. (1983): Changes in attitudes and behavior by using solar energy. *Journal of Economic Psychology*, 4,(1-2), 167-181.

Krause, Daniel (1993): Environmental consciousness: An empirical study. *Environment and Behavior*, 25,(1), 126-142.

Kuhlemeier, J.-B. & Van den Bergh, H. (1992): Environmental knowledge, attitudes, and behavior and their interrelationship in secondary education. *Pedagogische Studien*, 69,(6), 438-452.

Lansana, Florence, M. (1992): Distinguishing potential recyclers from non-recyclers: A basis for developing recycling strategies. *Journal of Environmental Education*, 23,(2), 16-23.

Leeming, Frank, C.; Dwyer, William, O.; Porter, Bryan, E. & Cobern, Melissa, K. (1993): Outcome research in environmental education: A critical review. *Journal of Environmental Education*, 24,(4), 8-21.

Lord, Kenneth R. (1994): Motivating recycling behavior: A quasi-experimental investigation of message and source strategies. *Psychology and Marketing*, 11,(4), 341-358.

Lynne, Gary, D. & Rola, Leandro. R. (1988): Improving attitude-behavior prediction models with economic variables: Farmer actions toward soil conservation. *Journal of Social Psychology*, 128, (1), 19-28.

Maule, A.-J. (1985): The importance of an updating internal representation of the environment in the control of visual sampling. *Quarterly Journal of Experimental Psychology Human Experimental Psychology*, 37A,(4), 533-551.

McCarthy, John, A. & Shrum, L.-J. (1994): The recycling of solid wastes: Personal values, value orientations and attitudes about recycling as antecedents of recycling behavior. *Journal of Business Research*, 30,(1), 53-62.

McGuinness, James; Jones, Allan, P. & Cole, Steven, G. (1977): Attitudinal correlates of recycling behavior. *Journal of Applied Psychology*, 62,(4), 376-384.

McQuire, Randall, H. (1984): Recycling: Great expectations and garbage outcomes. *American Behavioral Scientist*, 28,(1), 93-114.

Messick, David, M. (1984): Solving social dilemmas:Individual and collective approaches. *Representative Research in Social Psychology*, 14,(2), 72-87.

Midden, Cees, J. & Ritsema, Beatrijs, S. (1983): The meaning of normative processes for energy conservation. *Journal of Economic Psychology*, 4,(1-2), 37-55.

Milliken, Frances, J. (1987): Three types of perceived uncertainty about the environment: State, effect, and response uncertainty. *Academy of Management Review*, 12,(1), 133-143.

Mio, Jeffery, S; Thompson, Suzanne, C. & Givens, Geoffrey, H. (1993): The common dilemma as metaphor: Memory, influence, and implications for environmental conservation. *Metaphor and Symbolic Activity*, 8,(1), 23-42.

Mosler, Hans-Joachim (1993): Self-dissemination of environmentally responsible behavior: The influence of trust in a commons dilemma game. *Journal of Environmental Psychology*, 13,(2), 111-123.

Newhouse, Nancy (1990): Implications of attitude and behavior research for environmental conservation. *Journal of Environmental Education*, 22,(1), 26-32.

Nietzel, Michael, T. & Winett, Richard, A. (1977): Demographics, attitudes, and behavioral responses to important environmental events. *American Journal of Community Psychology*, 5,(2), 195-206.

O'Brian, Thomas, P. & Zoumbaris, Sandra, J. (1993): Consumption behaviors hinge on financial self-interest. *American Psychologist*, 48,(10), 1091-1092.

O'Connor, Brian, P. & Tindall, David, B. (1990): Attributions and behavior in a commons dilemma. *Journal of Psychology*, 124,(5), 485-494.

Oskamp, Stuart; Harrington, Maura, J.; Edwards, Todd, C. & Sherwood, Deborah, L. (1991): Factors influencing household recycling behavior. *Environment and Behavior*, 23,(4), 494-519.

Ostman, Ronald, E. & Parker, Jill, L. (1986-87): A public's environmental information sources and evaluations of mass media. *Journal of Environmental Education*, 18,(2), 9-17.

Ostman, Ronald, E. & Parker, Jill, L. (1987): Impact of education, age, newspapers, and television on environmental knowledge, concerns and behaviors. *Journal of Environmental Education*, 19,(1), 3-9.

Parthasarathy, R. (1989): Psychological or attitudinal factors which influence the introduction of energy conservation technologies. *Abhigyan*, 36-47.

Pearson, Jane, L. & Ialongo, Nicholas, S. (1986): The relationship between spatial ability and environmental knowledge. *Journal of Environmental Psychology*, 6,(4), 299-304.

Perkins, Helena, M.; Crown, Elizabeth, M.; Rigakis, Katherine, B. & Eggertson, Bertha, S. (1992): Attitudes and behavioral intentions of agricultural workers toward disposable protective coveralls. *Clothing and Textiles Research Journal*, 11,(1), 67-73.

Pettus, Alvin, M. & Giles, Mary, B. (1987): Personality characteristics and environmental attitudes. *Population and Environment Behavioral and Social Issues*, 9,(3), 127-137.

Pierce, John, C.; Lovrich, Nicholas, P.; Tsurutani, Taketsugu and Abe, Takematsu (1987): Environmental belief systems among Japanese and American elites and publics. *Political Behavior*, 9,(2), 139-159.

Powers, Richard, B. (1985-86): The Commons Game:Teaching students about social dilemmas. *Journal of Environmental Education*, 17, (2), 4-10.

Prester, Georg; Rohrmann, Bernd & Schellhammer, Edith (1987): Environmental evaluations and participation activities: A social psychological field study. *Journal of Applied Social Psychology*, 17(9), 751-787.

Ray, John, J. (1981): Are environmental activists middle class? *Tableaus*, 152, 6-7.

Rozendahl, P.-J.; Ester, P. & Van der Meer, Fr. (1983): Environmental attitude as a determinant of individual environment-related behavior. *Gedrag Tijdschrift voor Psychologie*, 11,(2-3), 122-134.

Rutte, Christel, G., Wilke, Henk, A. & Messick, David, M. (1987): Scarcity or abundance caused by people or the environment as determinants of behavior in the resource dilemma. *Journal of Experimental Social Psychology*, 23,(3), 208-216.

Ryan, Chris (1991): The effect of a conservation program on schoolchildren's attitudes toward the environment. *Journal of Environmental Education*, 22,(4), 30-35.

Samdahl, Diane, M. (1989): Social determinants of environmental concern: Specification and test of the model. *Environment and Behavior*, 21,(1), 57-81.

Samuelson, Charles, D. & Biek, Michael (1991): Attitudes toward energy conservation: A confirmatory factor analysis. *Journal of Applied Social Psychology*, 21,(7), 549-568.

Satow, Aiko (1987): Four properties common among perceptions confirmed by a large sample of subjects: An ecological approach to mechanisms of individual differences in perception. *Perceptual and Motor Skills*, 64,(2), 507-520.

Schahn, Joachim & Holzer, Erwin (1990): Studies of individual environmental concern: The role of knowledge, gender, and background variables. *Environment and Behavior*, 22,(6), 767-786.

Scott, David & Willits, Fern, K.(1994): Environmental attitudes and behavior: A Pennsylvania survey. *Environment and Behavior*, 26,(2), 239-260.

Shepard, Clinton, L. & Speelman, Larry, R. (1985-86): Affecting environmental attitudes through outdoor education. *Journal of Environmental Education*, 17,(2), 20-23.

Sherkat, Darren,E. & Blocker, T. Jean (1993): Environmental activism in the protest generation:Differentiating 60's activists. *Youth and Society*, 25,(1), 140-161.

Shrum, L.-J. (1994): The recycling of solid wastes: Personal values, value orientations, and attitudes about recycling as antecedents of recycling behavior. *Journal of Business Research*, 30,(1), 53-62.

Sia, Archibald, P.; Hungerford, Harold, R. & Tomera, Audrey, N. (1985-86): Selected predictors of responsible environmental behavior: An analysis. *Journal of Environmental Education*, 17,(2), 31-40.

Siegfried, William, D.; Tedeschi, Richard, G. & Cann, Arnie (1982): The generalizability of attitudinal correlates of proenvironmental behavior. *Journal of Social Psychology*, 118,(2), 287-288.

Simmons, Deborah & Widmar, Ron (1990): Motivations and barriers to recycling: Toward a strategy for public education. *Journal of Environmental Education*, 22,(1), 13-18.

Simmons, Deborah, A. (1991): Are we meeting the goal of responsible environmental behavior? An examination of nature and environmental education center goals. *Journal of Environmental Education*, 22,(3), 16-21.

Smith, Jeffrey, M. & Bell, Paul. A. (1992): Environmental concern and cooperative-competitive behavior in a simulated commons dilemma. *Journal of Social Psychology*, 132,(4), 461-468.

Smith, Stephen, M.; Haugtvedt, Curtis, P. & Petty, Richard, E. (1994): Attitudes and recycling: Does the measurement of affect enhance behavioral prediction? *Psychology and Marketing*, 11,(4), 359-374.

Stahl, Abraham (1993): Educating for change in attitudes toward nature and environment among Oriental Jews in Israel. *Environment and Behavior*, 25,(1), 3-21.

Steininger, Marion & Voegtlin, Kathleen (1976): Attitudinal bases of recycling. *Journal of Social Psychology*, 100,(1), 155-156.

Stern, Paul, C.; Dietz, Thomas & Black, J. Stanley (1985-86): Support for environmental protection. The role of moral norms. *Population and Environment Behavioral and Social Issues*, 8,(3-4), 204-222.

Syme, Geoffrey,J.; Beven, Cynthia, E. & Sumner, Neil, R. (1993): Motivation for reported involvement in local wetland preservation: The roles of knowledge, disposition, problem assessment, and arousal. *Environment and Behavior*, 25,(5), 586-606.

Synodinos, Nicolaos, E. (1990): Environmental attitudes and knowledge: A comparison of marketing and business students with other groups. *Journal of Business Research*, 20,(2), 161-170.

Thompson, John, C. (1985): Environmental attitude survey of university students: 1971 vs. 1981. *Journal of Environmental Education*, 17, (1), 13-22.

Ungar, Sheldon (1994): Apples and oranges: Probing the attitude-behavior relationship for the environment. *Canadian Review of Sociology and Anthropology*, 31,(3), 288-304.

Van der Pligt, Joop (1985): Energy conservation: Two easy ways out. *Journal of Applied Social Psychology*, 15,(1), 3-15.

Van der Pligt, Joop; Eiser, J., Richard & Spears, Russell (1987): Comparative judgements and preferences: The influence of the number of response alternatives. *British Journal of Social Psychology*, 26,(4), 269-280.

Verplanken, Bas (1989): Involvement and need for cognition as moderators of beliefs-attitude-intention consistency. *British Journal of Social Psychology*, 28,(2), 115-122.

Vining, Joanne (1987): Environmental decisions: The interaction of emotions, information, and decision context. *Journal of Environmental Psychology*, 7,(1), 13-30.

Vining, Joanne (1992): Environmental emotions and decisions: A comparison of the responses and expectations of forest managers, an environmental group, and the public. *Environment and Behavior*, 24,(1), 3-34.

Vining, Joanne & Ebreo, Angela (1992): Predicting recycling behavior from global and specific environmental attitudes and changes in recycling opportunities. *Journal of Applied Social Psychology*, 22, (20), 1580-1607.

Weigel, Russel, H. & Weigel, Joan (1978): Environmental concern: The development of a measure. *Environment and Behavior*, 10,(1), 3-15.

Weigel, Russel, H. & Newman, Lee, S. (1976): Increasing attitude-behavior correspondence by broadening the scope of the behavioral measure. *Journal of Personality and Social Psychology*, 33,(6), 793-802.

Westphal, Joanne, M. & Halverson, Wesley, F. (1985-86): Assessing the long-term effects of an environmental education program: A pragmatic approach. *Journal of Environmental Education*, 17,(2), 26-30.

Williams, Elizabeth (1991): College students and recycling: Their attitudes and behaviors. *Journal of College Student Development*, 32,(1), 86-88.

Wysor, Martha, S. (1983): Comparing college students environmental perceptions and attitudes: A methodological investigation. *Environment and Behavior*, 15,(5), 615-645.

Yount, James, R. & Horton, Phillip, B. (1992): Factors influencing environmental attitude: The relationship between environmental attitude defensibility and cognitive reasoning level. *Journal of Research in Science Teaching*, 29, (10), 1059-1078.

Zube, Ervin, H.; Vining, Joanne; Law, Charles, S. & Bechtel, Robert, B. (1985): Perceived urban residential quality: A cross-cultural bi-modal study. *Environment and Behavior*, 17,(3), 327-350.

3

MODERATING FACTORS
IN AN ENVIRONMENTAL CONTEXT

Changing societal structures through education and opportunity

Even though the environmental crisis might currently seem to be a modern-day problem and, in this respect, prompt, under specific circumstances, demands for a return to olden and more "natural" ways, we tend to forget that even ancient society produced environmental catastrophies, as the following quotation - from a well-known authority - shows: *"The present Attica can only be seen as a relict of the original land. Beginning at their summits, the mountains have withered and what is left of their original substance is akin to a body that has been weakened by disease"* (Homer, 2500 B.C.).

In the middle ages - and, in some places up to now, or now again - (Verne, 1984), waste and sewage was led or put into the streets, with garbage lining the sidewalks and heaped up against the houses. Excrements from horses and other beasts of transport and labour filled the streets and when rain or snow fell, they became dangerous and slippery. Under such circumstances it is understandable that the wealthy class, especially its female members, would be tremendously dependent upon a whole array of servants just to live comfortably and safe. Moreover, the idea generally put forward by the church that wealth was a special favour that God gave to His chosen ones (something not reflected in the writings of Christ and misinterpreted by the clergy) must have helped such discrepancies function. There were large periods of time when it was generally accepted that washing was bad for your health and the poor must have had an awful time of it, considering that cities at that time were places of filth and stench, where sickness and the black plague (Ehrlich, 1976) were the order of the day.

Perhaps we give too little thought to it, that our present-day circumstances are not so much the result of people generally becoming more noble (although wide-spread education has helped to make us more aware and given us new opportunities before unbeknownst to man), but are mostly the outcome of a restructuring of society. If one follows developments in such war-ravaged places as Bosnia, Afghanistan and places in Africa, it becomes clear that primitive conditions can return quite easily to the most modern and beautiful of societies. A case in point in the importance of societal influence is a famous German politician. It is said of Bismarck, that he single-handedly forced the German people - up to that time reportedly bearded and good-natured but messy people - to become as clean, efficient and well-functioning a society as they are known to be today. His idea was literally breathtakingly simple. A special task-force would patrol the streets and, wherever they would find waste, would pick it up and throw it into the house nearest the heap. People very quickly learned to clean up the garbage adjacent to their homes.

Perhaps at some time in the future, mankind will look back on today and find it incomprehensible how we as a society could have had such a puzzling relationship to the environment, just as today we look back to the Middle Ages and find it hard to understand how people managed on a daily basis. Of course, then as now, there were alternatives. Poor country dwellers, for example, must have had less of the discomfort of poor city dwellers, have eaten mostly their own produce (even in the most oppressive systems) and have had more natural waste-recycling. Today, a citizen aware of environmental practices, has access to quite a few options, including - although often at an additional price - the use of alternative energies - lately and more increasingly - even outside of the Western countries. In his choices however, he is quite dependent upon industrial development and innovations. Whereas he can, if his finances allow it, or he is willing to make some sacrifices, buy many energy-efficient products, install wind- or solar energy into his house and even feed his surplus energy into the municipal circuit, studies show, as mentioned in Chapter Two, that generally only the well-to-do opt for any of these possibilities. The not so well off resident puts other priorities first (such as putting shoes on his children's feet!) and is dependent upon the system in order to be able to make his own meaningful contribution. To those with money, the use of the newest equipment and household apparatus can help to reduce energy and, of course, the monthly bill. It has been calculated that use of all available modern appliances could (in the USA) reduce electricity output by roughly 25% (Samuelson, 1991). Interestingly enough, the gadgets that fill out the modern kitchen and make it look elegant and busy are destined to help us conserve energy. Whereas a coffee machine saves 50% and an egg-cooker also 50% energy compared to a regular stove, a toaster even saves 70% compared to the oven (Middel, 1990). A new washing machine saves roughly 60% of the water and 45% of the energy of a ten year old machine (Hillebrand, 1991). The new equipment available in Germany is even estimated to allow for as much of a savings as 40% (Hessisches Ministerium, 1989). With time, of course, these new developments will become available to all.

However, many changes and innovations are not only conditional upon industrial improvements but upon the reorganization of societal and industrial institutions. For roughly 20 years the US invested 80% of its research money only into nuclear science and energy. However, this large amount of capital resulted, - with the advent of nuclear power plants - in the end, in an energy technology that did not even cover 20% of the energy needs of the United States (Vester, 1980).

At roughly the same time, industry reduced its specific energy requirements. In Germany, for example, the requirement was cut by 43% from 1955 to 1973 and by 33% from 1973 to 1988 (Necker, 1989) largely by increasing efficiency. Germany - having the most stringent environmental regulations for power stations in the world (Lennings, 1989) - also has the capacity to generate twice as much electricity today from a kilogram of coal as it did in 1950 (Schröder, 1987).

In order, however, to utilize alternative energies such as sun and wind, it was important to change the emphasis from centralized maintenance to decentralized solutions (Vester, 1980). First begun in the United States, with time this was even taken into consideration in city planning (O'Neill, 1981). For this, the concept of the net was changed from the design of supply only to a mixture of supply and receive, where sun or wind energy users were even able to feed their surplus energy back into the net and receive electricity when they needed it on cold or windless days. The money they were able to save made installation of alternative energy feasible. Through modern long-term storage of the energy (Vester, 1980) even a relatively cold country such as Germany could cover roughly half (Schmidtz, 1990) of its heating needs. This possibility is now beginning to be offered in Germany, with some cities even providing special programs for the installation of sun-energy collectors. Aachen for example, is helping its citizens install collectors with government funding and promises of tax-exemption and Potsdam is building housing-units incorporating alternative energy. Coupled with such auto-makers as Toyota, who is reportedly preparing to make an electric car available (now being tested in Japan) that can be charged at any household outlet, making it possible - in the near future - to keep your car in the garage while it is being recharged, such possibilities could mean very real changes for our global society. And, considering that the automobile is coupled with some of the worst environmental pollution (Evans, 1984; Sheeky, 1984; Thurau, 1991), with gasoline stations providing - through the cumulative effect of year-long spillage of oil-products - some of the most permanently damaged terrain in Germany (Miller, 1991), resistant even to most of the newer washing and treatment methods being specifically devised, any alteration would bring about much-needed change. That is, at least the many larger areas of permanently damaged soil at or surrounding these gas-station sites, could conceivably be avoided were we to power our cars entirely differently - not to mention the markedly lessened air-pollution resulting from this.

Beyond this relationship however, it is important to remember, that the use of the automobile extorts a high price from local communities and is often responsible for high municipal indebtedness (Vester, 1980) - creating thoroughfares becomes a priority where, instead, the building of a viable inner-city transportation net would be needed more, as oftentimes is the case when the amount of cars exceed the limited road space. Furthermore, production, dealership and use of the automobile represent a cycle which is only slowly accessible to innovations (Vester, 1980), due to the complexity not only of the automobile itself, but to its production, presentation and sale.

Moreover, the over-use of the automobile is not efficient. Trams are capable of carrying 20 times as many passengers as a tightly packed freeway with 1,5 passengers per car at a speed of 130 kilometres per hour and 80 meter distance between the cars (Vesster, 1980). In addition to this, most cars stand idle in driveways, parking lots or garages a good deal of the day. Statistically (according to an unpublished study by Daimler-Benz) the largest amount of driving is done within 50 kilometers of the home, and within the speed of 25-50 kilometers per hour, making this type of transportation expensive and inefficient, both for the individual and the community. Even in Germany however, where there is a large and efficient public-transportation net, many drivers still find it inconvenient to use (Muscheid, 1989) and would support its expansion and reduction of prices (Muscheid, 1989). Arguably however, perhaps drivers are waiting for an alternative as comfortable as the automobile and will take nothing less than luxury in order to be weaned from the use of the car.

For, instead of the public being responsible for environmental protection, it rather needs to be educated to utilize the possibilities inherent in every situation or process. When it is, the prospects sometimes surpass even the most optimistic prognosis. Such is, for example, the case regarding the recycling of goods in Germany. For the past several years, the disposal of waste has been a difficult problem for Germany, with some of the material being dumped into poorer countries - such as Poland. Lately, however, it has been reported, that, in some cases, and particularly in some cities, where recycling functions better than in others, the demand exceeds the supply. That means therefore, that there is not enough waste to fuel the existing recycling programs. In lieu of the shortage, it has even been reported that some cities are threatening suit of those companies that regularly export their excess pulp etc., claiming that local needs are more important and should be served first! If the trend continues, Germany could be importing waste to fuel its extensive recycling projects, which often utilize old and used material instead of raw natural resources (Schaible-Rapp, 1988; VEBA, 1990) for production, or which refashion or remake the same products again from waste (such as glass etc.) or even convert used matter into energy. This type of action shows some very forceful examples of successful waste and recycling programs and of what good reorganization, municipal regulation and consolidation - coupled with innovative technology - can do.

Cultural, social and functional units and their influence upon environmental habits [1]

Environmental degradation in Poland

In the past few years, Poland has taken great steps to control the terrible environmental destruction that was largely incurred during the period of Soviet ideology, (Kramer, 1993; Peitsch, 1991 and Pietras & Pietras, 1991). Unfortunately, in areas such as Tarnobrzeg, in the southern part of Poland, landscapes that look like the surface of the moon are not so easily and cheaply transformed into lush gardens. Particularly strip mining and the burning of coal with a high content of sulfur have contributed much to the overall damage, but the list is long. Where plants have not been modernized, production - with old, sub-standard equipment - can take as much as 30% more energy than capitalistic production (Öschlies, 1987). Indeed, where there is a shortage of ecological re-use of such main elements of life such as air, water and land - to which such problems as the lack of filters as well as the need of clean and efficiently distributed technology and energy contribute their part - the poignant truths of the importance of ecological balance have unfortunately needed to be made clear to the concerned residents (Biela, 1991). At present, over 300 established non-governmental environmental groups and institutions, frequent coverage in the media and international concern of groups such as Greenpeace are doing their best to place the train of ecological soundness back on its tracks.

Issues of pollution

Unfortunately, in the present era of political changes, much decision-making is often left directly to the development in industry itself, which has oftentimes dismissed the effects of the more efficient use of filters and more modern methods of production (Ochrona Srodowiska, 1992) as well in the new areas of production and the manufacture of polluting products. Oftentimes, money is spent at the wrong end, for example, in the proportionately high wages of managing personnel or according to the personal whims of directors. Too often, because of government subsidies, resources are exploited at market prices lower than the real value of the item (Jarzebski, 1985; Öschlies,

---

[1] The pages in the following section are part of an article printed in the conference proceedings of ELMECO, (International Conference on Environmental Protection), held in Kazimierz 8-9 September, 1994.

1987). Product management is often either not well organized or nonexistant and, as a result, money for re-investment, such as in modern technology, is not made available. Also, as a result of western influence in media and consumption, some products that are "recognized" as being ecologically sound, renewable or recyclable and are advertised as such, do not find the necessary facilities for their proper utilization present in Poland yet. There has, for example, been a steady increase in the use of plastic materials in the last four years, most notably replacing a well-functioning recycling system using glass bottles. While technically these products are recyclable, to date only two of the necessary facilities exist at this point in the whole of Poland and much of the waste material ends up in public dumps contributing to the problem of waste.

Still, it is hard to condemn the above development, for the products at present available in plastic containers are produced and manufactured according to higher standards of cleanliness and hygiene than was true of the older versions. These were sometimes extremely unhealthy and unfit for immediate consumption: In the beginning of the 90's it was still necessary, for example, to boil all water and milk. Even a small amount of un-boiled milk added to coffee could bring on severe stomach/ intestinal pains and complications. This has changed since then and milk is now fit for consumption directly at purchase.

In Germany however, particularly efforts toward unification of Europe have been an important motor for environmental rehabilitation (Umweltbewußtes Europa, 1990). Often, advancement was made especially through new and innovative laws that sought to encompass European problems (Umweltbewußtes Europa, 1990). Indeed, it seems that environmental laws have been more effective than specific consumer awareness efforts in bringing forth positive results (Preuss, 1991), although generally a certain level of awareness must be present in society in order to force judicial action, which again is often dependent upon legislature periods and political popularity (Stölting, 1991). It is unfortunate that, within this context, effective action has taken so long in forthcoming, as societal awareness and even the establishment of scientific research dates back at least to the 1970's (Grob, 1991). However, just as political impulses seem at present to produce the most effective movements, they can also become a hindrance to effectual action (Ausubel, 1980; O'Neill, 1981; Rhode, 1987; Seibold, 1985; Tomain, 1989; Vester, 1980 and Walter, 1984).

As in many areas, so also in environmental protection, mankind sometimes must be forced to do what is for their own good. Greater efforts towards ecological conservation have thus produced the effect that the utilization of new appliances generally saves money (Hessisches Ministerium, 1989; Hillebrand, 1991 and Samuelson, 1981) and has allowed industrial production to increase without a comparable increase in the use of energy (Vester, 1980). An emphasis on savings and conservation has also recently characterized the use of the utilities (Necker,

1989; Economic Commission for Europe, 1985; Lennings, 1989; Schröder, 1991; Vereinigung Deutscher Elektrizitätswerke, 1989 and Anderson, 1981) such as electricity and heating etc.

Unfortunately, judging from the literature (Holzapfel & Vahrenkamp, 1993), for every environmentally affirmative action, there are changes in the advancement of technology, the structure of production or political reversals of attitude that seem to bestow us with other dilemmas. Wheras in Germany the green recycling circle has put pressure on industry to change its means of production, causing some very effective changes (see last section) dangerous waste is often still - for a price - dumped into the foreign harbors of poorer countries, ignoring the fact that pollution knows no borders. Furthermore, in the same context, the circle of production suppliers keeps increasing, for industry has found it cheaper to delegate tasks and assign materials to suppliers and then to assemble or gather, distribute and market themselves (Holzapfel & Vahrenkamp). That this causes more need for transportation of materials and thus more pollution and obstruction of roads and passages, seems of secondary concern. An energy tax that would compensate for this movement would seem to need to be calculated separately for every firm. Also, unfortunately, to date, most transportation in Europe is still done by private trucking, as trains are not as efficient, fast or direct as private forms of transportation. These however, especially through the continued expanse of their use, are still very far from their optimal environmental rehabilitation.

Lastly, both countries suffer from what is perhaps one of the underlying factors of pollution and environmental degradation. Regardless of whatever form of political commitment the two countries might have, common to both capitalism and socialism is that they are merely two variants of a materialism in which natural elements such as air and water and land are still free to be used and degraded and where often too little responsiblity is taken by the user (Peitsch, 1991), be he private, public or industrial [2].

Patterns inherent in capitalistic societies

Many western societies, although by law conceived of as democratic, have since succumbed more fully to capitalism and in many instances, democracy has led to structures supporting the status quo of society and the making of wealth. In many countries, if the poor are lucky, some small amount filters down to them eventually. In many respects, European citizens are luckier than this and through the fact that existent programs are slowly being extended to the Central European states, both Germany and Poland face a more stable future than many countries do.

---

[2] This concluds ELMECO, 1994.

Equally, in much of Western Europe and certainly in Germany, there is not the degradation of whole landscapes, as is characteristic of many societies (including the United States and Russia for example), as forestry, mining and other uses of natural resources are done using the principles of gardening - the balance of nature is taken into account at all times. Moreover, the poor, who have access to many societal programs are not necessitated - as they are still in Poland - to use natural resources for their heating, thus also contributing to natural devastation (as is also the case in Africa, for example). Nevertheless, there are certain problems in European societies that still cause predicaments for environmental protection. Although many of them have more recently received a more mixed form of government, utilizing many principles of industrialism and socialism together, still structures do not allow for much real exercise of the principles of democracy, even in most of the more modern European systems.

Many programs for example, although helpful to parts of society, such as the agricultural or health sector, in utilizing resources and money that is not dependent upon market regulations or accessible to more control, are capable of existing only for the benefit of a small amount of people and not society as a whole. These need to be changed into programs responsive to the good of all people. Moreover, while many products are manufactured at society's expense - the agricultural sector of many countries, while, as mentioned, heavily subsidized, uses products that have been proven harmful to health, are polluting air, water and land and offer us fruit, vegetables and meat that are often harmful to consumption - as the recent beef scandal in England has proven - they are independent of society's control. Thus, in many respects, it is unreasonable to demand that the consumer become an active agent for the promotion of ecological products, because he has no real control over what is being produced, while often, what he doesn't buy is subsidized anyway (Tomain, 1987). Also, for many products the market price does not reflect the natural price (Levin, 1986). While the market price mostly reflects the value of the labor and capital that go into its production, the natural price would include the calculation of the recyclability of the natural resources that the product has used, the amount of pollution it has generated and the amount that the quality of life has suffered in the immediate area surrounding the production site. Agriculture is no exception to this, sometimes creating extreme pollution in ground and water through excess fertilization and other modern methods of husbandry. Perhaps a good way to increase awareness in this respect is to begin to calculate the "per capita environmental harm" (Yearley, 1996) that is done. This needs then to be assigned to either the areas of industry, private persons, technology and the state itself, making it clearer who is responsible, who benefits financially, who is the user or consumer of the product and who suffers from the pollution, because in many cases these are all different groups or individuals. Then, a comparison between countries would be possible and we could finally not only calculate the amount of pollution but also its economic as well as human aspects.

Work paradigms and the environment in Poland

Early in the 1990's, it was very apparent that Poland had undergone an intense and prolonged period of exposure to pollution. Although most large firms had their own departments for the environment, ergonomics, and work hygiene, with one specialist of each allocated from one to several thousands of workers, the extent of the damage told quite another story. Furthermore, at the beginning of the transformation, the old socio-political structures prevented any effective change from taking place. These, and many additional predicaments, were the legacy of the communists and their nearly 50 years of mismanagement.

It is believed that the published literature in the field of work psychology to some extent reflects the reformations that have taken place, both in the mentality of the Polish people and in their various institutions. For a specifically compiled review of Polish literature on the environment, please turn, in addition, to Chapter One.

Although even the 1980's saw a significant number of publications on topics familiar to the western reader, the larger amount has been published in the last five years. Whereas such typically capitalistic themes as the "psychology of serving clients" was researched as early as 1985 by Wlodzimierz, and Ratajczak published her research on honesty and conscientiousness at the work-place in 1988, the majority of articles at this time, such as "Units and groups in the work process", Karpowicz, (1986); "Fundamentals of work psychology", Pietrasieski (1988); "Influences of groups on the work process", Daszkowski, (1988); "Man and his work environment" Karney, (1988); "The work situation and its psychological consequences", Somczynski (1988); and "Psychological functions of an electrical plant", Geras (1987) did not particularly reflect more western ideas of the work-place and still contained an aura of the research typical for communism. Even further works such as, the "Humanization of highly complex work-tasks", Szmidt (1987); "Formal signs of the system as a measurement of the development of the individual", Gasiul, 1987; "Work-groups and motivation", Kozdrzaj, (1988); "Work stress and its signs", Barczyk (1988); "Psychology of work and management", Bartkowiak et al., (1989); "Psychosocial acitivity in work", Milczarek, (1989); "Problems of general psychology and work psychology", Duralska et al., (1989); "Directors in 1988", Biedermann et al., (1989); "Operationalizing psychology", Hornowska (1989); "Organizational stress", Borucki (1988);

"Empirical research", Noworol (1989); "Psychology and sociology of work", Manek (1989); "Elements of psychology and sociology of work", Ityk (1989) and "Study of the fundamentals of psychology, sociology and organization of work", Kowalczuk (1989), could be considered rather interim and not yet completely westernized.

For all of the other faults of western societies, the literature, research and application of findings in the area of work-psychology have, since the days of its inception, contributed much to the alleviation of human suffering and have, likewise, added a significant contribution to the humanization, organization and workability of the everyday work-place.

Whereas from the beginning, work-science in the West was used directly in an engineering context and - albeit at first needlessly embellished and ornate, hence rigid and inflexible - it has since become a tool of benevolent influence in many different areas. In the East however, communist ideology oftentimes supplanted important findings and, where this was not true, the unfortunate limitations of everyday life and the narrowness forced upon it by the inelasticity of central planning did not permit it to become any instrument of real change in the work-place; this is why current western work-analysis questionnaires that were translated into Polish proved to be ineffective (a fact that is shown in the content of the literature as well as the lack of progress in the industry of that time - well known from the tales of the frustration that work-psychologists had to cope with): paradigms and settings of work-places were so dissimilar to the West. Anyone who has attempted to compare work-places in, let us say, the US, Germany and Holland, to those of Poland, the Czech Republic and Bulgaria, will verify how fundamentally different work-places were, even of the very same branch of industry.

Up to the present day in certain firms - whereas privatization has, to a great extent, been allowed to fundamentally change industrial complexes - one can still find production units that look like bad reproductions of western units as they did 50 years ago. It must be said that in Poland, although public opinion varies on this matter, it has been primarily attempted to let privatization change as many industrial firms as possible, where changes have not taken place, it has often been a lack of money and/ or offers from the West. Yet even in those units that have been changed by Western companies, much of the old mentality is still prevalent. Many work-places - up until 1997 - did not provide for any ordered breaks from work, did not provide for places of refreshment and leisure and generally, although, as mentioned above, departments for environment, work hygiene and ergonomics existed, these were not able to make significant contributions to the course of the average work-day. Moreover, continuing education is neither viewed nor provided for in the same way, as it is, for example, in Germany.

Although the Poles have speedily incorporated new ideas of capitalism such as community and corporate bonds and stocks, the options of re-funding that this generally provides cannot necessarily be accessed by those responsible for the humanization of work-places, exchange of machinery, or indeed, of a change of workers rights, all of which often still need to be fought for. In the present situation of everyday economic reality in Poland however, workers, at present, only demonstrate, lobby and strike for more money or stabilization of their work-places.

The 1990's have, so far, added a good amount of new ideas to the literature. Such titles as "How to become a manager tomorrow", Karney (1991); "The psychological problems of choosing a job", Czerwieska (1991); "Shaping work elements in a firm", Gruszczieska-Malec (1991); were among the first titles published. Of further interest are such titles as: "Hazards of the work place", Tyszki (1992); "Lublin questionnaire of work-place analysis", Biela (1992); "Dinosours in our midst - or the remnants of communism" Bernstein et al., (1992); "Special problems of methods and research", Aranowski (1992); "Self-process and change within work tasks", Gaz (1993); "Managers in a process of change", Karczmarczuk et al., (1993) and "Three steps to a career", Makowski (1995). Additional titles include such topics as morality in politics, (Dabrowski, 1991); social perceptions, (Golieska, 1993); psychological methods, (Sosnowski et al., 1993); success and careers, (Gondzik, 1993); mechanisms of motivation in work, (Hirszel, 1993); management (Cenin, 1990; Tokarski, 1990; translation from the English by Stewart, 1992 and translation from the English by Conor et al., 1992; Kozusznik, 1994); sociology and psychology of work, (Bugla, 1990; Witkowski, 1990; Bugiel et al., 1993; Manek, 1994); stress in professional work, (Biela, 1990); humanization and architecture, (Sparkowski, 1990); a psychological model of the effectivity of work, (Gliszczieski, 1991); psychogy of work, (Dudek, 1992; Ratajczak, 1991); social elements of work places, (Jacher, 1992; Januszek, 1992); psychohygienics of work, (Kaliciuk, 1991); perception in social situations, (Golieska, 1993); liking business, (Sedlaka, 1994); organizational aspects of the work process, (Gros, 1994; Tokarski, 1994); adaptation of a questionnaire on personality, (Drwal, 1995); psychology of work and unemployment, (Terelak, 1993); playing and working, (Jachimska, 1994); controlling work and one's own life, (Lakein, 1994, translation from the English) and how to interest students in the psychology of work, (Ludkiewicz, 1994).

Whereas Germany has experienced several decades of humanization of the work-place, both in word and in deed, many elements of the work-place are new in Poland and just beginning to be introduced. Such Polish industry as is dependent upon an image of cleanliness and must take a standpoint of environmental benignancy - as, for example, the manufacturers of cosmetics - is, of course, advancing more rapidly in its progress than other branches, but, in general, especially as far as small and middle-sized firms are concerned - whether newly privatized or still state-owned - environmental, as well as humanization and work-task concerns are among the last points to be taken seriously. In a country where thousands of trees are felled illegally each year, most often taken from conservation areas where the object has been to preserve especially rare timber, because many people are unable or unwilling to pay the price of coal, let alone electricity or gas, perhaps the quickest methods of general education will be via television, bringing these issues home to the everyday individual. Poland is still, in many respects, especially as far as the mentality of the average person is concerned, a poor country and it will take at least one generation in order to create a new understanding in the average Pole in this respect.

Components of the environmental crisis in Poland

Estimates - according to the World Bank - of environmental damage in Poland can be summarized to include mainly six different areas:
– safe water and sanitation;
– poor management of solid and hazardous wastes;
– inadequate control of pollution from vehicles and industrial facilities;
– accidents due to congestion and crowding;
– occupation of environmentally sensitive lands; and finally,
– a loss of cultural resources and open space (Environmental Department Dissemination Notes, 1995).

Specifically concerning the third item, in Poland, the **"health costs of air pollution are estimated to be at least 1 to 1.5 percent of the GDP"** (Environmental Department Dissemination Notes, 1995). In addition to the above mentioned points, indoor air pollution from the burning of coal is still a severe health hazard in Central and East European Countries, including Poland, (Environmental Department Dissemination Notes, 1995).

Specific difficulties relating to further urbanization

From the beginning of the communist influences, Poland has seen an increase in urban population. The 1950's saw many changes in policy toward agrarian areas, such as the formation of the PGR or collective farms. When Polish farmers, especially in the central and eastern regions of Poland, boycotted these types of establishments, they were largely resolved into smaller farms (except in the formerly German areas) and mostly turned over to individual farmers (Nagiecki, 1996). With restructurization however, had come an influx in the population of urban areas, a trend that has continued until today.

Estimates are, that this will increase within the context of expanding capitalization. Whereas western investment has brought mixed blessings, new standards for products and produce have influenced many market areas (Nagiecki, 1996). However, as the trend continues, increasingly, small farmers will find their financial limits, forcing them off the land and into the cities: a progress that will favor larger farms and more mechanization in the outcome. This tendency is well under way in Lublin, a city traditionally surrounded by farm-land. Estimates are that the city may have increased by as much as one-fourth within the last six years, although the large number of illegal workers from the Ukraine make the exact figures difficult to calculate.

Within this context it is important to remember that such trends not only increase the costs of urban developmental pollution, but also tend to swell the ranks of the unemployed. In a mileu where many are seeking employment and not all finally find a place to work - and that in a country where employment was seen as a basic human right for roughly three generations (Poles marry and establish families rather early in life: whereas the WW2 generation is still alive, their grandsons and daughters are now starting to - or seeking - work) - one cannot reasonably expect workers to care about environmental standards. As was mentioned before, they are careless about work safety, largely unaware of health requirements and receive little compensation for damage to their health. It is one of the ironies of history that capitalism has proved to be more benevolent to its working population than communism ever was; indeed, health statistics prove disparaging differences in disease and mortality (with Polish men dying an average of 10-15 years earlier than Germans do).

The following two studies however, should show whether Polish workers, although confronted with the reality of everyday circumstances, do inform themselves on environmental topics, have hopes for improvement in the future and, given half a chance at increasing the quality of their life, are willing to comply with new standards. Perhaps then, they are just as upset about environmental degradation as their German counterparts but must contend with different socio-political realities to deal with their environment.

Pertinent environmental issues concerning local industry

Inspection of several local plants in the beginning of the 1990's, including, among others, the Power Plant, the local car factory, the tractor and farm instruments factory and the municipal bus and transportation facility, showed a severe simplicity and outmodedness in the instruments and work tools used, an aura of untidiness, stain and squalidness of the work context and, in many areas, a lack or inefficiency of work organization. Thus, very often piles of finished pieces could be found lying in the middle of production areas, silently rusting.

Whereas work organization seems to have changed in all factories that were privatized, where one can no longer find such things as rusting parts and there is an atmosphere of sometimes frenzied production, some factories have, of course, remained state-owned. To illustrate the differences more closely, let us compare two of the above mentioned factories in Lublin: the car factory and the tractor and farm parts factory.

Lublin Car Factory - FS (now Daewoo)

Even in the beginning of 1994, an inspection of the car factory, as had been possible one and two years before, was impossible. New investments from the West defined an atmosphere of secrecy, with guards standing their shift even in the main office building, where primarily secretaries and clerks worked in the offices adjacent to the senior directors of the company. Entrance was conditioned upon personal contact or context of the visit, whereas before, visitors, especially from the West had been welcomed and provided with careful and considerate hospitality. The change had come about with the beginning of more close cooperation of FS with its partner plant Fiat in Italy, and the change to more modern production. With the advent of Daewoo however, a South Korean mega-company, two years later, and their millions of investment, with an additional billion promised in the future, has caused another generation of significant changes to influence the already existing alterations.

Like in the other major Daewoo investment in Warsaw, the Korean company has brought many new innovations in management, organization and production. New models are already starting to be sold now, after most of the present stock of Fiat models has been reduced, and, with them, there has been restructuring of entire work stations. New and modern technology has replaced aging, old-fashioned and out-of-date equipment and with it comes a more efficient use of energy and raw materials. It has been estimated that "**production processes in these countries have a relatively high raw material and energy intensity, compared with relevant technologies in developing countries**" (Nowak, 1993). Therefore, economical feasibility dictates many changes right at the beginning of a takeover by a Western company. Indeed, in relation to big industry, most of the impact made upon the environment is made by Western financing, cross-cultural cooperation, joint-venture business dealings or environmental projects, usually also funded by the West (if anything, Poland only matches funding to some percent).

In this respect, Poland is in the fortunate position to be one of the Central European Countries courted by the West, providing it with the possibility to join - at least theoretically - as many Western Capitalistic unions, institutions, joint interest groups and clubs as there are in existence. Thus, from the requirements of the European Bank for Reconstruction and Development, used to determine environmental impact assessments in relevant legislation, through the demands of the World Bank for certain environmental standards, to OECD (Organization for Economic Cooperation and Development) and European Union directives for legislation from banking, to requirements for measurably cleaner air and water, waste-management programs and other municipal actions related to environmental standards set by these groups, Poland has a variety of standards to meet, all designed to make it a cleaner, more efficient country.

The profits for the workers are often immediate. Because of pressure from the West, Poland is rapidly undergoing legislative changes. One of these is the new law going into effect in 1997, that for the first time guarantees a break during the working day. Not previously regulated by the Labor Code, (Fogelman, 1996), it guarantees 15 minutes of rest where the work day lasts at least 6 hours. New vacation, overtime and worker benefits are also included in this legislation.

As far as companies are concerned however, different firms can profit in very contradicting ways. As, for example, certain consumer products such as the automobile have become as expensive in Poland as they are anywhere else in the world, a marked difference exists now from the roughly $800 needed to buy a Polish made car five years ago. This makes a firm producing such products more interesting for Western investments and thus, internal restructuring. In addition, consumer demands for gas, electricity and other services has also prompted an adjustment of prices to a more Western niveau. The companies concerned with such production are the most likely to be financed in joint-venture and unfortunately, in today's market realities of the present-day Poland, this also means the most effective and fastest change in every regard, including aspects of the environment.

Lublin tractor factory - URSUS

Tractors are certainly not as widely in use as cars are and consumer demand is undoubtedly not as high: thus, the marketability of this product may not completely be compared to that of the automobile. Moreover, as mentioned above, Polish farms, traditionally never high in technology-use, are undergoing changes, whereby the large PGRs no longer function the way they used to and the small farms are going through their own metamorphosis, not a very stable market under the best of conditions. However, internal as well as external factors have contributed to the fact that this factory is not producing on the same standard as the above-mentioned car factory. One of the problems lie in the fact that it is still state-owned, but privatization of firms has come about directly as a result of their attractiveness to outside buyers.

Of comparable size to FS, Ursus was an important firm in the communist era, producing within a certain market where it monopolized manufacture and clientele was guaranteed. What has happened since the change however, is typical of many - to date - state-owned firms: where the jobs of thousands of workers are at stake, the state (and particularly the city of Lublin) is reluctant to close down a large factory, even in the face of large financial losses. At Ursus however, the change in Polish politics was never accompanied by a change in management and production and, for at least the last few years, the company has had to compete against smaller and more efficient up-starts. One competing company for instance, manufacturing largely the same kind of material but with more Western style models and more reliable products, has largely turned development and construction over to the Ukrainians, who are cheaper than the Poles and only assembles the parts in Poland. They sell at competitive prices largely taking the market away from such large, inefficient firms as Ursus. Unfortunately however, as mentioned, a company such as this is forced to keep producing because of the jobs at stake, and, in addition to this must be supported by government financing because of the politics of seeking the least embarassing solutions to problems, especially where a large amount of workers are concerned. As a result, this firm keeps producing in an outmoded, polluting way.

Conclusion

Work content and context can not even now be compared in the two neighboring countries of Germany and Poland - Polish employees are only now starting to work in more modern, safer, more humane jobs and are beginning to see worker benefits and rights such as have been common in Germany for decades. Several years ago, even this was not true.

It must be noted within this context, then, that Poles, caught up in the much higher risks of everyday life in Poland, would likely respond to environmental risk differently than the Germans. In order to make a case in point: the Dowayo people of Cameroon, for example, are completely assured - to the point of not understanding white anthropologists reactions - that cobras are entirely harmless (Berreby, 1996). Within the theory of cognitive dissonance, there could be several explations for this: two come to mind immediately. First, peoples immediately confronted with danger on a daily basis, generally develop coping strategies and capacities for reducing fear that others who are not confronted with these dangers - logically - do not have. This in itself reduces fear of impending danger. Action would be one capacity that would be a sensible solution. In the second case however, where the risk is too high and action is almost inevitably doomed to failure, that is, the risk cannot be influenced by human action, it must then be minimized in order to reduce the stress of everyday life to a point where life again becomes liveable. There is ample evidence in the risk literature for this kind of relationship pertaining to pollution and environmental hazards.

This kind of relationship exists also in Poland: tall stories abound to illustrate the physical prowess of Poles, especially of those who live in the country. That a man can carry a horse home on his shoulders seems to come as no surprise and is - to date even - easily believed. One must of course argue that the population in Lublin - surrounded by country - and a part of what the Poles themselves call the second Poland, or Poland category B, have a different mentality than those living in Warsaw, Cracow or in those cities bordering the West.

This type of belief, however, seems to be just another example of how people, having to cope with unknown and relatively high risks, not only negate these risks but invent life strategies that in reality are totally ineffective in dealing with these risks. Must not such type of mentality, however, especially in lieu of the changing structures of modern society and the necessity of coping with entirely different problems today, be understood and if possible changed in order to guarantee all peoples a more satisfactory existence within the possibilities of a life that would guarantee prosperity and happiness for all humans on this planet if we could only utilize what we know.

REFERENCES

Allport, G.W. (1935): Attitudes. In: C. Murchison (Ed.): Handbook of social psychology. Worcester: Clark University Press, 798-844.

Anderson, J. M. (1981): Ecology for Environmental Sciences: Biosphere, Ecosystems and Man. New York: John Wiley.

Auhagen, Ann, Elisabeth & Neuberger, Karin (1994): Verantwortung gegenüber der Umwelt: Eine Studie über umweltbewusstes Handeln. Gruppendynamik, 25,(3), 319-332.

Ausubel, J. (1980): Economics in the Air - An Introduction to Economic Issues of the Atmosphere and Climate. In: J. Ausubel & A. K. Biswas (Eds.): Climatic Constraints and Human Activities. Oxford: Pergamon Press, 13-59.

Bernstein, Janis (1995): The Urban Challenge in National Environmental Strategies. Environment Department Dissemination Notes, Number 31, August.

Berreby, David (1996): Bushed. The Sciences, July/August, 41-46.

Biela, Adam (1991): Initiating of the local ecological activity (Sejmik) at heavily polluted areas. Lublin: Catholic University of Lublin.

Biela, Adam (1993): Reakcje psychiczne w sytuacji globalnych zmian w środowisku. Kosmos, 42,(1), 187-198.

Cramer, Manfred (1989): Umweltkrise und der psychosoziale Bereich. In: W. Stark (Ed.): Lebensweltbezogene Prävention und Gesundheitsförderung. Konzepte und Strategien für die psychosoziale Praxis. Lambertus.

Dąbrowski, Dorota (1996): Muni property market starting to boil. Warsaw Business Journal, May 6-12, 13.

Diekmann, Andreas & Preisendorfer, Peter (1992): Persönliches Umweltverhalten. Diskrepanzen zwischen Anspruch und Wirklichkeit. Kölner Zeitschrift für Soziologie und Sozialpsychologie, 44,(2), 226-251.

Economic Commssion for Europe (1985a): Impact of non-conventional sources of energy on water. New York: United Nations.

Environmental Impact Assessment Legislation: Czech Republic, Estonia, Hungary, Latvia, Lithuania, Poland, Slovak Republic, Slovenia. UNEP Industry and Environment, April - September, 1995.

Fogelman, Lejb (1996): Grappling with the ins and outs of Polish public procurement law. Warsaw Business Journal, May 27-June 2, 11

Fogelman, Lejb (1996): The new labor code: changes in vacations, work hours, overtime. Warsaw Business Journal, April 15-21, 11

Grob, Alexander (1991): Meinung - Verhalten - Umwelt. Frankfurt: Peter Lang.

Haigh, N; Bera, G. & Zentain, V. (1987): The Background to Environmental Production in Market and Planned Economy Countries. In: G. Enyedi; A. J. Gijswijt & B. Rhode (Eds.): Environmental Policies in East and West. London: Taylor Graham, 22-29.

Hammerl, Barbara, Maria (1994): Umweltbewusstsein in Unternehmen. Eine empirische Analyse des Umweltbewusstseins im Rahmen der Unternehmenskultur. Lang.

Hessisches Ministerium für Wirtschaft und Technik (1989): Gesparte Energie - Gespartes Geld. Wiesbaden: Hessisches Ministerium für Wirtschaft und Technik.

Hillebrand, D. (1981): Waschtechnik im Wandel. Strom Praxis, 20-23.

Holzapfel, H. & Vahrenkamp, R. (1993): Bemerkungen zum Zusammenhang der steigenden Arbeitsteilung mit dem Verkehrsaufwand Informationsdienst. Institut für ökologische Wirtschaftsforschung GmbH, Vereinigung für ökologische Wirtschaftsforschung E.V., (2), 8, 6-7.

Janiszewski, Wiesław (1973): Ochrona przyrody w Polsce na tle sytuacji międzynarodowej. Warszawa: Liga Ochrony Przyrody.

Jarzębski, Stefan (1985): O środowisku naturalnym bez emocji. Polityka, 12.10.1985.

Kramer, Heinz (1993): The European Community's Response to the "New Eastern Europe". Journal of Common Market Studies, Vol.31. No.2, June 1993.

Kuldiński, A. (1989): Ecological Renaissance. The first milestone on the way to the United Europe. Warszawa: University Press.

Lennings, M. (1989): Energie im Blickfeld. Jahresbericht, 1989, Vereinigung Deutscher Elektrizitätswerke, Frankfurt.

Mosler, Hans-Joachim (1990): Selbstorganisation von umweltgerechtem Handeln: Der Einfluss von Vertrauensbildung auf die Ressourcennutzung in einem Umweltspiel. Universität Zürich, Philosophische Fakultät 1.

Nagiecki, Janusz (1996): Bread and Freedom. Agriculture in Poland. The Ecologist, Vol.26, No.1, January/February.

Necker, T. (1989): Für eine realistische Energiepolitik - wider energiepolitische Illusionen. Vortrag beim zwölften Workshop "Energie" des RWE am 08.11.1989 in Braunlage.

Nowak, Zygfryd (1993): Polish Cleaner Production Programme - NGOs in action. UNEP Industry and Environment, October - December, 33-36.

O'Neill, G. K. (1981): 2081. A hopeful View of the Human Future. New York: Simon and Schuster.

Öschlies, W. (1987): Bald ist Polen doch verloren. Köln: Böhlau Verlag.

Peitsch, Heike (1991): Umweltkatastrophe Mensch. Heidelberg: Roland Ansanger Verlag.

Pietras, Z. J. & Pietras, M. (1991): International Ecological Security. Marie Curie-Skłodowska University.

Preuss, Sigrun (1991): Umweltkatastrophe Mensch. Heidelberg: Roland Ansanger Verlag.

Protecting Polands Forest Biodiversity. Biodiversity Portfolio Review, September 1995-January 1996, 6-7.

Rhode, B. (1987): The United Nations Economic Commission for Europe. In: G. Enyedi; A. J. Gijswijt & B. Rhode (Eds.): Environmental Policies in East and West. London: Taylor Graham, 388-395.

Samuelson, R. J. (1991): Tinkering with Energy. Newsweek, March 4, 1991, 38.

Schahn, Joachim (1993): Die Kluft zwischen Einstellung und Verhalten beim individuellen Umweltschutz. In J. Schahn & T. Giesinger (Eds.): Psychologie für den Umweltschutz. München: Psychologie Verlags Union.

Schahn, Joachim; Dinger, Johanna & Bohner, Gerd (1994): Die Rolle von Rationalisierungen und Neutralisationen für die Rechtfertigung umweltschädigenden Verhaltens. Universität Saarbrücken, Psychologisches Institut, Diskussionspapier Nr. 80. Thommen, B.; Ammann, R. & von Cranach, M. (1988): Handlungsorganisation durch soziale Repräsentationen. Bern: Huber.

Schröder, N. (1991): Die Sonne als Energiespender. Der EAM Bote, 2, 91, 42 ,4-5.

Seibold, E. (1985): Fördern durch Fordern. Weinheim:VCH Verlagsgesellschft mbH.

Stölting, E. (1990): Zeit, Kompetenz & Ressort. Bürokratische Probleme bei der Bewältigung von Umweltkrisen. In: H. P. Dreitzel & H. Stenger (Hgs.): Ungewollte Selbstzerstörung. Frankfurt: Campus Verlag, 62-87.

Tomain, J. P. (1987): Nuclear Power Transformation. Bloomington: Indiana University Press. Umweltbewußtes Europa. Presse und Informationsamt der Bundesregierung. Bonn.

Vereinigung Deutscher Elektrizitätswerke VDEW e.V. (1989): Die öffentliche Elektrizitätsversorgung im Bundesgebiet 1989.

Vester, F. (1980): Neuland des Denkens. Vom technokratischen zum kybernetsichen Zeitalter. Stuttgart: Deutsche Verlags-Anstalt.

von Cranach, M.; Kalbermatten, U.; Indermühle, K. & Gugler, B. (1980): Zielgerichtetes Handeln. Bern: Huber.

Walter, H. (1984): Vegetation und Klimazonen. Stuttgart: Eugen Ulmer.

Bibiliography from Polish Computer System:

Aranowski, Elżbieta (1992): Wybrane problemy metodologii badań. Warszawa: Wydawnictwa Uniwersytetu Warszawskiego.

Barczyk, Joanna (1988): Stres zawodowy i jego skutki. Katowice: TNOIK.

Bartkowiak, Grażyna & Nowodworski, Zbigniew (1989): Psychologia pracy i kierownictwa. Poznań: Wydaw. AE.

Bernstein, Albert, J. & Rozen, Sydney, C. (1992): Dinozaury są wśród nas. Warszawa: Wydaw. Naukowe.

Biederman, Viktoria & Dąbrowska, Ewa (1989): Dyrektorzy. Warszawa: IOPM.

Biela, Adam (1990): Stres w pracy zawodowej. Lublin: Redakcja Wydawnictw KUL.

Biela, Adam (1992): Kwestionariusz lubelski analizy stanowiska pracy. Lublin: Katolicki Uniwersytet Lubelski.

Borucki, Zenon (1988): Stres organizacyjny: mechanizm, następstwa, modyfikatory. Gdańsk: Uniwersytet Gdański.

Branders, Donna & Philips, Howard (1994): Grupa bawi się i pracuje. Wrocław: UNUS. Translation from the original English.

Bugiel, Julian (1990): Socjologia i psychologia pracy. Kraków: Wydawnictwo AGH.

Bugiel, Julian & Haber, Lesław, H. (1993): Zarządzanie a socjologia i psychologia pracy. Kraków: Wydawnictwo AGH.

Cenin, Mieczysław (1990): Psychologiczne determinanty i metody doskonalenia kierowniczej kadry oświatowej. Kalisz: CDN.

Conor, Hannaway & Hunt, Gabriel (1994): Umiejętności menadżerskie. Warszawa: Kopia.

Czerwińska-Jasiewicz, Maria (1991): Psychologiczne problemy wyboru zawodu. Warszawa: Wydawnictwa Uniwersytetu Warszawskiego.

Dąbrowski, Kazimierz (1991): Moralność w polityce. Warszawa: BIS.

Daniluk, Włodzimierz (1985): Psychologia obsługi konsumentów. Warszawa: IRWIK.

Daszkowski, Julian (1988): Wpływ pracy grupowej na wysiłek w realizacji zadań. Wrocław: Zakład Narodowy im. Ossolińskich.

Drwal, Radosław, L. (1995): Adaptacja kwestionariuszy osobowości. Warszawa: Wydaw. Naukowe PWN.

Dudek, Bohdan (1992): Psychiczne obciążenie prac. Łódź: IMP Sekcja Wydaw.

Duralska, Hanna & Obacz, Andrzej (1989): Zagadnienia psychologii ogólnej i psychologii pracy. Warszawa: ZETDEZET.

Gasiul, Henryk (1987): Formalne cechy systemu wartości jako wskaźniki rozwoju osobowości. Toruń: UMK.

Gaz, Stanisław (1993): Poczucie zmiany siebie w okresie stworzenia się osobowości dojrzałej. Kraków: Wydział Filozoficzny.

Geras, Gocimierz (1987): Czynna elektroskarnia i jej znaczenie w badaniach psychologicznych. Gdańsk: Wydawnictwo UG.

Glieszczyński, Xymen (1991): Psychologiczny model efektywności pracy. Warszawa: Wydaw. Naukowe PWN.

Golińska, Lucyna (1993): Temperamentalne uwarunkowania percepcji społecznej. Łódź: Wydawnictwo Uniwersytetu Łódzkiego.

Gondzik, Erwin (1993): Sukces i kariera człowieka. Katowice: Uniwersytet Katowice.

Gros, Urszula (1994): Organizacyjne aspekty zachowań ludzi w procesach pracy. Katowice: AE.

Gruszczyńska-Malec, Grażyna (1991): Kształtowanie treści pracy w przedsiebiorstwie przemysłowym. Katowice: AE.

Hierzel, Krzysztof (1993): Mechanizmy motywacyjne w pracy. Warszawa: Wydawnictwa Akademii Teologii.

Hornowska, Elżbieta (1989): Operacjonalizacja wielkości psychologicznych. Wrocław: Zakład Narodowy.

Iżyk, Wanda (1989): Socjologia pracy z elementami psychologii pracy. Wrocław: Wydaw. Uczelniane AE.

Jacher, Władysław (1992): Społeczność w zakładzie pracy. Katowice: Prace Naukowe.

Januszek, Henryk (1992): Społeczności zakładowe. Poznań: Wydaw. AE.

Kaliciuk, Stanisław (1991): Psychohigiena pracy. Warszawa: Wydaw. Ośrodka Badań Społecznych.

Karczmarczuk, Kryspin (1993): Kierownicy w procesie zmian. Łódź: Przedsiebiostwo Specjalistyczne Absolwent.

Karney, Janina, E. (1988): Człowiek w środowisku pracy. Warszawa: Instytut Wydawniczy.

Karney, Janina, E. (1991): Osobowość menadżera czyli jak zostać dyrektorem jutra. Warszawa: Międzynarodowa Szkoła Menadżerów.

Karpowicz, Ewa & Szaban, Jolanta (1986): Jednostka i grupy w procesie pracy. Warszawa: Instytut Organizacji.

Kowalczuk, Rajmund (1989): Podstawy psychologii socjologii i organizacji pracy. Warszawa: Wydawnictwa Szkolne.

Kozdrój, Alicja (1988): Grupa pracownicza jako przedmiot i podmiot motywowania. Wrocław: Polska Akademia Naukowa.

Kożusznik, Barbara (1994): Psychologia w pracy menadżera. Katowice: Wydaw. UK.

Król, Tadeusz, Z. (1989): Psychologiczne i sytuacyjne uwarunkowania efektywności przedsiębiorstwa. Gdańsk: Uniwersytet Gdański.

Lakein, Alan (1994): Być panem swego czasu i swego życia. Warszawa: Ethos. Translation from the original English.

Ludkiewicz, Zofia (1994): Zainteresowanie studentów studiowaniem i pracą zawodową. Warszawa: Wyższa Szkoła Pedagogiki Specjalnej.

Makowski, Tadeusz (1995): Trzy kroki do kariery. Warszawa: ABC.

Manek, Anna, M. (1989): Ćwiczenia z psychologii i socjologii pracy. Lublin: Wydawnictwa Uczelniane PL.

Manek, Anna, M. (1994): Ćwiczenia z psychologii i socjologii pracy. Lublin: Politechnika.

Milczarek, Stanisław (1989): Psychospołeczne uwarunkowania aktywności w zakładzie pracy. Warszawa: Ośrodek Badań Społecznych.

Noworol, Czesław (1989): Analiza skupień w badaniach empirycznych. Warszawa: Państwowe Wydaw.

Pietrasieski, Zbigniew (1988): Podstawy psychologii pracy: podrecznik dla technikum. Warszawa: Wydawnictwo Szkolne i Pedagogiczne.

Pietrasiewski, Zbigniew; Somczyński, Kazimierz, M. & Kohn, Melvin, L. (1988): Sytuacja pracy i jej psychologiczne konsekwencje. Wrocław: Zakład Narodowy im. Ossolińskich.

Ratajczak, Zofia (1988): Niezawodność człowieka w pracy. Warszawa: Państwowe Wydawnictwo Naukowe.

Ratajczak, Zofia (1991): Elementy psychologii pracy. Katowice: Uniwersytet.

Schmidt, Czesław (1987): Humanizacja pracy wysoce podzielonej. Łódź: Politechnika.

Sedlak, Kazimierz (1994): Polubić biznes. Kraków: Wydaw. Profesjonalne.

Sosnowski, Tytus & Zimmer, Klaus (1993): Metody psychofizjologiczne w badaniach psychologicznych. Warszawa: Wydawnictwo Naukowe PWN. Translation from the original German.

Sparkowski, Zygmunt (1990): Architektura i humanizacja na tle rozwiązań przemysłowych. Warszawa: Wydawnictwa PW.

Stewart, Dorothy, M. (1994): Praktyka kierownia. Warszawa: Panst. Wydaw. Ekonomiczne. Translated from the original English.

Terelak, Jan, F. (1993): Psychologia pracy i bezrobocia. Warszawa: Wydaw. Akademii.

Tokarski, Stefan (1990): Studium sprawności i kierowania w przedsiębiorstwach. Gdańsk: Wydaw. UG.

Tokarski, Stefan (1994): Psychologia organizacji. Gdańsk: Wydaw. Uniwersytetu.

Tyszki, Tadeusz (1992): Psychologia i bezpieczeństwo pracy. Warszawa: IP.

Witkowski, Stanisław (1990): Z zagadnień psychologii społecznej i psychologii pracy. Wrocław: Wydaw. Uniwersytetu Wrocławskiego.

II

EMPIRICAL INQUIRY:
ASSESSMENT OF ENVIRONMENTAL
COMPONENTS

4

APPRAISING THE EXPLORATIVE RESULTS

Environmental questionnaires in the context of work-study in Germany

As mentioned above, many aspects of the environmental issue are not comparable in the neighboring countries of Poland and Germany. However, to resign because of this, from any attempt at analysis would be to question the validity of any cross-cultural comparisons. Most important in any investigation, is a recognition of the factors of inquiry and the difference of their relative possible framework and, accordingly, to adjust interpretations to this context.

If it were - because of various differences - thought to be impossible to compare the Germans with the Poles in these issues, it must be pointed out that even the populations of Western European countries are very dissimilar in many ways. The English, for example, are unable to cope with various aspects of the environment in the same way the Germans are because of an entirely different system of further education, or work accompanying education. The different approach to this has influence on the preparedness of various workers in many industries. One of such areas where changes have come about rapidly, in accordance with more pro-environmental thinking, is the quarrying and extraction of gypsum, in itself a major industry. Because however, gypsum has now become a by-product in the generation of electricity from coal, as is happening in most major new plants, the structure of an entire industry needs to be changed. Thus, where entire branches of industry are threatened, re-schooling workers becomes an important part of stabilizing economies. Germany, where these needs are met on an institutional level and re-schooling is a part of the everyday work-life, thus has a good way of coping with this kind of development.

In another example: In France, forests are not as integral a part of the culture as in Germany, to the extent that the French have imported the concept of "Le Waldsterben" (the dying of forests) in order to somewhat convey the phenomenon of vast amounts of trees and forest areas dying. Nevertheless, complete comparability should be hard to reach and even more difficult to quantify. However, although cross-cultural studies always leave some questions unanswered and their reliability is hard to establish, they are nevertheless considered to be an important part of research.

To show a further discrepancy, in Germany, there have been quite a number of questionnaires on environmental issues from a psychological perspective. This development is far ahead of Poland. As the following shows, the topics covered in Germany - those to some extent of relevance to the present study - were in such areas as the separation of garbage (Herr, 1988; Raab et al., 1992; Schahn et al., 1994); rationalization (Schahn et al., 1994); cognition (Schahn et al., 1989; Schahn et al., 1990); responsibility (Auhagen et al., 1994); politics (Wessner, 1992; Riemann et al., 1993); youth (Graudenz et al., 1988; Unterbruner, 1993); home-environment (Winter et al., 1984; Peter et al., 1984; Miller, 1985; Strebl, 1986;Reichel, 1987; Fink et al., 1992); playgrounds (Fritz, 1984); judgement (Borcherding et al., 1991); attitude and behavior (Kley et al., 1979; Grob, 1990a; 1990b; 1991; Hippler et al., 1993); transportation (Klaedtke et al., 1991); noise (Guski et al., 1978; Namba et al., 1986; Müller-Andritzky, 1990); space (Molt, 1986); risk (Ruff, 1990a; 1990b); Czech Republic (Rosova et al., 1990); coping (Kraemer, 1989); Tschernobyl (Lukesch et al., 1986); nuclear power (Peters, 1979); offices (Wutzl, 1976); power-plants (Kasper et al., 1987); urban settings (Lalli, 1992; Kaiser et al., 1990); tourism (Haimayer, 1986); ethics (Sieloff, 1987) and stressors (Rohrmann, 1986). However, since they did not contain items directly concerned with work psychology, they were of no further use in the present study and will not be discussed further in the following pages (see Bibliography at the end of this chapter for further reference).

Development of a work-environment questionnaire

As already mentioned in Chapter Two, cognitive dissonance in relation to environmental topics is an important subject in German psychological literature. Although there have been quite a number of studies concerning information use and processing, fewer have been made on the relationship between attitude and behavior. Again, the English literature has made this more of a topic of research, limiting, however, the discussion mainly to research on attitude and behavior itself and not to, for example, the field of cognitive dissonance, as was shown more specifically in Chapter Two.

The forming of hypotheses for the attitude/behavior relationship in work settings for the two populations

Upon looking closer at most environmental issues, it becomes clear that many of the difficulties that arise, come from the complexity of the issue itself. Market forces, for example, have been good for many environmental problems, in providing for newer, more efficient, non-polluting, biodegradable or just plain "natural" products. For that reason, these forces often do have a good influence. On the other hand, these same forces can provide formidable obstacles to the prevention of pollution or, indeed, to any attempt to ameliorate the so prevalent afflictions the environment has had to cope with. There are quite a number of examples for this, but one salient one concerns water pollution through detergents. This example also shows that consultation and cooperation can often have just as important as, or more of an effect, than technological, scientific, or industrial advancements. When it became apparent that cleaning liquids and detergents were polluting bodies of water to the extent that fauna and flora were in terrible danger, water-recycling attempted to extract many of the most harmful elements from sewerage water before it was recycled into streams; in all, the effects were very positive. Meanwhile however, industry, aware of the problems it was creating with the addition of harmful chemicals that produced many unwanted side-effects, sought to rid detergents of harmful elements, by substituting them with others, often not aware that they were quite as noxious and that, moreover, existing recycling and cleansing plants and facilities were not longer capable of coping with them and eliminating them. So the poisonous cycle would start anew and all advances made in one field were undermined by advances made in another.

In many new developments however - as is reflected in the present literature - an understanding of the complex, interrelated problems has spread. As, however, the risk literature of the last two decades has shown, it has become increasingly hard for the average citizen to calculate the elements of risk involved, let alone to try to balance the needs of the ecology with his own. The visions and ideology of man harmonizing with his surroundings, often depicted by ecological psychology (much of it influenced by architecture and design) are beautiful but very hard to realize in all of its final implications. A creation of harmony and balance, although wonderful aspirations, can sound simple, but is one of the most difficult challenges that life has to present.

The occurrence of cognitive dissonance

The more than ample literature available on the subject of cognitive dissonance, postulates that where cognitive elements of a belief or behavior cannot be logically connected, a state of being - called cognitive dissonance - occurs especially where and/or when the irrational elements are or become particularly relevant to thought or action. In order to mitigate this type of state of being, persons concerned will ignore information, disregard obvious facts and warnings and even change behavior in order to prove to themselves that all is still logical and relevant in their lives.

As mentioned above, cognitive dissonance has not come under fire in Germany as it has in the United States, (it is interesting to see how just one journal, perhaps in an attempt to provide for controversy, or just to fill its pages, can contribute so much to debate within the scientific community). Because of this, suffice it to say, that, in this context, the biggest problem to be faced in the next pages is one of defining just how cognitive dissonance can be measured in a questionnaire. For questions on the nature of the cognitive dissonance controversies, please turn to Chapter Two.

Barring the use of complex questions relating to the illogical nature of many environmental issues, the questionnaires now presented were designed to determine dissonance by a correlation of different items, especially concerning those relating to attitudes and behavior, consciousness and action.

Cognitive dissonance in hypothetical analysis

In order to begin with the most simple, obvious subject of investigation, let it be assumed that:

H_1

> **Cognitive dissonance - as rationalization and balancing of cognition with attitudes and behavior - can be found within both of the two groups under investigation, to be proven by statistical outcomes, correlations and results.**

H_0

Outcomes will not show statistically valid relationships. Of further interest within this context, are hypotheses concerning the differences within and between the two populations under consideration in Germany and Poland. Thus, a further hypothesis to be formulated should read:

H_2

> **The two populations measured in Germany and Poland will show statistical differences and different correlations.**

H_0

The two populations will present similar tendencies.

Lastly, pertaining to the differences within populations, the hypothesis should be formulated thus:

H_3

> **There are in-country differences according to place of work, sex, education and work-task.**

H_0

There are no differences within country.

A discussion of the two questionnaires presented

Following, will be a presentation of the time and location of the questionnaires used in the two populations in Germany and in Poland. For the exact wording of the first questionnaire, please turn to the Appendix. The second questionnaire can be found in: Grob, Alexander (1991): Meinung, Verhalten, Umwelt. Bern: Peter Lang.

The first questionnaire was developed by this author, taking the most salient questions out of the environmental pollution literature. However, particularly in Germany, contacts to industry were very difficult to make. Attempts to match the number finally received in Germany by a somewhat equal number of workers in Poland proved to be relatively easy in Poland because, at that time, cooperation with industry was relatively easy.

The second questionnaire used, was developed by Alexander Grob in Switzerland and distributed in the Swiss city of Bern, with the outlying country also used in the initial distributions. These findings have been published (Grob, 1991) and will only be further referred to briefly in this context. Please see Chapter Six, Seven and Eight for results from this.

Table 1 shows the exact distribution of the questionnaires taken into the final evaluation.

As Table 1 shows, in Germany, the questionnaires were distributed in Berlin (B); Bremen (HB) and Giessen (G). In Poland, questionnaires were only distributed in Lublin. $Q_{Distrib.}$ signifies the amount of questionnaires distributed and Q_N, the amount received.

Table 1. Distribution of questionnaires

Q_{Time}	Q1	Q2	$Q_{Distrib.}$	Q_N	$Q_{Location-Place}$
11.,1990	GR		100	10	HBVulkan
12.,1990	GR		100	12	G-Voko
06.,1991	PL		30	30	L-EPlant
03.,1992		PL	500	397	L-B; C; F; P
06.,1992		GR	200	8	B-Private; HB-Private
09.,1992		GR	200	31	HB-Klöckner
02.,1996	PL		100	28	L-D; E; M; P
03.,1996		GR	450	102	HB-IGMetall;S;P

Comments: Q1, or Questionnaire 1 was called "Industrial Aspects of Environmental Protection"; Q2, or Questionnaire 2, was called "Measures of Environmental Attitudes and Behavior". GR, signifies the German version; PL, the Polish one.

Table 2. Reliability Analysis for Invariant Factors

Factors	Item Number	Alpha	
		Germany	Poland
Factor 1	9,10,13,23,	.85	.75
Affective Reaction	24, 31 , 32, 33, 36		
Factor 2		.18	.71
Perception of Discrepancy	3,7,16,19,39		
Factor 3		-.05	.77
Commercial Operants	6,20,34,35		
Factor 4		.18	.68
Singularity	1,14,22,25,37		
Factor 5		.76	.62
Ethical Constituents	2,4,5,12		
Factor 6		.40	.60
Technological Components	8,11,28,38		
Factor 7		.73	.16
Commitment to Production	15,17,18,27		
Factor 8		.40	.23
Personal Responsibility	21,26,29,30		

Table 3. Reliability Analysis for Variant Factors

Factors	Item Number		Alpha	
	Germany	Poland		
			Germany	Poland
Factor 1	8,9,13,16, 23,24,36	4,9,10,12 32,36,39	.88	.78
Factor 2	12,26,29,30 37,38	6,20,23,24 33,34,35	.80	.81
Factor 3	1,10,31,32, 33,39	3,5,7	.41	.72
Factor 4	2,3,4,5, 19,21	8,11,14,18 31,38	.80	.69
Factor 5	6,7,22,34	1,22,25,29	.71	.77
Factor 6	15,17,18 20,27	13,15,17,21 27,30	.80	.46
Factor 7	11,25,35	2,19	.60	.35
Factor 8	14,28	16,26,28,37	.74	.50

Questionnaire 1

Interpreting first results from the German and Polish populations (n = 52), of questionnaire 1, a reliability analysis showed discrepant Alpha values for the German and Polish population in most factor groups for the invariant sample, as Table 2 shows.

Contrary to this, reliability was higher where the two populations were treated as variant samples.

The spread of the invariant factor analysis was then correlated, once for Germany and twice for Poland. Figure 1 shows the correlations for Germany.

As Figure 1 shows, the highest correlation for Germany was between commercial operants and commitment to production: .56 with a significance of < .01. The two highest negative correlations were between affective reaction and technological components: -.60, again with a significance of <.01 as well as between commercial operants and personal responsibility: -.51, with a significance of <.05. Especially the two negative correlations allow for interesting interpretations in light of the above hypo-

Figure 1. Correlation of Factors for Germany

Factors	Factor 1	Factor 2	Factor 3	Factor 4	Factor 5	Factor 6	Factor 7
Factor 1							
Factor 2	-.12						
Factor 3	.36	-.18					
Factor 4	-.10	-.37	-.06				
Factor 5	.32	.03	.34	-.08			
Factor 6	-.60**	.36	-.01	-.36	.01		
Factor 7	.21	.15	.56**	-.26	.37	.15	
Factor 8	-.26	.21	-.51*	-.03	-.15	-.03	-.30

* p<.05; **p< 01; ***p<.001

Figure 2. Correlation of Factors for Poland

Factors	Factor 1	Factor 2	Factor 3	Factor 4	Factor 5	Factor 6	Factor 7
Factor 1							
Factor 2	.15						
Factor 3	.25	.00					
Factor 4	.11	.14	-.27				
Factor 5	.47**	.32	.26	-.11			
Factor 6	.35	.04	.17	.41*	-.02		
Factor 7	.13	-.19	.18	-.29	.20	-.28	
Factor 8	.12	-.20	-.03	.21	-.21	.35	-.19

*p<.05; **p<.01 ; ***p<.001

Figure 3. Correlation of Factors for the second Polish group

Factors	Factor 1	Factor 2	Factor 3	Factor 4	Factor 5	Factor 6	Factor 7
Factor 1							
Factor 2	.02						
Factor 3	.12	.07					
Factor 4	.63***	-.17	.33				
Factor 5	.49**	.16	.19	.33			
Factor 6	.21	.08	.26	.47*	.12		
Factor 7	.13	.22	.14	.05	.13	.18	
Factor 8	.16	.12	.18	.30	-.25	.27	.15

*p<.05; **p<.0; ***p<.001

theses and would tend to support H_1. The same factors showed different correlations in the Polish population however, in itself then tending to support H_2. Figure 2 shows the correlations for Poland.

Here, the highest correlation was between affective reaction and ethical constituents: .47, with a significance of <.01 and singularity and technological components: .41, with a significance of <.05. Although this represents interesting findings concerning the belief in technology not found in the German population, the first correlation is particularly interesting, as will be shown further on.

As Table 1 shows, a more recent study was done in Poland, with the same questionnaire. Workers filling the questionnaire out, were attending courses (at the Polytechnical University in Lublin). Interestingly enough, they show almost the same findings as those above, that is, a positive correlation between factors 1/5 and 4/6 and that five years later. Now however, there is the interesting addition of factors 1/4. The exact results are given in Figure 3.

Factor 4, here designated as singularity, seems to contain those questions that are related to rather ambiguous feelings toward the environment and it is interesting that it has correlated so highly with affective reaction. When the means of the two studies in Poland (P_1 and P_2) were compared, (see Chapter Five for a comparison of the means of P_1 with those of the German workers), they were very close. There were several salient exceptions. One was item number 36, showing quite a contrast of means (5.63 (1) to 3.04 (2)) between the two samples. As the content of the item reads "The production of my firm causes environmental pollution; this is harmful to me", this is quite an important finding. There could be several reasons for this change. One might be the variety of firms that the workers came from (of which the large majority however, have high potential for pollution), as opposed to the fact that the first round of questionnaires was given out only to the Lublin power plant. A closer look at the worker affiliation, educational background and present job status should show relevant interconnections more clearly.

Upon perusing the questionnaires more closely however, we find the two samples to be very comparable to each other, except for the homogeneity of place of work in the first study and that the differences in evaluation is more likely to be due to other considerations. Like in the first study, the mean age is in the 30's, the workers have completed some form of secondary education and are placed in better positions in their firms, such as instructor, specialist and computer analyst. The firms they work for include a printing shop, Daewoo, the Lublin power plant, the local mine etc.- characteristic polluters in the past.

Another reason could be that, as discussed, pollution, has been cut drastically in the years following the political changes - that is, the 90's have brought great structural changes in production and management in Poland. A third reason could be the relative inconsequence - to the workers - of the question of environment. That this is not very likely, is shown by the following two items. Item 3, concerning the question of ethics in politics and economics showed a lower mean (3.23) in 1991 than in 1996 (5.21). Another difference - in item 19 - relates to the responsibility of the consumer and shows a change from 1991 (3.87) to 1996 (5.07).

An additional interesting difference, but one that is not likely to throw much light upon the findings discussed above, is the question of ethics (item 4). Whereas the response was 4.43 in 1991, it was only 2.89 in 1996. Apparently, there have been some overall changes in mentality in the meantime. Especially interesting is the fact that ethical dealings are expected of others (Item 3) and not of oneself (Item 4). This reflects the popular opinion in media and even in research psychology (books written in the US 20 years ago are now being translated into Polish, the newer findings have seemingly not found their way to Poland yet), that aggression and unethical behavior are the most sure means to material prosperity and thus, happiness. Politics, apparently, is expected to stand above that, although politicians of course, known to be only human.

In this light, there have - recently - been many discussions in the media about the changes in Poland and whether, even in the light of the enormous material benefits of capitalism, the change of politics has been so beneficial to the country. This has been pondered, not only by those groups as pensioners, disabled, women, the 15% of the population seeking work and, in a lesser but even more tragic sense, the vast amount of jobholders in state-employment. Also, and more importantly for the stability of the country, many of those who more recently qualify as the new middle class, but are still earning now more than the equivalent of $200-300 dollars per month, have joined this discussion. In contrast to the Czech Republic and Hungary, this is luckily (percentage-wise) the largest income group in Poland today, whereas in those countries, rich and poor are even more polarized; therefore it seems logical, that as this group is influenced, changes affecting this class will come to Poland first.

Although Poland is seeking and awaits shortly, (2001), a place in the European Community, there are signs that they will become a member determined to find and ready to define their own personality within the circle of their new family of nations.

Questionnaire 2

Please turn to Chapter Six, for this text.

Conclusion

As the above figures show, the results for the Polish, compared to the German population, are exactly opposite to each other in the cases specified. However, it must again be stated that:

1. Work content and context can not even now be compared in the two neighboring countries of Germany and Poland,
2. Polish employees are only now starting to work in more modern, safer, more humane jobs, and
3. Polish workers are beginning to see worker benefits and rights (starting in the year 1997), such as have been common in Germany for decades.

Several years ago, all this was different. However, and as will be further discussed in the next Chapter, Poles seem to be open to discussions on the environment and a harried life-style has not prevented them from dreaming of better opportunities. Such differences as could be found no doubt stem from varied exigencies of life for the two populations.

Therefore, it would seem that, whereas the German population, in order to live in consonance with their behavior, negate the possibility of other behavior, the Polish population, caught up in the much higher risks of everyday life in Poland, respond as a risk sample might, that is, risk of any kind is completely negated. It stands to reason that, where overall risks are higher, methods for coping are different and living with daily risk is done completely differently than in those cases where risks are lower and can be differentiated.

Thus, while it may be concluded that the Polish and German populations do not show evidence of cognitive dissonance regarding pollution in the same way, there could be evidence that it does exist - albeit in different forms - in both populations researched.

The next chapter, comprising an article that was published in 1994, shows further correlations between the two populations.

REFERENCES

Allport, G. W. (1935): Attitudes. In: C. Murchison (Ed.): Handbook of social psychology. Worcester: Clark University Press, 798-844.

Auhagen, Ann, Elisabeth & Neuberger, Karin (1994): Verantwortung gegenüber der Umwelt: Eine Studie über umweltbewusstes Handeln. Gruppendynamik, 25,(3), 319-332.

Bernstein, Janis (1995): The Urban Challenge in National Environmental Strategies. *Environment Department Dissemination Notes*, Number 31, August.

Berreby, David (1996): Bushed. *The Sciences*, July/August, 41-46.

Biela, Adam (1993): Reakcje psychiczne w sytuacji globalnych zmian w środowisku. *Kosmos*, 42,(1), 187-198.

Cramer, Manfred (1989): Umweltkrise und der psychosoziale Bereich. In: W. Stark (Ed.): Lebensweltbezogene Prävention und Gesundheitsförderung. Konzepte und Strategien für die psychosoziale Praxis. Lambertus.

Dąbrowski, Dorota (1996): Muni property market starting to boil. *Warsaw Business Journal*, May 6-12, 13.

Diekmann, Andreas & Preisendorfer, Peter (1992): Persönliches Umweltverhalten. Diskrepanzen zwischen Anspruch und Wirklichkeit. *Kölner Zeitschrift für Soziologie und Sozialpsychologie*, 44,(2), 226-251.

Environmental Impact Assessment Legislation: Czech Republic, Estonia, Hungary, Latvia, Lithuania, Poland, Slovak Republic, Slovenia. *UNEP Industry and Environment*, April - September, 1995.

Fogelman, Lejb (1996): The new labor code: changes in vacations, work hours, overtime. *Warsaw Business Journal*, April 15-21, 11.

Fogelman, Lejb (1996): Grappling with the ins and outs of Polish public procurement law. *Warsaw Business Journal*, May 27-June 2, 11.

Grob, Alexander (1991): Meinung - Verhalten - Umwelt. Frankfurt: Peter Lang.

Hammerl, Barbara, Maria (1994): Umweltbewusstsein in Unternehmen. Eine empirische Analyse des Umweltbewusstseins im Rahmen der Unternehmenskultur. Lang.

Mosler, Hans-Joachim (1990): Selbstorganisation von umweltgerechtem Handeln: Der Einfluss von Vertrauensbildung auf die Ressourcennutzung in einem Umweltspiel. Universität Zürich, Philosophische Fakultät 1.

Nagiecki, Janusz (1996): Bread and Freedom. Agriculture in Poland. *The Ecologist*, Vol.26, No.1, January/February.

Nowak, Zygfryd (1993): Polish Cleaner Production Programme - NGO's in action. *UNEP Industry and Environment*, October - December, 33-36.

Protecting Polands Forest Biodiversity. *Biodiversity Portfolio Review*, September 1995-January 1996, 6-7.

Schahn, Joachim (1993): Die Kluft zwischen Einstellung und Verhalten beim individuellen Umweltschutz. In J. Schahn & T. Giesinger (Eds.): Psychologie für den Umweltschutz. München: Psychologie Verlags Union.

Schahn, Joachim; Dinger, Johanna & Bohner, Gerd (1994): Die Rolle von Rationalisierungen und Neutralisationen für die Rechtfertigung umweltschädigenden Verhaltens. Universität Saarbrücken, Psychologisches Institut, Diskussionspapier Nr. 80.

Thommen, B.; Ammann, R. & von Cranach, M. (1988): Handlungsorganisation durch soziale Repräsentationen. Bern: Huber.

von Cranach, M.; Kalbermatten, U.; Indermühle, K. & Gugler, B. (1980): Zielgerichtetes Handeln. Bern: Huber.

Bibliography of environmental questionnaires available in Germany:

Auhagen, Ann, E. & Neuberger, Karin (1994): Verantwortung gegenüber der Umwelt: Eine Studie über umweltbewußtes Handeln. *Gruppendynamik*, 25,(3), 319-332.

Battmann, Wolfgang (1984): Der jugendliche Motorradfahrer zwischen Hedonismus und Ökologiebewußtsein. In A. Stiksrud (Ed.): Jugend und Werte. Beltz, 289-299.

Bernhardt, Ursula; Hauke, Gernot; Graf-Hoyos, Carl & Wenninger, Gerd (1984): Entwicklung eines Verfahrens zur Diagnose von Mensch-Umwelt-Systemen. München: Technische Universität.

Boehnke, Klaus (1982): Zur Erhebung von Sozialdaten im Berliner Jugend-Längsschnitt. Berlin: Institut für Psychologie.

Borcherding, Katrin; Eppel, Thomas & von Winterfeldt, Detlef (1991): Der Vergleich von gewichteten Urteilen in der multiattributiven Nutzenmessung. Management Science, 37,(12), 1603-1619.

Fink, Benedykt & Forster, Pit (1992): Die Bedeutung materieller Dinge in der häuslichen Lebensumwelt: Eine Pilotstudie. *Zeitschrift für Pädagogische Psychologie*, 6,(2), 115-131.

Fritz, Elke (1984): Stadtranderholung als betreute Kinderfreizeit. Innsbruck: Naturwissenschaftliche Fakultät.

Graudenz, Ines & Randoll, Dirk (1988): Erleben der atomaren Bedrohung bei jungen Erwachsenen. *Psychologie in Erziehung und Unterricht*, 35,(3), 180-187.

Grob, Alexander (1990): Meinungen im Umweltbereich und umweltgerechtes Verhalten. Bern: Dissertation.

Grob, Alexander (1991a): Einstellungen und Verhalten im Umweltbereich. *Psychoscope*, 12,(9), 13-17.

Grob, Alexander (1991b): Meinung - Verhalten - Umwelt. Lang.

Guski, Rainer; Wichmann, Ulrich; Rohrmann, Bernd & Finke, Hans-Otto (1978): Konstruktion und Anwendung eines Fragebogens zur sozialwissenschaftlichen Untersuchung der Auswirkungen des Umweltlärms. Zeitschrift für Sozialpsychologie, 1,(9), 50-65.

Haimayer, Peter (1986): Gletscherskigebiete in Österreich. Vorträge zur Fremdenverkehrsforschung. Berichte und Materialien.

Herr, Dieter (1988): Bedingungsmodell umweltbewußten Handelns. Nürnberg: Wirtschafts- und Sozialwissenschaftliche Fakultät.

Hippler, Hans-J.; Schwarz, Nobert & Sudman, Seymour (1987): Social information processing and survey methodology. Recent research in psychology.

Kaiser, Klaus; Gunderlach, Robert & Berger, Gerhard (1991): Ergebnisse der Stuttgarter Bürgerumfrage. Statistischer Informationsdienst, Sonderheft 4.

Kasper, Elisabeth; Sieloff, Ulrike; Nieder, Anita & Eckensberger, Lutz-H. (1987): Entwicklung eines Tests zur Erfassung des Wissens über die Kraftwerksproblematik. Universität Saarbrücken: Fachbereich Sozial- und Umweltwissenschaften.

Klädtke, Anja & Schneider, Hans-Dieter (1991): Welche Beziehungen bestehen zwischen Umweltorientierung und Verkehrsverhalten? Fortschritte der Verkehrspsychologie, Vol.27, 265-271.

Kley, J. & Fietkau, H.-J. (1979): Verhaltenswirksame Variablen des Umweltbewußtseins. *Psychologie und Praxis*, 23,(1), 13-22.

Krämer, Michael (1989): Problembewältigungsstrategien und politisches Engagement. *PP-Aktuell*, 8,(3), 111-123.

Lalli, Marco (1992): Stadtbezogene Identität: Theorie, Messung und empirische Ergebnisse. Journal of Environmental Psychology, 12,(4), 285-303.

Lukesch, Helmut; Nöldner, Wolfgang & Kischkel, Karl-Heinz (1986): Die Reaktorkatastrophe von Tschernobyl in psychologischer Sicht. Regensburg: Arbeitsberichte zur Pädagogischen Psychologie.

Miller, Rudolf (1985): Wohnsituation und Umweltwahrnehmung. In A. Dietrich (Ed.): Bericht über den 34. Kongress der Deutschen Gesellschaft für Psychologie in Wien, 1984. Vol.2, 849-851.

Molt, Walter (1986): Identität und Raumerleben. *PP-Aktuell*, 5,(1), 21-30.

Müller-Andritzky, M.; Chassein, J. & Schick, A. (1990): Interkulturelle Studien zur Erfassung selbstproduzierten Lärms sowie von Nachbarn produzierten Lärms in Wohngebieten. Oldenburg: Institut zur Erforschung von Mensch-Umwelt-Beziehungen.

Namba, Seiichiro; Kuwano, Sonoko & Schick, August (1986): Eine kulturvergleichende Studie zu Lärmproblemen. Journal of the Acoustical Society of Japan,(E), 7,(5), 279-289.

Peter, Jochen & Witte, Erich, H. (1984): Wohnform und Partnerschaft. Hamburg: Fachbereich Psychologie.

Peters, Wolfgang (1979): Haben Sie Angst vor Ihrem Kernkraftwerk? *Bild der Wissenschaft*, 16,(11), 96-105.

Raab, Erich & Jimenez, Paul (1992): Einstellungen zu Müllvermeidung, Mülltrennung und Biomüll. Eine psychologische Studie. Saarbrücken: Berichte aus dem Institut für Psychologie.

Reichel, Wolfgang (1987): Wahrnehmung und Beurteilung von Wohnhäusern. Bochum: Fakultät für Psychologie.

Riemann, Rainer; Grubich, Claudia; Hempel, Susanne; Mergl, Susanne & Richter, Manfred (1993): Persönlichkeit und Einstellungen gegenüber aktuellen politischen Themen. *Personality and Individual Differences*, 15,(3), 313-321.

Rohrmann, Bernd (1986): Probleme der Vergleichbarkeit bei der Gestaltung sozialwissenschaftlicher Forschung zu Umweltstressoren. In A. Schick, H. Hoege & G. Lazarus-Mainka (Eds.): Contributions to psychological acoustics. Oldenburg: Universität Oldenburg, 285-298.

Rosova, Viera; Bianchi, Gabriel & Sladekova, Lubica (1990): Sozopsychologie - Methoden und Ergebnisse für die Grundlagen-Forschung sowie Anwendung. In: S. Höfling & W. Butollo (Eds.): Psychologie für Menschenwürde und Lebensqualität. München: Deutscher Psychologen Verlag, 99-108.

Ruff, Frank, M. (1990a): Dann kommt halt immer mehr Dreck in den Körper. *Psychologie Heute*, 17,(9), 32-38.

Ruff, Frank, M. (1990b): Ökologische Krise und Risikobewußtsein. Berlin: Technische Universität.

Schahn, Joachim & Holzer, Erwin (1989): Untersuchungen zum individuellen Umweltbewußtsein. Bericht aus dem Psychologischen Institut, Diskussionspapier Nr. 62.

Schahn, Joachim & Holzer, Erwin (1990): Konstruktion, Validierung und Anwendung von Skalen zur Erfassung des individuellen Umweltbewußtseins. *Zeitschrift für Differentielle und Diagnostische Psychologie*, 11,(3), 185-204.

Schahn, Joachim; Erasmy, Petra; Trimpin, Andrea & Ditschun, Kersten (1994): Psychologische Massnahmen zur Förderung von Hausmüllvermeidung und Hausmülltrennung. Bericht aus dem Psychologischen Institut, Diskussionspapier Nr. 78.

Schahn, Joachim, Dinger, Johanna, Bohner, Gerd (1994): Die Rolle von Rationalisierungen und Neutralisationen für die Rechtfertigung umweltschädigenden Verhaltens. Bericht aus dem Psychologischen Institut, Diskussionspapier Nr. 80.

Sieloff, Ulrike; Nieder, Anita; Kasper, Elisabeth & Eckensberger, Lutz-H. (1987): Development of a questionnaire for the assessment of ethical orientations in an environmental dilemma. Universität Saarbrücken: Fachbereich Sozial- und Umweltwissenschaften.

Strebl, Gabriele (1986): Gesundes Wohnen - physische, psychische und soziale Aspekte. Salzburg: Naturwissenschaftliche Fakultät.

Timp, Detlef, W. & Fietkau, Hans. J. (1993): Kognitionen gegenüber Umweltrisiken und Belastung im Gefahrguttransport. *Umweltpsychologische Mitteilungen*, 1, 33-45.

Unterbruner, Ulrike (1993): Sehnsüchte und Ängste - Naturerleben bei Jugendlichen. In H. J. Seel, R. Richter & B. Fischlehner (Eds.): Mensch - Natur. Zur Psychologie einer problematischen Beziehung. Westdeutscher Verlag, 164-174.

Wessner, Rolf (1992): Der Widerstand gegen die Startbahn-18-West – ein komplexes Erfahrungsfeld. *Zeitschrift für Sozialpsychologie und Gruppendynamik in Wirtschaft und Gesellschaft*, 17,(3), 37-50.

Weyer, Geerd & Hodapp, Volker (1978): Eine deutsche Version der Work Environment Scale. *Diagnostica*, 24,(4), 318-328.

Winter, Gerhard & Church, Stephen (1984): Ortsidentität, Umweltbewußtsein und kommunalpolitisches Handeln. In H. Moser & S. Preiser (Eds.): Gesellschaftliche Herausforderungen an die Politische Psychologie. Beltz, 78-93.

Wutzl, Elizabeth (1976): Eine architekturpsychologische Untersuchung von Büroräumen. Wien: Grund- und Integrativwissenschaftliche Fakultät.

5

UNDERSTANDING THE ENVIRONMENT: A COMPARISON OF WORKERS IN GERMANY AND POLAND [1]

Abstract

In fall 1990 and summer 1991 respectively, German and Polish industrial workers (n = 52), were given thirty-nine item questionnaires containing issues of environmental import from behavioral/attitudinal standpoints. Measurements tended to reflect dimensions of location divergence.

In German modal results, type of transportation used, reflected the extent of personal and political commitment to environmental protection. This corroborates results found by Grob, 1990, that attitudes are related to behavior.

Results from Polish workers showed a different effect. Whereas behavior did predict attitudes, type of transportation reflected a reversed commitment to environmental protection.

Introduction

In Poland, the mechanisms of communism have left some very devastated areas in its wake - more than 10% of the country has been so ravished, that critics speak of environmental disaster and it has been estimated that 30% of the inhabitants live in dangerously polluted areas.

The city of Lublin, close to the Ukrainian border and located in a traditionally cleaner area because of the relative sparsity of industrial plants, yet has air with such a high content of soot and particles, that it leaves traces on skin and clothing and often, in the right climatic circumstances, the smog at face level takes on a light brown or light-gray color directly visible to the eye. Especially in winter, when energy use increases and

---

[1] This article was published in Psychology: A Journal of Human Behavior, 1994, Vol.31, (2),1-6

particles and fumes are not easily dispersed (Starzewska, 1987) due to their amount as well as weather conditions, but often remain in suspension at ground level, cars are covered with a smeary dirt - a large part of this is from the exhaust of their own making.

Many citizens still burn coal in their own homes and virtually all of the electricity produced in Poland is generated with coal of a relatively high sulfur content. In most cases this occurs without filters: fumes emerging from most factory chimneys are of a deep, dark black.

Innovations such as that at the Zabrze Chemical Institute - located near the highly polluted city of Katowice - are being made, whereby coal is combined with natural salts to decrease emissions. Immediate implementation is, of course, hindered by financial and socio-economic factors typical of the present-day Poland.

In some respects, the process of privatization in Poland has left little room for questions of environmental impact. Privately, citizens are more concerned with rampant inflation, increasing living costs and insufficient wages. Roughly one-third of apartments in Lublin are not paid for each month by their occupants. Communist law still applies regarding this: there is practically no justification for eviction - even of private property - at present possibly still a major source of social stability.

General Work Context

Until 1994, the time-frame for the study, some twenty-five percent of state industry was in private hands and this had changed agonizingly slowly since 1991. Foreign firms often found themselves needing to offer plans of complete modernization and worker compensation for less than 50% ownership in return and negotiations could take several years to complete. Newer joint-ventures generally considered environmental standards in addition to worker needs. Guarantees of compensation were especially significant in the face of roughly 15% jobless and the prevalent tendency to allot directors and those with higher company functions up to 100 times more pay than the worker - in many cases the former communists profiting the most. Typical of the extent to which "pure" capitalism has proliferated, even the media has been critical of this.

In addition to the changes in larger industrial firms, many smaller ones had by then newly come into being and more than 30% of the labor force was then employed in some form of private firm. From an environmental standpoint, privatization had been more successful in larger firms: access to foreign know-how had mainly concerned them, although several pilot-projects had concerned joint ventures or exchange of knowledge with small industry, so in the future, this promises to be different.

At that time and even until now however, in state-owned firms, workers still come into direct contact with materials such as asbestos without having the use of protective clothing or devices. The degree or noxiousness merely determines their length of paid vacations: on the average, they receive an additional week to three weeks, in order to provide for a "cleansing" of the organism.

Whereas difficulties in the work-context can also arise in Germany (Weber, 1990; Müller, 1985), the difference is one of degree, especially concerning the extent of government control curtailing rampant capitalism, through the social free market - "soziale Marktwirtschaft" - system.

At that time and still up to the present, issues of health had relatively low value among Polish workers (Ratajczak, 1993). A brief encounter with Polish work-places makes this attitude and their high-risk behavior at work (Ratajczak, 1993) plausible: many are daily and continually confronted with danger. Reflection on this fact would tend to invoke a high amount of dissonance regarding work. Totally disregarding danger of any type precludes having to face the outcome of years of exposure to noxious agents before it inevitably emerges.

Research Question

The environment has been a viable issue in Poland at least since Solidarity was able to force, in the early 1980's, the closure of several of the most polluting factories through strikes and demonstrations. To date, the more than 300 environmental non-governmental organizations and groups through the country, are largely a development of post-communism.

Whereas - where water-recycling, energy and many other factors are concerned - quantifiable differences can be made between the technology and its relation to the social structure of the two countries of Poland and Germany, placing the latter into a more favorable position, attitudes are harder to measure.

The environmental issue is one with many potentially dissonant aspects, for often decisions made in favor of the environment presuppose personal discomfort of some sort. However much we as a society have not learned to put our knowledge to environmental use and have created a certain context, the individual constrained by this lack and making a decision, often finds his actions curtailed and thus continually needing to rationalize his behavior in some way. In the questions proferred, it was sought to define this in terms of affirmation or denial in regard to the measurement of the relationship between behavior and attitude.

Cognitive dissonance (Aronson, 1980; Frey, 1984) - in relation to the environment - (Schaible-Rapp, 1988; Wortman, Stahlberg & Frey, 1988), can be seen in the light of commitment. Specific behavior creates its own ideals, its constraints in processing information and even in relating to other people. More recently, Ernst et al. (1992), has found that information was processed according to environmental behavior and behavior that was environmentally damaging tended to evoke a disregard even of objective information.

Data and Methods

The present study was conducted during the period of late 1990 in Bremen, Germany and in the summer of 1991 in Lublin, Poland. Although support was given by the local works-council, for Bremen the rate of return was 22 out of 200. In Lublin, where the vice-director distributed the questionnaires, the rate of return was 30 out of 30; each firm was given roughly one week to complete the questionnaires.

In the sample, age ranged from roughly 20 to 60 years and was rated in single digits (e.g. 31 - 40 = 3), with the mean falling at 3 for Polish workers and at 4 for German workers.

Four of the fifty-two workers were women, 1 in Germany, 3 in Poland: none of the salient outcomes measured, reflected a difference in sex: for example all of the car drivers (see Table 4) were male. Level of education was rated on a five-point scale ranging from primary through secondary and preparatory school and according to type and presence of diploma; generally, Polish workers tended to be better educated, the mean in Bremen being German primary whereas the mean in Lublin was Polish lower secondary school.

Work status was rated on an eleven-point scale, ranging from white to blue-collar activity. Correspondingly, on the average, Polish workers had better positions, such as foreman etc. than the German workers, although even then of course, their compensations were on a scale of less than 1:10 (Polish: German); this has only changed in small degrees since that time.

Results

In the following table, the resulting means and other results are given. These will be interpreted further, before a discussion of the import of these results is given.

In the distributed questionnaire, the multiple r for those German workers who drove cars - item 29 - and were not wiling to be involved in any kind of environmental activity, was .42 - with a significance of .053 - although n = 22. It is expected that stronger results will be forthcoming in a second larger study now almost completed (see Chapter 6 for this larger study). The mean results are more specific (see Figures 4 and 5) and show the tendency for German workers- who, on a rated scale from 1 to 8, were given 1, meaning that they exclusively drove cars and did not even try to avail themselves of public transportation - not to want to involve themselves in environmental activity.

In the Polish sample, interpretation of the mean allowed for the opposite effect.

Table 4. Analysis of Variance for behavioral and attitudinal environmental items

Variables	G-worker Mean	P-worker Mean	F-Ratio	R
"Ethics/good life"	4.27	4.40	.07	.04
"Attend cultural events"	4.45	4.33	.12	.05
"Religion & ethics"	4.09	3.23	3.35	.25
"Understanding ethics"	4.95	4.43	1.27	.16
"Ethics interesting"	4.14	3.27	5.08*	.30
"Work most important"	2.23	3.07	3.56	.26
"I'm worried about the above"	2.23	2.97	3.31	.25
"Work makes me happy"	3.32	4.23	6.32*	.34
"Worry abt. environment"	5.95	6.13	.39	.09
"Products not eco-sound"	5.45	5.83	.88	.13
"Anger"	4.23	5.17	3.54	.26
"Introspection abt. ecology"	5.18	4.87	.46	.10
"My firm is eco-sound"	3.50	3.90	.99	.14
"My firm does not listen"	3.91	2.93	5.51*	.32
"Products could be changed"	3.36	3.33	.00	.01
"Ecology threat to modern society"	4.77	3.53	8.45**	.38
"Society needs modern products"	4.59	3.63	4.15*	.28
"Issue too one-sided"	3.55	4.50	4.42*	.29
"User responsibility"	5.68	3.87	13.73**	.46
"Production cannot change"	4.14	3.93	.14	.05
"Quality should be changed"	3.91	2.77	5.01*	.30
"Product dependent on fashion"	2.18	1.60	2.89	.23
"User should think"	6.14	6.10	.01	.02
"Anger over threats"	5.59	5.27	.59*	.11
"Problems wide-spread"	3.41	2.83	1.04	.14
"Worry about products"	4.00	3.47	1.49	.17
"Costs of change too high"	3.64	4.50	2.84	.23
"Belief in Technology"	3.41	4.37	4.03*	.27
"Transportation"	3.50	4.30	1.65	.18
"No interest in ecology"	3.14	2.90	.21	.07
"Society is in danger"	4.86	4.43	.74	.12
"Products should be more eco-sound"	4.50	4.30	.15	.05
"Self-blame"	4.23	3.90	.56	.11
"Eco-work groups"	3.91	3.73	.12	.05
"I work only for the money"	5.14	4.73	.61	.11
"Production is harmful to me"	4.59	5.63	4.78*	.30
"Future-oriented"	3.55	2.30	8.81**	.39
"Eco-soundness is difficult"	5.18	5.20	.00	.01
"Too many unknowns"	4.73	4.97	.20	.06

Note * p<.05 ** p<.01

Figure 4.

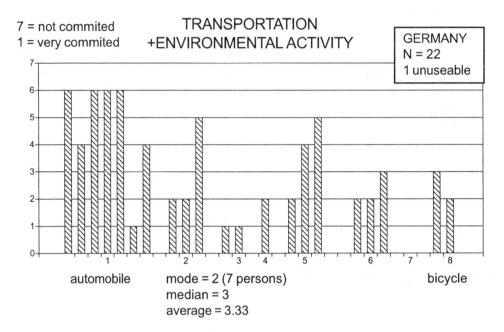

Figure 5.

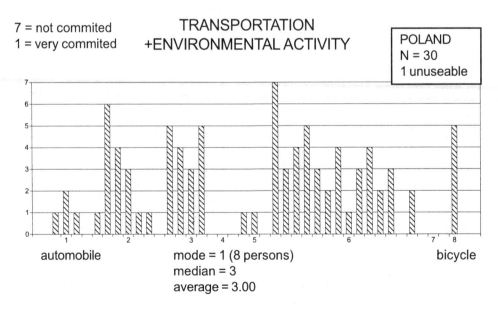

Figure 6.

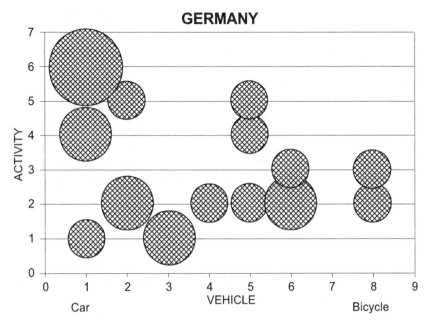

Figure 7.

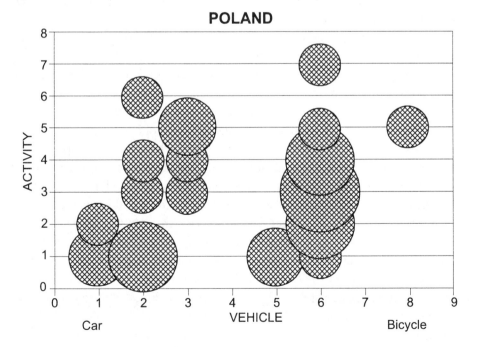

Further, item 29, the use of transportation and item 31, which questions if present society has a future, resulted in r = .48 with p < .01. Item 29, again transportation and items 1-5, relating to questions of ethics, were multiple r = .65 and p < .05; item 35, a question whether worker is only done for money, with item 1-5 ethics, resulted in a multiple 5 = .65 and p < .01.

Among the mean ratings listed in Table 4, particularly item 16, 19, 21 and 37 - with their higher German means - are of interest. Among other significant ratings, item 36 - evaluating the harmfulness of production - is significantly higher in Poland.

Further, the next figures will show differences even more exactly.

Here, the distribution allows the reader to see where preferences are made. The Polish sample shows quite the reverse picture on the one hand and, on the other, a two-peaked distribution.

Discussion

With a total n = 52, this study can only serve as a preliminary attempt to clarify relative interrelationships concerning the content specified above. Given n = 22 in Germany, the Polish study was accordingly kept small: Walters et al. (1993) corroborate in their research and correspondence the difficulties of conducting research of this type in Germany, especially for a resident of a foreign country. One positive aspect of the size is the possibility of analyzing each worker and correlating item scores more exactly.

The mean results in Figures 4 and 5 show a practically opposite tendency for German and Polish workers to be commited to environmental activity when driving cars. For German workers, this agreed with the findings of Ernst et al. (1992), that namely those without a positive commitment to the environment negated the whole issue and with those of Grob, (1990) who related attitudes to behavior.

The Polish workers, on the other hand, showed more of a willingness to be environmentally active when they drove cars. In Poland, where public transportation is neither as efficient, nor as clean as in Germany, the attitude seems to be that cars provide the better and more environmentally sound alternative to public transportation. This is reflected by the slightly higher but significant mean for Polish workers in item 28, which concerns itself with a belief in technology and in its ability to eventually solve the crisis entirely. As further reflected by item 36, where both German, but even more so Polish workers, significantly answered that production in their firm causes pollution and that ultimately this is to their own personal disadvantage, one must remember that most Polish firms use outdated equipment, which often installed already used parts (some equipment dates back to the turn of the century). It is plausible that, to the Poles, anything new is bound to be better, as indeed is often quite true.

In Germany, as overall in the West, restructuring of the economy due to economic crises has generally reduced a reliance on heavy industry and a concentration on new technologies (Kinnear et al., 1987). Furthermore, much has been done to reduce pollution in heavy industries, whereas the Poles - and this often with German technologies - are just at present beginning to reduce adverse effects on the environment when planning production. Concern about pollution dates back to communist times, as reflected in the laws dating back to the beginning '70s, but these were rarely put into effect until now.

The correlation of item 29 - transportation - with item 31, where doubt is expressed whether society can continue in its present form, seems to, according to individual measures, reflect that those driving cars have less hope for the future, indicating a more critical evaluation of the present situation. The respective high correlations of item 29 with items of ethics 1-5 and item 35 where the workers were asked to rate if they only worked because it enabled them to have money, with items of ethics 1-5, show car drivers to be more ethically concerned but also with a tendency to do their work largely for financial reasons (any visit to an industrial plant in Poland should make clear that there are few intrinsic pleasures present.)

Further significant respective means can be taken from Table 4. By way of an explanation, item 16 "ecology threat...", was the question of whether society can afford to strive for ecological soundness, without risking all modern comforts: interestingly, in light of above, results were (highly) significantly higher in Germany than in Poland: that is to say, Germans were more convinced that an enhancement of ecological measures was a threat to modern society. Item 37, where individuals were asked to rate their own willingness to sacrifice their cars for the sake of the environment, was again (highly) significantly higher in Germany than in Poland: in Poland car drivers do not associate cars with the worst pollution and indeed, the majority did not drive cars but seemed to feel - according to individual low scores - that if they had one, they would not give it up. The higher mean in Germany reflects the non-drivers - for the drivers had a lower score by one point - with generally those using the most environmentally sound vehicle most willing to give up cars. The rest of the items in Table 4 would seem to be self-explanatory and ultimately reflect quite a difference of attitude between German and Polish workers.

REFERENCES

Aronson, E. (1980): The social animal. San Francisco: W. H. Freeman & Company.

Ernst, A. M., Bayen, U. J., & Spada, H. (1992): Informationssuche und - verarbeitung zur Entscheidungsfindung bei einem ökologischen Problem. In K. Pawlik & K. H. Stapf (Eds.), *Umwelt und Verhalten*. Göttingen: Hans Huber, 107-127.

Frey, D. (1984): Die Theorie der kognitiven Dissonanz. In D. Frey & M. Irle (Eds.), *Theorien der Sozialpsychologie*. Band I. Stuttgart: Hans Huber, 243-293.

Grob, A. (1990): Relevanz von Einstellungen im Umweltbereich und umweltgerechtes Verhalten. Bern: Universität Bern.

Kinnear, R., & Rhode, B. (1987): Europe: Its Environmental Identity. In G. Enyedi, A. J. Gijswit & B. Rhode (Eds.), *Environmental Policies in East and West*. London: Taylor Graham, 5-21.

Müller, R. (1985): Grenzen und Reichweite der Arbeitsmedizin. Zu ihrer Geschichte, ihren Konzepten und Praktiken. In R. Müller (Ed.), *Arbeitsmedizin in sozialer Verantwortung*. Bremen: Zentraldruckerei der Universität Bremen, 39-71.

Ratajczak, Z. (1993): Conflicting Perspectives on Health Promotion in the Work Place. *Polish Psychological Bulletin*, 24(1),75-81.

Schaible-Rapp, A. (1988): Das Entsorgungsproblem. In D. Frey, C. G. Hoyos & D. Stahlberg (Eds.), *Angewandte Psychologie*. München: Psychologie Verlags Union, 283-297.

Starzewska, A. (1987): The Polish People's Republic. In G. Enyedi, A. J. Gijswijt & B. Rhode (Eds.), *Environmental Policies in East and West*. London: Taylor Graham, 294-310.

Walters, D., Dalton, A., & Gee, D. (1993): Worker and Trade Union Representative on Health and Safety in Europe: The Theory, the Practice and the Potential. London: Centre for Industrial and Environmental Safety and Health.

Weber, K. (1990): Der Asbestose Skandal. Hamburger Stiftung für Sozialgeschichte des 20. Jahrhunderts: Arbeitsschutz und Umweltgeschichte. Köln: Volksblatt Verlag.

Wortmann, K., Stahlberg, D., & Frey, D. (1988): Energiesparen. In D. Frey, C. G. Hoyos & D. Stahlberg (Eds.), Angewandte Psychologie. München: Psychologie Verlags Union, 298-316.

6

PREDICTING ATTITUDES ON THE ENVIRONMENT FROM BEHAVIOR: DIFFERENCES IN POLISH AND GERMAN INDUSTRIAL WORKERS [1]

Abstract

Between spring and fall of 1992, a questionnaire containing items on environmental issues with public, private and industrial content were distributed to Polish and German industrial workers. The questionnaire featured items on behavioral and information dissonance as well as environmental knowledge and attribution. In a previous study done with a similar questionnaire (Meseke, 1994), scaled results on behavioral items were correlated with those of attitudinal ones. While German results reproduced previous findings by Grob (1991), Polish ones did not. This second set of findings however, produced more similarities between Poles and Germans. Differences between German and Polish workers were especially pronounced when technological behavior was compared to attitudes towards the environment. In addition, some of the other findings of the first study could be replicated. In the following, further results are differentially listed according to country, firm, occupation and gender.

Introduction

Increasingly, the complexity of modern life is so high, that many work elements are becoming smaller, more compacted (Friedrichs, 1981) and more specialized; the time where man could calculate the societal impact of his own work is in many cases long past. In

---

[1] The following text was presented in an article (of the same title) in the Polish Psychological Bulletin, 1995, 26, (1), 43-56. The research was carried out with the assistance of Grant Nr. NIMG 91-D 0079 from the European Tempus Fund in Brussels, Belgium.

the same way, it is often difficult to recognize the different elements of impact in environmental destruction. Moreover, our faculties are rather more designed to notice immediate danger and to avoid it, but they are not competent at calculating statistically, especially since this often implies contra-intuitive thinking, (Fietkau, 1988; Flohr, 1988 & Preuss, 1991).

Regarding the environment, people are generally dependent upon the information available at the time and within their societal context in order to come to conclusions, as the contexts of many environmental problems are very specific and not easily understood. Even where specific studies are made and results are known, much of the information filtered to the public is unuseable for their daily lives and thus has small immediate behavioral and learning, i.e. knowledge, impact and is, even where easily interpreted, not readily translated into action.

All of the above contribute to a rather unfortunate situation. It often leaves producer and customer alike frustrated at the lack of unified pro-environmental action, as the solution of one problem seems to bring other problems in its wake or ignore those that otherwise occur (Holzapfel & Vahrenkamp, 1993). Indeed, this kind of framework, or more specifically, the lack of one, might be destined to evoke cognitive dissonance (Frey, 1985; Rohrmann, 1988; Wortmann, 1988) of some kind, as action strategies - especially because of the uncertainty factor - are not easily put into congruence with ideals and mental attitudes. Often the only alternative left open for people is to defend the choices they made, in order to achieve mental and overall internal stability.

In addition, because of the lack of clarity over what really constitutes pro-environmental action, very often the present environmental circumstances evoke behavioral compensation that is aimed at solving the problem individually but instead just contributes to the general confusion and does not provide for environmental rehabilitation at all.

Also, in making decisions, one is most likely to receive information from what one feels and sees as the most immediate form of feed-back. Often, one is confronted with environmental contamination only in a very general form and even where, as in some heavily industrial cities, one can barely breathe the air, daily necessities of life take on more importance than the environment: their neglect often proves more life-threatening than even the most contaminated air, water or land surface.

If however, because of a lack of concerted, definite action, we must rely on personal decision-making and individual behavior regarding the environment, we almost condemn ourselves to a lack of real progress. Such complicated decision-making must be based on real behavioral choices, many of which are just not present for the average person because they depend upon an entirely new organization of society.

Therefore, effective environmental action must at least be based on information, options and the chance for concerted behavior. In many ways, industry has more access to these than private persons - or consumers - do: oftentimes, the bulk of research money comes from industry: at present, at least in Europe, some of the most effective measures are actually being taken by them, (often under pressure of government sanctions). Certainly their monetary presence is one of the most forceful and potentially effective, especially when compared to the limited possibilities of the consumer. That, of course, does not exhonerate private persons and neither negates or further seeks to discuss the power of consumer purchasing, it only differentiates - for the time being - between the roles in which they should be made responsible for their actions. It is in the capacity of their public role as agents of the production process where most of the difficulties arise and where they can most directly be solved! The workers themselves, of course, have very limited opportunities to directly change the production process but they, as an active part of a specific industrial entity, often have quite a few options presented to them. In this context, it is interesting to compare the different attitudes of the two groups.

Previous findings

In research done with industrial workers in the period of late 1990 to early 1991, (Meseke, 1994, see Chapter Five) evaluations pointed to differences in the ratings of the German vs. the Polish group studied. Calculations showed, that the same behavioral patterns led to different attitudes of the German and Polish workers.

In Germany, those who were rated as high to middle frequency drivers, were more convinced than any other group that the advancement of technology would provide the impetus for environmental improvement. This was not true in the same sense in Poland, where however, modal results indicated an overall slightly higher belief in technology than in Germany, at a statistical significance of $p < .05$. Concerning stability of society however: in Germany, those representing a high modal distribution could be found in all but those who exclusively drive cars, whereas in Poland car drivers had the most faith in the stability of society.

The differences between Germany and Poland, related to the above items, throw an interesting light on research done previously. German workers, for example, confirm such research as that done by Ernst et al., 1992 and Grob, 1991 (see also Frey, 1981 and Preuss, 1991) the former of which specifically found environmental behavior to predict that a specific behavior - according to the theory of cognitive dissonance - tends to reinforce people to be committed to a prior choice they have made and to, within this context, ignore or negate other possibilities. In this respect, the work done in Switzerland by Grob was also significant, who found users of private transportation to be notably less involved in behavior that was rated by him as being environmental than those who used public transportation, even when he excluded car-related items in his final analysis of variance (Grob, 1991 pg. 110-113). Lyons and Breakwell, (1994) on the other hand, have found information to be a good predictor of environmental attitudes, which might be one of the contributing factors involved in the differential Polish and German findings found here.

Research Design

The following research shows the results of a questionnaire distributed to a Polish and a German population. It was constructed by Alexander Grob of the University of Bern in Switzerland in the late 80's and his findings have been presented in his dissertation and a later publication (see Grob, 1991).

Hypothesis

The initial hypothesis made before the two studies were undertaken, was that findings would be the same in Germany and in Poland, especially as far as cognitive dissonance, measured in relating attitudes to behavior, was concerned. This hypothesis was made before the results of any of the other (Grob, etc.) studies were known, as comparison of the dates can show. As mentioned above however, the findings of the first study pointed to such items as a: "I drive a car", and b: "I am willing to be actively politically involved in the environment" as being positively linked in Poland but negatively in Germany, pointing to two very different relationships toward the environment and thus different outcomes of cognitive dissonance.

This study seeks to, again, compare the different groups involved in this research with each other and, where possible, to replicate the findings.

Sample

As can be seen in the following figure, the Polish sample of n = 397 workers included a great percentage of managing technical and mechanical tasks. The majority of the workers were in their 30's. Of the total n = 397, 147 were women and 245 were men.

The smaller German sample consisted of n = 39 - also of various professions - the majority of which were again in their 30's and of which 16 were women and 23 were men.

Figure 8.

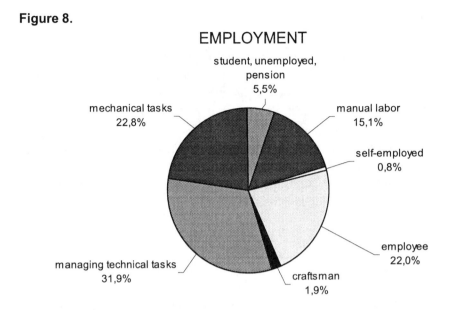

Figure 9.

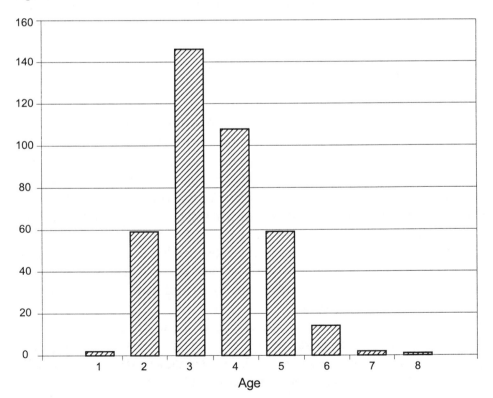

Procedure

Participation in this study was voluntary. Subjects were asked to fill out the Grob questionnaire (1990, in German or Polish) entitled "*Measures of environmental attitudes and behavior*". In Germany, two industrial firms were given some 200 questionnaires. In addition, a total of 200 questionnaires were given out to private households in worker districts of Berlin and Bremen. The end results of these distributions was a resulting sum of 43 returned questionnaires, of which 39 could be used in the final calculation.

In Poland, a total of 500 questionnaires were distributed, of which 160 were given out to private households and the rest to three different firms. The resulting total feedback was n = 397.

The Questionnaire

For the construction of his questionnaire, Grob presented a previously carefully selected pool of items to environmental experts and psychologists to review, and used various statistical methods to insure that those items used in the final questionnaire had received the highest of several approval ratings (Grob, 1991, pg.65-67). An additional total of three reliability testings produced an instrument that fulfills the criteria given by classical test theory (IBID, pp. 65-99).

Results

Some salient results follow, which are taken from the analysis of variance for the 1991 population (n = 52) and compared to the 1992 study (n = 436). There was a lapse of approximately one year between the two studies for Poland and two years for Germany. Because of the differences of rating, only the first 38 questions of the second questionnaire are used in the first two tables. Whereas the first table is a comparison of the means of the two studies: the second one is a comparison of the means for the Polish population only and compares the firms to each other.

As one may note, in Table 5, many of the item results have remained the same and show replicability of the data. Of special interest are the differences in user responsibility and - one may note - this relationship remains the same even when the wording of the question is changed.

A closer look at the Polish data in a more specific analysis of variance between the three firms and private households shows most Total Standard Deviations to be around 1.00 and Cochrans C Max. Variance to be at or below .5. The following table shows where Total SD is above 1.50 and thus means may more significantly differ from each other.

Table 5. Analysis of Variance for Environmental Items in the German and Polish Population: Differences and Similarities 1991/1992

	G-worker Mean	P-Worker Mean	F-Ratio	R
1991				
- Anger	4.23	5.17	3.54	.26
- Anger over threat	5.59	5.27	.59*	.11
1992				
- Feelings of anger	5.38	5.76	2.56	.08
- Anger	5.90	5.78	.29	.03
- Anger at threat for future	5.90	5.64	1.34*	.06
1991				
- Belief in Technology	3.41	4.37	4.03*	.27
1992				
- Technical progress needed	4.23	6.17	93.30***	.42
- Problems will be solved w/ technol.	4.13	6.02	77.61***	.39
- Technical appliances would help	4.41	5.65	31.12***	.26
- More investm. in techn. needed	5.54	6.02	4.58*	.10
- Science and technology can solve problems	5.37	6.26	21.68***	.22
1991				
- Ecology threat to modern society	4.77	3.53	8.45**	.38
1992				
- Eco-info is threat to society	2.30	3.36	12.28***	.17
1991				
- User responsibility	5.68	3.87	13.73**	.46
1992				
- Solution in technology rather than personal responsibility	2.97	5.47	89.68***	.42

Table 6. Analysis of Variance between the four Polish groups (Total Standard Deviation and Cochrans C Max. Variance for the firms Brewer = B; Canalization = C; Car factory = F and private households = P)

Item	B	P	C	F	TSD	CMax
Media exagg.	4.32	3.70	3.68	3.82	2.04	.26
Bad company policy	4.71	3.98	3.74	4.09	1.90	.31
E. threat for society	3.78	3.16	3.16	3.19	1.79	.30
Need more techn.	5.17	5.63	5.75	5.40	1.90	.28
Work valuable	4.56	3.56	4.35	4.30	1.68	.29
Don't see pollution	5.44	5.18	4.47	3.90	2.52	.29
Industry is respon	4.52	3.52	3.70	3.79	1.83	.31
Don't like change	5.00	4.87	4.82	4.94	1.79	.30
Trees not polluted	4.98	4.45	4.49	4.06	2.03	.31
Work more impt.	4.93	4.04	4.44	4.61	1.65	.31
Stop driving	4.98	4.55	4.68	4.16	1.87	.30
Techn. is solution	5.28	5.71	5.29	5.62	1.52	.30
Noise pollut. bother	5.65	5.55	5.73	5.32	1.58	.31
Pers. freedom impt.	4.57	4.29	4.29	3.63	1.95	.29
Government helps	4.33	3.38	3.60	3.50	1.68	.27

Figure 10. POLISH POPULATION All Item Groups

	Knowl.	Perc.	Disc.	Aff.r.	Pv	Inf.	Tech.	Beh.	Trans.
Perception	-.05								
Discrepancy	.15	.14							
Affective react.	.02	.22***	.02						
Personal values	-.12*	.57***	.20*	.14**					
Information seek.	-.03	.30***	-.02	.54***	.37***				
Technology	.05	.24***	.19*	.47***	.13*	.45***			
Behavior	-.08	-.10	-.17	-.02	-.22**	-.01	-.07		
Transportation	-.12*	.03	-.42***	.03	.10	.09	-.10	.42***	
Personal comm.	.07	.17*	.20	.21**	.22**	.28***	.15*	.09	.05

'p<.05 **p<.01 ***p<.001

Figure 11. GERMAN POPULATION All Item Groups

	Knowl.	Perc.	Disc.	Aff.r.	Pv	Inf.	Tech.	Beh.	Trans.
Perception	-.15								
Discrepancy	-.19	.18							
Affective react.	.09	.25	.29						
Personal values	-.10	.48***	.13	.13					
Information seek.	.14	-.12	.16	.41**	-.24				
Technology	.08	.58***	.11	.13	.52**	.14			
Behavior	-.11	-.06	.03	.27	-.13	.07	-.08		
Transportation	-.12	-.08	.33	.23	.04	.10	-.15	.54***	
Personal comm.	.27	-.13	.33	.09	-.09	.42**	-.04	-.24	-.24

Even though the above ratings are not characterized by as much homogeneity as the rest, one cannot find great differences between them. This is of particular interest because one of the firms - the car factory - was regarded (by environmental experts here in Lublin) to be by far the most polluting of the various firms.

The following two figures show the factors Grob derived and correlations for both groups provide some interesting similarities as well as differences. In the Polish group, transportation correlated with environmental behavior at a value of .42 at the .001 level, which does not conform to the results of the first study, where a low correlation was shown in the Polish population.

Among the German workers, the correlation found between transportation and environmental behavior was .54, also at the .001 level, a finding much comparable to the previous one. Finally, these same item groupings were also used to rate professional groups and compare the results of gender.

Great differences cannot be found between the various professional groups depicted here. Perhaps the most salient difference consists of the self-employed group, who several times have higher means, sometimes of several points. Interesting is their high personal perspective toward commitment and their rather low comparative rating of environmental behavior. The high mean that craftsmen (6) have in regard to transportation, shows them to utilize the least polluting forms of public transportation. Because differences are so small however, these findings would need to be replicated in an even larger population in order to be of further interest.

The final table, shows differences of gender. These are not particularly salient throughout.

Table 7. Analysis of Variance between different task groups with Total Standard Deviation (TSD) and Cochrans C Test for Homogeneity of Variance (CM = CMax)

1*	2	3	4	5	6	7	TSD - CM
Knowledge:							
1.43	1.51	1.14	3.89	1.36	.67	1.40	1.56 - .20
Perception:							
4.98	4.38	5.00	5.80	4.83	4.26	5.16	1.16 - .20
Discrepancy:							
3.65	3.59	3.48	---	3.91	3.13	3.81	.59 - .38**
Affective Reaction:							
6.15	6.15	6.19	6.28	5.98	5.81	6.58	.83 - .57***
Personal Values:							
4.56	4.22	4.41	4.87	4.68	4.31	4.66	.93 - .23*
Seeking Information:							
5.33	5.30	5.45	6.17	5.32	4.76	5.73	.87 - .39***
Belief in Technology:							
6.07	5.88	6.04	6.50	5.75	5.69	5.98	.81 - .59***
Environmental Behavior:							
1.97	2.15	2.75	2.10	2.32	2.90	2.42	1.00 - .21
Transportation:							
3.30	3.20	3.72	3.00	3.92	4.86	3.13	1.63 - .18
Personal Committment:							
4.26	4.14	3.90	6.19	4.48	3.73	4.28	1.17 - .24

*p<.05 ** p<.01 ***p<.001

* Key:
1= mechanical tasks; 2=managing technical tasks; 3=employee; 4=self-employed; 5=manual labor; 6=craftsman; 7=other - student, unemployed, pensioner

Table 8. Independent Samples of Gender for Item Groups Pooled Variance Estimate for T value and Degrees of Freedom

	Male	SD	Female	SD	F	T	DF
Knowledge							
	1.74	1.60	.78	1.29	1.53**	6.21***	390
Perception							
	4.76	1.56	4.84	1.15	1.01	-.65	363
Discrepancy							
	3.60	.52	3.63	.69	1.77*	-.24	113
Affective Reaction							
	6.06	.90	6.27	.65	1.96***	-2.42*	375
Personal Values							
	4.46	.93	4.49	.93	1.01	-.27	369
Seek. Information							
	5.27	.90	5.52	.76	1.43*	-2.78**	381
Belief in Techn.							
	5.94	.86	5.93	.70	1.51**	.14	376
Environm. Behav.							
	2.11	.94	2.63	1.06	1.28	-3.01**	141
Transportation							
	3.32	1.69	3.76	1.52	1.24	-2.47	366
Pers. Committment							
	4.38	1.11	3.85	1.18	1.13	3.03**	184

*p<.05 ** p<.01 ***p<.001

Discussion

Any research on environmental attitudes and behavior must needs be characterized by change according to the vast societal responses to this area of human activity and their relative impact on existing problems. This is true of both Germany and Poland because the time-period in question encompasses much environmental activity in Germany as well as societal and political changes in Poland - both of these carrying many positive effects on environmental issues with them.

In the past 20 years, Germany has meaningfully changed its emission and pollution level in a vast amount of industries. In addition, even though industry has greatly increased production over the past 30 years, the use of and direct need for energy has decreased! This is true in part due to alternative energy - such as solar heat and energy generation - being directly used by plants, to better energy relays and to re-structuring of firms as well as utilization of environmental experts (who usually tend to save the firms so much each year, that the income of the experts is small in relation to savings).

Environmentalism in Germany has been slow to touch the consumers favorite object: the car. While 3-way-catalysers are decreasing exhaust, more cars are being registered each year and the real output of emissions is increasing. Meanwhile, public transportation has, not only because of pollution, but out of a lack of space - especially within inner-city-limits - become a real alternative for most commuters. In addition, many city-dwellers - and visitors - now prefer shopping areas to be car-free (grocery markets as exceptions are usually located in car-accessible places), thus taking away one of the arguments for using the car in the first place. In the past years, there has been a series of smog-alerts, especially in larger cities, where private vehicles were principally not allowed to be driven during a certain time (with the exception of police, ambulances etc.) It was possibly due to this and the attempts of mass-media that the findings in Germany were so salient. As the results of the second study now point to the same type of behavior existing in Poland, one might interpret this to have come about through an access to more information in Poland in the interim between the two studies. Another reason for the differences in the two studies however, might be found in semantics and the higher relative importance assigned to political activity in Poland than in Germany. In this context it is interesting to look at the differences of ecological organization in the two countries - whereas in Germany ecological behavior has almost become mandatory, a large part of behavior is still left up to the individual in Poland. Additionally, whereas in Germany, the perceived threat ecology poses for the organization of society changed, it remained the same in Poland (see Table 5): ecology is seen as less of a societal threat than it was two years ago. That the correlation between behavior and transportation was still so high in Germany seems to isolate transportation from the other dimensions. These findings seem to indicate a dissonance accompanying environmental behavior in both countries, where one type of behavior strongly reinforces or negates the next one.

Again, these findings are especially surprising when one considers that many changes in industry and aspects of environmental social re-organization are just beginning to start in Poland; yet Poland is already so similar to Germany. To be considered however, is that the Poles are beginning with technology at a point where it is well-developed and can possibly do a great deal to help in problems of environmental pollution, thus making the finding of their higher belief in technology, which paradoxically was never as high among drivers (Meseke, 1994) in Poland, perfectly plausible within the societal situation.

As one notes, the tables present differences to be greater between the two populations than between either professional groups, gender or different firms.

Conclusion

Many of the findings from the 1994 study could be replicated (Table 5). In the second study, drivers in Poland also replicated the findings made by Grob (1991) and Ernst (1992), where cognitive dissonance seemed to account for behavior influencing attitudes to the effect that a person negates or ignores issues that provide a dissonant relationship to their daily behavior. Perhaps the widespread use of catalyzers has made drivers believe that they are driving environmentally friendly vehicles and their argument is, that some simple solution will come for all the other problems as well.

The findings are especially interesting in light of the fact that many forms of what was considered to be part of environmental behavior by Grob, (those forming the group of items used in the questionnaire), have become organizational social reality in Germany and have become an accepted part of responsible human behavior, such as taking a daily shower or bath and brushing one's teeth. The fact that drivers still do not conform to this is an almost astounding verification of cognitive dissonance.

REFERENCES

Ernst, A. M., Bayen, U. J. and Spada, H. (1992): Informationssuche und - verarbeitung zur Entscheidungsfindung bei einem ökologischen Problem. In: K. Pawlik & K. H. Stapf (Eds.), Umwelt und Verhalten (pp.107-127). Göttingen: Hans Huber.

Fietkau, H.-J. (1984): Bedingungen ökologischen Handelns. Weinheim-Beltz.

Flohr, H. (1988): Ideen oder Gene? Politisches Handeln zwischen Biologie und Kultur. In S. Bachmann, M. Bohnet & K. Lompe (Eds.), Industriegesellschaft im Wandel. Chancen und Risiken heutiger Modernisierungsprozesse (pp. 57-75). Hildesheim: Georg Olms AG.

Frey, D. (1984). Die Theorie der kognitiven Dissonanz. In D. Frey & M. Irle (Eds.), Theorien der Sozialpsychologie, 1, (pp 243-292). Stuttgart: Hans Huber.

Frey, D., Heire, C., Stahlberg, D., and Wortmann, K. (1987): Psychologische Forschung zum Energiesparen. In J. Schultz-Gambard (Ed.), Angewandte Sozialpsychologie (pp. 275-289). München: Psychologie Verlags Union.

Grob, A. (1991): Meinung, Verhalten, Umwelt. Bern: Peter Lang AG.

Haigh, N., Bera, G., and Zentain, V. (1987): The Background to Environmental Production in Market and Planned Economy Countries. In G. Enyedi, A. J. Gijswijt & B. Rhode (Eds.), Environmental Policies in East and West (pp. 22-29). London: Taylor Graham.

Holzapfel, H., & Vahrenkamp, R. (1993): Bemerkungen zum Zusammenhang der steigenden Arbeitsteilung mit dem Verkehrsaufwand. Informationsdienst. Institut für ökologische Wirtschaftsforschung GmbH, Vereinigung für ökologische Wirtschaftsforschung e.V., 2, 8, 6-7.

Janiszewski, W. (1973): Ochrona przyrody w Polsce na tle sytuacji międzynarodowej. Warszawa: Liga Ochrony Przyrody.

Jarzębski, S. (1985): O środowisku naturalnym bez emocji. In Polityka, 12.10.1985.

Kramer, H. (1993): The European Community's Response to the 'New Eastern Europe'. *Journal of Common Market Studies*, 31, 2, June 1993.

Kruse, L.; Graumann, C.-F. & Lantermann, E.-D. (1990): Ökologische Psychologie. München: Psychologie Verlags Union.

Kuldiński, A. (1989): Ecological Renaissance. The first milestone on the way to the United Europe. Warszawa: University Press.

Lazarus, R. S.; Launier, R. (1978): Stress-related transactions between person and environment. In L. A. Pervin & M. Lewis (Eds.), Perspectives in interactional psychology. New York.

Lewin, K. (1963): Feldtheorie in den Sozialwissenschaften. Stuttgart: Huber.

Lyons, E. & Breakwell, G. M. (1994): Factors predicting environmental concern and indifference in 13- to 16-year-olds. *Environment and Behavior*, 26, 2, 223-238.

Meseke, M. (1994): Understanding the environment: A comparison of workers in Germany and Poland. Psychology: *A Journal of Human Behavior*, 31, 2, 1-8.

Mogel, H. (1990): Umwelt und Persönlichkeit. Göttingen: Hogrefe

Müller,G. F. & Crott, H. W. (1984): Gerechtigkeit in sozialen Beziehungen. In D. Frey & M. Irle (Eds.), Theorien der Sozialpsychologie, 1 (pp.218-241). Stuttgart: Hans Huber.

Ochrona Środowiska (1992): Materiały i opracowania statystyczne. Warszawa: Główny Urząd Statystyczny.

Öschlies, W. (1987): Bald ist Polen doch verloren. Köln:Böhlau Verlag.

Pawlik, K. & Stapf, K. H. (Eds., 1991): Umwelt und Verhalten. Göttingen: Huber.

Peitsch, H. (1991): Kooperation zwischen Ost und West im Umweltbereich. Dissertation. Köln.

Preuss, S. (1991): Umweltkatastrophe Mensch. Heidelberg: Roland Ansanger Verlag.

Rohrmann, B. (1988): Gestaltung von Umwelt. In D. Frey, C. G. Hoyos & D. Stahlberg (Eds.), Angewandte Psychologie. München: Psychologie Verlags Union.

Schott, E. (1991). Psychologie der Situation. Heidelberg: Roland Asanger Verlag.

Sharp, M. & Pavitt, K. (1993): Technology Policy in the 1990s: Old Trends and New Realities. *Journal of Common Market Studies*, 31, 2, June 1993.

Szczepański, J. (1989): Poland: Facing the Future. Warszawa: University of Warsaw, Faculty of Geography.

Tymowski, A. W. (1993): The Unwanted Social Revolution. *East European Politics and Societies*. Vol. 7, Nr.2, Spring 1993, pg. 169-202.

Wortmann, K.; Stahlberg, D. & Frey, D. (1988): Energiesparen. In D. Frey; C. G. Hoyos & D. Stahlberg (Eds.), Angewandte Psychologie (pp. 298-316). München: Psychologie Verlags Union.

7

ENVIRONMENTAL ATTITUDES
AND BEHAVIOR OF GERMAN WORKERS [1]

Abstract

In March, 1996, questionnaires were distributed to German industrial workers in cooperation with the IG Metall in Bremen and to some private households as well, returns totaled n = 126. These were compared to some results done in a previous study in 1992, where n = 397. Items measured attitudinal as well as behavioral aspects of different environmental issues. Results showed that environmental behavior was to some extent positively correlated to attitudes. It was also, in several cases, a strong predictor of further environmental behavior in various contexts.

Introduction

It is difficult to quantify the progress that has been made in relation to environmental issues. The duration of mankind's abuse has been long-standing - the first historically documented smog alerts dating from the time when larger agglomerations of people abused firing, heating and refining processes by merely being too industrious - for example in London. This same assiduity brought forth forest spoilation in large areas covering Greece, the former Yugoslavia and areas surrounding Rome, to mention only a few in Europe.

When one considers the longevity of the environmental movement, it is quite heartening to find that many structural and attitudinal changes have come about within the last twenty years. Judging by the strength of the environmentally engaged groups and their ability to force reversals because popular opinion supported them (in Poland, among other things, the closure of extremely hazardous production plants

---

[1] The following chapter was presented as a paper at the conference "Crossroads in Cultural Studies" in Tampere, Finland, in June, 1996. It was modified somewhat to change the context of this text.

was affected; in Germany many developments can be traced to engaged - and often politically active - nature and environmental groups) there has been an immense change in popular sentiment in this time-period on both sides of the Odra River.

Unfortunately, judging from the literature (Petschow, 1993; Antes, 1993), for every environmentally affirmative action, there are changes in the advancement of technology, the structure of production or political reversals that seem to bestow us with other dilemmas. On the one hand, for example, the circle of production suppliers keeps increasing, for industry has found it cheaper to delegate tasks and assign materials to suppliers and to assemble, distribute and market themselves (Holzapfel & Vahrenkamp, 1993); on the other hand however, this causes more need for transportation of materials and thus more pollution and obstruction of roads and passages: unfortunately, this seems of secondary concern.

General work context

When one considers the availability of health care, the daily life of the Polish worker was organized very similarly to that - for example - of the average German one, even before the change in 1989. One need only consider the accessibility of works councils and medical personnel present in representation of size in factories and firms of both countries to appreciate their far-reaching potential influence, although the practical possibilities of the Poles were always much poorer than those of the Germans.

However, a very major difference between the two countries is the general standard of technology in state industrial firms. Whereas the German government has treated investment into public property as a real financial asset, directly involving itself in many and various market areas, the principles of Marxist communism (Helfgott, 1992) and a "big brother" mentality of the Soviet states have never allowed effective modernization, even where Polish political visionaries tried to effect changes throughout the years. In seeing the struggle that the Poles are going through today, one must never forget how many years of difficulties they have behind them, where change was made impossible or slow because of a lack of political understanding as well as consensus in international legislation and socio-economic regulations. Sadly enough, they have been left with the bill for all of this.

Certainly in Soviet times and in all too many cases still now, workers often faced excruciating muscle-work in industrial units and not seldomly the work-schedule was very heavy; both of which were exacted by a machinery that had numerous ergonomic deficiencies and often was simply very old and used. To some extent, that has changed since then, both in private and in state firms. Not even now however, are the work situation and the practical implications of the social and legal insurances the Polish worker enjoys comparable to those of the German one, albeit Germany has lost and

Poland has gained some ground in the last two years and both are structurally similar: a situation which has increasingly proven to make changes easier and faster.

Research Problem

The question of a sound natural and physical environment is a problem of increasing viability on the entire European continent and one that, of course, makes no hold at borders. In attempting to look for similarities and differences in attitudes and behavior toward the environment, questionnaires were distributed in Bremen, Germany.

Method

A multidimensional environmental questionnaire (Grob, 1991), was distributed. Participation in this study was voluntary. Returns were n = 126.

Sample

As can be seen in the following figures, the tasks of the n = 126, included a great percentage of students and mechanical tasks.

Figure 12. Distribution of Tasks

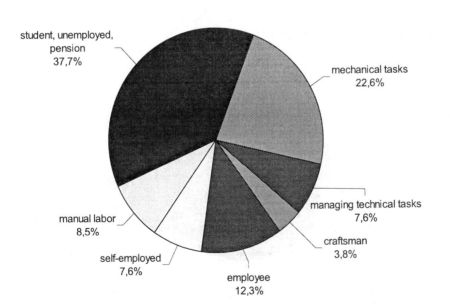

Figure 13. Distribution of Age

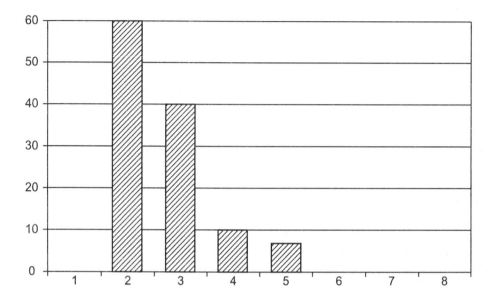

The majority of those questioned were in their 20's.

Of the total n = 126, 43 were women and 83 were men: the exact distribution can be seen in the following.

Figure 14. Distribution of Gender

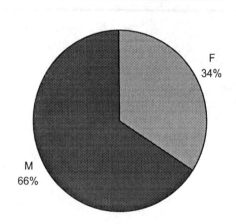

Results

The following Table recapitulates some results from the 1992 study in comparison to the one done in 1995.

As this table shows, feelings of anger have lowered in the German population and there is also less belief in the capacity of technology to solve all problems. The feeling that personal responsibility is more important than technological advances is still as high in Germany as it was in 1992, varying largely from the Polish population. Further differences in the means of the two populations can be seen in Appendix One.

Table 10 shows a comparison of different task groups to the factors already mentioned in the last chapter.

These values show very small differences, as was the case with the Polish study mentioned in Chapter Six.

Table 9. Analysis of Variance

Items	Means		
	G-1992	P-1992	G-1996
Feelings of anger	5.38	5.76	4.39
Anger	5.90	5.78	4.13
Anger at threat for future	5.90	5.64	3.53
Technical progress needed	4.23	6.17	3.71
Problems will be solved w/techn.	4.13	6.02	4.58
Technical applications would help	4.41	5.65	3.87
More investm. in techn. needed	5.54	6.26	4.24
Science and technology can solve probl.	5.37	6.26	3.82
Eco-info is threat to society	2.30	3.36	3.53
Solution in technology rather than personal responsibility	2.97	5.47	2.76

Table 10. Analysis of Variance between different task groups

1	2	3	4	5	6	7	TSD-CM
Knowledge							
1.17	3.79	1.08	2.04	---	1.75	.93	1.74-.48***
Perception							
3.69	4.47	3. 38	3.70	3.58	3. 55	3.26	.81-.29*
Discrepancy							
3.67	4.40	3.60	4.13	4.00	---	---	.46-.66
Affective Reaction							
6.05	5.14	6.11	5.65	5.83	5.13	5.10	1.15-.56***
Personal Values							
3.77	4.17	3.45	3.53	3.51	2.65	3.15	.93-.19
Seeking Information							
5.07	4.77	4.96	5.19	5.09	4.83	4.74	.92-.40***
Belief in Technology							
4.88	4.85	4.22	3.75	4.76	4.96	4.45	1.07-.37**
Environmental Behavior							
3.30	2.55	3.43	2.30	1.50	---	3.48	1.17-.66*
Transportation							
1.56	1.33	2.11	1.50	1.67	2.00	3.39	1.49-.22
Personal Commitment							
3.60	3.48	2.81	4.94	3.23	3.69	4.29	1.10-.29

*$p<.05$; **$p<.01$; ***$p<.001$

Total Standard Deviation (TSD) and Cochrans C Test for Homogeneity of Variance (CM=CMAX)

Key:
1 = mechanical tasks;
2 = managing technical tasks;
3 = employee;
4 = self employed;
5 = manual labor;
6 = craftsman;
7 = student

Table 11. Independent Samples of Gender

Male	SD	Female	SD	F	T	DF
Knowledge						
1.24	1.76	1.23	1.58	1.23	.05	115
Perception						
3.55	.81	3.49	.79	1.05	.40	114
Discrepancy						
3.82	.52	3.67	.09	30.43	.41	11
Affective Reaction						
5.58	1.15	5.63	1.06	1.16	-.23	113
Personal Values						
3.68	.93	3.15	.82	1.28	2.98**	111
Seek. Information						
5.00	.81	4.86	1.05	1.67	.76	110
Belief in Technology						
4.79	1.00	4.18	1.03	1.06	3.13**	115
Environm. Behav.						
2.39	1.21	3.24	1.08	1.26	-1.66	18
Transportation						
2.33	1.55	2.54	1.48	1.10	-.55	71
Pers. Commitment						
3.76	1.09	3.54	.99	1.22	.44	29

*p<.05; **p<.01; ***p<.001
Item Groups Pooled Variance Estimate for T Value and Degrees of Freedom

Discussion

The above findings are especially interesting in light of those mentioned in Chapter Six, where few differences were found between the various professions and the genders. A further comparison of the findings will be found in Chapter Eight.

While this adds interesting aspects to the question of German vs. Polish worker attitudes towards the environment, it should be underscored that, in the long run, a change in attitude should come with a changing system and technological innovations which will then be available to both countries.

By and large, when considering the volume of environmental damage or environmentally contaminating products - as already mentioned - the most effective environmental behavior can be made by industry within the productional process (Preuss, 1991). To argue that individual buying behavior and consumption and with it the market controls that could lever and evoke changes are able to form and shape this gigantic area of activity, is to ignore several points.

Most importantly, it is time that regulation must be passed and this especially on an international level. Every other major activity of man is regulated, airplanes and cars cannot move without ignoring the many constraints on their activities and yet, within the many-faceted area of pollution, we happily act in further unconstraint - in ignorance of the most simple relationships, oftentimes forgetting to simply organize ourselves better: much of pollution can be alleviated by doing just that. Processes must be changed, if society is to be capable of functioning for very much longer.

Individuals are much more helpless in their fight against pollution than institutions or firms (Mogel, 1990). To make individuals responsible for what they have little control of is to blatantly ignore the fact that many of the most polluted environments in the world are in areas where the poor abound, those characteristically unable to withstand many forces of society and endowed with very little buying power in order to make their needs felt (Rosen, 1994).

Unfortunately, many times the poor are at fault for environmental damage and must be educated and shown alternatives: in Poland, this is manifested in the fact that oil pipelines running through very poor urban or rural areas are systematically drilled into and millions of liters per year are lost, not through robbery, but in further and steady leakages after these drillings take place. Much of this is done in the countryside, where 40% of Poles live as farmers (compared to 6% in Germany, Mach, 1994) and often make their living by selling the agricultural products they can grow on one or two acres: people are not only poor but very simple.

Real change will come then, through an interaction between growing political concern (Joppke, 1994), a change of legislature and enforcement (Bohling, 1992; Cairncross, 1994) and in education and the offering of alternative structures (Masberg, 1992). At least a part of the energy expended in enforcement must be directed and addressed to the lack of moral principles: this is particularly true of Poland, where bribing of officials is necessary even to those who have the law on their side.

Finally, in the wake of European integration, which should also have positive monetary effects on Poland (Richter, 1994; Christou, 1994), standards need to be internationalized (Yeager, 1992), also encouraging international policing institutions, with a real calculation of the costs involved (Qayum, 1994).

REFERENCES

Arrous, J. (1994): The Leontief Pollution Model. A Systematic Formulation. *Economic Systems Research*, 6, 1, 105-107.

Bell, A. (1994): Climate of opinion: public and media discourse on the global environment. *Discourse and Society*, 5, 1, 33-64.

Biela, A. (1984): Stres psychiczny w sytuacji kryzysu ekologicznego. Badania z zakresu sociopsychologii. Lublin: Wydawn. Tow. Nauk. KUL.

Bohling, W. (1992): Probleme und Auswirkungen einer Verankerung des Umweltschutzes in der Verfassung der Bundesrepublik Deutschland. In M. v. Hauff & U. Schmid (Eds.), Ökonomie und Ökologie (pp. 3-16). Stuttgart: Schäffer-Poeschel Verlag.

Cairncross, F. (1994): Environmental Pragmatism. *Foreign Policy*, 95, 35-52.

Christou, C. & Nyhus, D. (1994): Industrial Effects of European Community Integration. *Economic Systems Research*, 6, 2, 179-198.

Ernst, A. M., Bayen, U. J. and Spada, H. (1992): Informationssuche und - verarbeitung: zur Entscheidungsfindung bei einem ökologischen Problem. In K. Pawlik & K. H. Stapf (Eds.), Umwelt und Verhalten (pp.107-127). Göttingen: Hans Huber.

Frey, D. (1984): Die Theorie der kognitiven Dissonanz. In D. Frey & M. Irle (Eds.), Theorien der Sozialpsychologie (Vol. 1, pp.243-292). Stuttgart: Hans Huber.

Grob, A. (1991): Meinung, Verhalten, Umwelt. Bern: Peter Lang AG.

Helfgott, R. B. (1992): Labor Process Theory vs. Reform in the Workplace. *Critical Review* 6, 1, 11-27.

Joppke, C. & Markovits, A. S. (1994): Green Politics in the new Germany. *Dissent*, Spring, 235-240.

Kommission der Europäischen Gemeinschaften (1993): Gemeinschaftsrecht im Bereich des Umweltschutzes, Vol.1, Allgemeine Politik.

Krämer-Badoni, T. (1994): Life without the car: an experiment and a plan. *International Journal of Urban and Regional Research*, 18, 2, 347-356.

Lewin, K. (1963): Feldtheorie in den Sozialwissenschaften. Stuttgart: Huber.

Mach, B. W., Mayer, K. U., Pohoski, M. (1994): Job changes in the Federal Republic of Germany and Poland: a longitudinal assessment of the impact of welfare-capitalist and state-socialist labour-market segmentation. *European Sociological Review*, 10, 1, 1-28.

Marcinkiewicz, J. (1987): Pollution in the Heart of Europe. London: Polish Society of Arts and Sciences Abroad.

Masberg, D. (1992): Konzeptionen einer ökologischen Marktwirtschaft - Anmerkungen aus der Sicht einer Politik der Umweltvorsorge. In M. v. Hauff & U. Schmid (Eds.), Ökonomie und Ökologie (pp.17-38). Stuttgart: Schäffer-Poeschel Verlag.

Marody, M. (1994): In Search of Collective Sense. *Polish Sociological Review*, 1, 105, 17-22.

Meseke, C. (1994): Understanding the Environment: A comparison of workers in Germany and Poland. *Psychology: A Journal of Human Behavior*, 31, 2, 1-8.

Mogel, H. (1990): Umwelt und Persönlichkeit. Göttigen: Hogrefe.

Müller,G. F. & Crott, H. W. (1984): Gerechtigkeit in sozialen Beziehungen. In: D. Frey & M. Irle (Eds.), Theorien der Sozialpsychologie (Vol.1, pp.218-241). Stuttgart: Hans Huber.

Ochrona Środowiska (1992). Warszawa.

Preuss, S. (1991): Umweltkatastrophe Mensch. Heidelberg: Roland Ansanger Verlag.

Qayum, A. (1994): Inclusion of Environmental Goods in National Income Accounting. *Economic Systems Research*, 6, 2, 159-166.

Richter, J. (1994): Austria and the Single European Market. *Economic Systems Research*, 6, 1, 77-90.

Roller, E. (1994): Ideological Basis of the Market Economy: Attitudes Toward Distribution Principles and the Role of Government in Western and Eastern Germany. *European Sociological Review*, 10, 2, 105-117.

Rosen, R. (1994): Who gets Polluted? *Dissent*, Spring, 223-230.

Thorbrietz, P. (1986): Vernetztes Denken im Journalismus. Dissertation. Tübingen:Max Niemeyer Verlag.

Tymowski, A. W. (1993): The Unwanted Social Revolution. *East European Politics and Societies*, 7, 2, 169-202.

Yeager, P. C. (1992): The Politics of Efficiencies, the Effeciencies of Politics: States vs. Markets in Environmental Protection. *Critical Review*, 6, Nr. 2-3, 231-253.

8

SELF-PERCEPTION, IDENTITY
AND THE ENVIRONMENT

A Desideratum of environmental psychology

As the opening paragraph of Chapter One indicates, issues in psychology often fall short of treating contemporary problems, seeming not really to offer concrete and final solutions to human plights and predicaments.

Because psychology mostly offers many theories for the treatment of mankind's ills and falls short of providing for clear and proven methods, one may designate it as a yet growing science in its infancy. Although its beginnings can be traced back to the Greeks of 2000 years ago, who treated mental illness with music and verse in natural surroundings, much of the therapy that psychology offers today, can be likened to the blood-letting treatments of medical science in the Middle Ages and beyond. This was not because other treatments were not known and tried before, it just happened to be the accepted method of the time. Meanwhile, many people suffered and died a premature death - among others Mozart - because of the unqualified opinions of those in power. What a loss to mankind!

The last word has, by far, not been given in the field of medicine. But it is a realm open to development and experimentation. There are few overall theories provided, in which to subdivide all of the available treatments, but a skillful doctor must, both in practice and theory, base his therapy on his knowledge of relationships.

So it is with psychology - perhaps even more so. The largest development and advance of psychology comes, surely by no means accidentally, at a time when the realities of mankind are changing in ways never before known in all of its long history. Utilizing structures and institutions that mankind spent ages in developing, these changes nevertheless cannot be encompassed by them. Although, for example, riches have always been related to influence, power and authority, never before in all of recorded history, has its accumulation received its impulse, and been determined by, so many. This has even prompted the media, above all in the United States, to ponder about who really is in charge of modern policy and politics, since the wealth of individuals by far exceeds that of the government. This is not new, kingdoms were always supported by the rich and could fall at their discretion, what is new is that the wealth is concentrated in so many today.

And this is one of the developments modern psychology needs to understand because it is directly related to its growth and evolution and the continuing need for more theory and research. With the fall of communism, the accumulation of wealth in its most effective form has become the one leading impulse of most of the nations in the world. Whereas some are not yet as effective as others, much progress is made each and every year, placing riches and with them undreamt of possibilities into the hands of common people that were unheard of for kings even decades ago.

With this come new developments, such as the accessibility of leisure. That is not to say that those possessing wealth utilize this possibility, but it is at their disposal, if needed and sought for. One of the indications of its wide-spread use, theories of overwrought and overworked managers notwithstanding and the overused addage of modern man having "no time", is that travel constitutes the number one industry in the world, that is, wealth is provided through the transportation, and its accompanying needs and necessities, of masses of people from one place to the other.

This changes the way we interact with each other. And the condition of wealth as well as its spending makes a different kind of interaction necessary. Whereas, even decades ago, time was spent working and daily life constituted trudgery, we often, today, have too much leisure time on our hands. This, of course, while being an extreme test to some, is a boon to those creative people who always have one project or the other in the making and are fascinated by their own handiwork. If things continue at the present pace, it will, indeed make a change of mentality necessary to the extent that self-development should become one of the overlying goals of mankind.

Accommodating these changes and at an ever-advancing pace and with ever more forceful requisite, is the need for communication, classically a field of psychology but today receiving almost more impulse from business and economics. It is time for psychology to regain this and utilize its findings for such fields as ecological and environmental psychology as well.

As postulated in the beginning of this chapter, this is not to be accomplished by an overlying theory or even several of them. Therefore, as time comes, psychology will hopefully not spend its time in argumentation over which theory is more logical than the rest. Indeed, a theory such as cognitive dissonance, should be judged, not only by its theoretical perfection, the reliability of its methods, or the certainty of its position, but rather by how applicable it is in daily life and whether its understanding brings further relief to mankind in its daily use. Thus, an overall theory like that, becomes an accumulation of many mini-theories, all designed to explain human interaction more perfectly. This of course becomes a problem when one seeks to teach students route memorization rather than logical thinking and the over-use of one type of methodology in order to verify the truth (which only illusorily comes closer if we look for the truth where the light is better while it is yet covered with darkness in some other place).

Perhaps, as humankind learns more perfect ways of interaction and communication - in the sense of it being more useful, plentiful, effective and yielding - psychology itself will be influenced and changed. Hopefully, it will be a mutual development and not, as it threatens to be today, a rejecting of the use of this science in favor of more practical theories. Ecological psychology would be only one of the areas that would profit from this.

The crisis of environmental psychology

The above does not seek to negate the many excellent studies that are undertaken each year, but the findings of these, once reported are not very often incorporated into public and much less political policy. Perhaps it is this relationship that influences the very trendiness of psychological issues, both in the United States and in Europe. Because the policies of the scientific establishment are different in the States however, changes occur there much faster than in Europe, where, though its growth reflects the instability of an emerging field as well, there is a great deal more institutional stability in the area of higher learning, theory and science than in the United States, where even programs and findings of merit are subject to change according to political events. This has positive as well as negative sides.

Although much has been said about the theory of cognitive dissonance, this paper should not be seen as an attempt at its verification. Perhaps the past crisis that it is gone through is merely a sign of its development to an overall useage on a human and daily level. More than seeking to verify its methods, the application of which must needs deepen and vary the methodology of the original theory, the present trend of small studies utilizing its ideology should be continued in order to more clearly define its principles and more subtilely utilize its findings.

Environmental psychology must come to a recognition of this. As in the area of all environmental studies, mankind cannot expect quick and fast answers. Indeed, one of the largest contributions the many studies on psychological, environmental studies are having, is not the verification of any theory or the addition of information, but the fact that people are influenced and oftentimes change their coping styles into those that reflect more effective environmental habits.

At present, research seems to have come to a point where everything has been said before and environmental psychology, while not dead yet, has somewhat lost its popularity. This however, could prove to be a tragic loss to mankind. For it is the very development at present, that of small changes at a local level, that will surely prove to be the most effective counter-action to environmental pollution today. While difficult to summarize and to categorically press into one overall theory, yet this development and the impulses it sets free is the real contribution that modern psychology offers for the problems of this planet today.

Final results of the questionnaire series

As mentioned above, no attempts will be made to verify or negate the theory of cognitive dissonance with the results of the questionnaires proffered. As mentioned in the Introduction, this theory is only one of many used in the context of this paper, as discussed further in Chapter Two and the more recent controversy it has aroused was only mentioned in these pages, so that the argumentation as to the timeliness of this paper could be somewhat eased and limited in its extent and its content put into a more positive light.

Hypotheses, on the other hand, are more simply verified or discarded. Re-stating therefore, those proffered in Chapter Four, clear results can be put forth in the following pages. Each of the hypotheses will be stated here, with the evidence provided in turn.

H_1 **Cognitive dissonance - as rationalization and balancing of cognition with attitudes and behavior - can be found within both of the two groups under investigation, to be proven by statistical outcomes, correlations and results.**

Although the following results may not be over-interpreted, they are a first statistical outcome of those studies made and, as such, provide for a positive assumption that the hypothesis might be accepted.

A very interesting finding in Germany is highlighted by Figure 1, (Chapter Four), where the two highest negative correlations were found between emotions (Factor 1) and belief in technology (Factor 6), as well as between commercial operants (Factor 3) and personal responsibility (Factor 8). Paradoxically, those most interested in the money aspect of their job, had the least high sense of responsibility. The positive correlation between commercial operants (Factor 3) and commitment to production (Factor 7) just seems to highlight this fact. Among the Polish workers, as shown in Figure 2 and Figure 3 (Chapter Four) however, two of the highest correlations were between Factor 1 (emotions) and Factor 5 (ethical constituents) and Factor 4 (singularity) and Factor 6 (technological components), both of which could be replicated in the 1996 study. The second Polish group however, showed the highest correlations between Factor 1 (emotions) and Factor 4 (singularity).

A closer look at the means listed in Table 4 (Chapter Five) show these relationships more clearly. Beyond higher overall scores in the emotion items, they showed that Poles had significantly lower scores in user responsibility than Germans and a moderately higher belief in technology (to solve all problems of the environment) than the Germans had. Furthermore, the Germans were more quality-oriented and future-oriented than the Poles.

Furthermore, Figure 4 through 7 (Chapter Five) show a relationship that did not show up in either the means or the correlations, and which is surely one of the positive outcomes of a small exploratory study: while looking through the results, a correlation was noticed that is pictured by the graphs. Whereas environmental activity is high (1) to moderately high in the entire Polish population, it is lowest in that part of the German population that drives cars, particularly low in those driving cars to work and in their free time.

The above should then tend to show that aspects of dissonance would be present in the German workers but not in the Polish, or at least not to that extent. Going back to the findings of the higher belief in technology to solve environmental problems and the lower responsibility scores, would seem to shine some light on the discrepancy.

The second questionnaire underscores the higher belief in technology in Polish workers with 6 items, as shown in Table 5, Chapter Six. The second German population in 1996 showed essentially the same results, but even overall lower, as Table 9 (Chapter Seven) shows.

Again, in Table 5 user responsibility is higher in the German population as shown by the fact that Poles have a significantly higher mean score when asked if they see a solution in technology rather than personal responsibility. Table 9 shows that this relationship stayed the same in the German population in 1996.

Before, however, we reject H1 for the Polish population, a glance at Chapter Six Figure 10 shows a high correlation between affective reaction and information seeking, transportation and behavior and a negative correlation between transportation and discrepancy, the same positive correlations are shown in the German group.

Thus, the second population would tend to support H1 in both groups. So we may accept H1 while not rejecting H2 namely:

H_2 **The two populations measured in Germany and Poland will show statistical differences and different correlations.**

As the above shows, the findings in the 1991/1992 compared to the 1996 studies in the Polish as well as the German groups are more similar to each other than the findings are in the international Polish/German comparison. That is, in-country groups are more similar to each other throughout time than they are to the other-country groups.

The third hypothesis is easier to interpret. As Table 6 (Chapter Six) shows, no significant differences were found in the means of the four groups represented. While Table 7 (Chapter Six) shows means of the self-employed to be higher in their knowledge as well as personal commitment values, Table 8 shows no significant difference between the genders.

Table 11 (Chapter Seven) shows no significant Gender differences in the German population and Table 10 (Chapter Seven) shows the relationship between the task groups. Here, the only difference is the higher knowledge value in those employed in managing technical tasks and the self-employed.

Thus H$_3$, that there are in-country differences, cannot really be supported.

Conclusion

It is difficult to appraise studies that have reached out to hundreds of people, both in Germany and in Poland and have, in the end, put the results of 618 questionnaires at the disposal of this investigation, which must seek now to quantify the opinions in a comprehensive and meaningful way. Where outcomes are dependent upon subjective evaluations, both of attitudes and behaviors, a number of methodological faults might appear. That, nevertheless, some meaningful differences and similarities were found to be stable both through time and the proffering of two different questionnaires, should argue for their actual existence in the populations questioned. Further, it should point to the reliability and validity of the instruments used, without, of course, wanting to over-interpret the results.

Of foremost interest in this context, is that dissonance - as defined by the authors mentioned in Chapter Two - could be measured. As the following Table shows, there was a high correlation between environmental use of transportation and other pro-environmental behavior. Both populations also showed high correlations in perception and personal values.

Table 12. Factor correlation (1992)

	GERMANS	POLES
	Behavior	
Transportation	. 54***	.42***
	Perception	
Personal Values	.48***	.57***
	Affective Reaction	
Information Seeking	.41**	.54***
	Information Seeking	
Personal Commitment	.42**	.28***

However, as far as personal commitment and information seeking was concerned, the German population had higher, more significant results. Information seeking and affective reaction however, showed similar results again.

In the 1990/1991 study, the findings are more discrepant, as the following Table shows.

Table 13. Factor correlation (1990,1996/1991)

	GERMANS	POLES (P1, P2)	
		Affective Reaction	
Ethical Constituents	.32	.47***	.49***
		Affective Reaction	
Technological Components	-.60**	.35	.21
		Commercial Operants	
Commitment to Production	.56***	.18	.14
		Commercial Operants	
Personal Responsibility	-.51***	-.03	.18
		Singularity	
Technological Components	-.36	.41*	.47*

Table 14. Factor correlation (1992)

	GERMANS	POLES
	Perception	
Technology	.58***	.24***
	Affective Reaction	
Technology	.13	.47***
	Personal Values	
Technology	.52***	.13*
	Information Seeking	
Technology	.14	.46***

As one can see, results show technology neither to correlate positively with emotions nor with singularity of purpose for the Germans, whereas the Poles show a positive correlation in the second group. Interestingly enough, where commercial operants correlated significantly with commitment to production, it correlated negatively with personal responsibility, both for the German group.

Because this study was carried out with two different questionnaires, results are, of course, somewhat different. Whereas, as stated above and especially in Chapter Six, results of several questions were replicable (see especially Table 5), the above two Tables show a more diversified replicability.

One of the most interesting questions this study leaves open is the fact that the issue of technology, although so easily seen in the calculations of the means in Chapter Five and Chapter Six did not show themselves in the correlations of either study, especially those calculated in Figures 1-3 and Figures 10-11. This can be seen in the above Table, (Table 13), as well as in Table 14.

It would tend to seem more logical to find high correlations only in the Polish population, rather than the two-peaked highs in both populations.

It can only be hoped that this study contributes some meaningful findings to environmental problems in psychology in both countries. If anything however, it shows that, albeit the populations differ in some of their results, the fact that workers on both sides of the Oder River were willing to take the time to fill out these questionnaires in their free time, there are positive tendencies in both of the countries and that both Germans and Poles care about the environment enough to sacrifice some time for it.

Should following studies attempt to replicate these findings, they might not find such a cooperative atmosphere in Polish industry as that which allowed the large 1992 study here in Lublin. However, they could possibly, as this study did not allow, compare work-places in Germany and in Poland more readily, a theme that was largely ignored in this paper because of its infeasibility.

The most important question however is, if dissonance towards the environment exists in both populations, how might it be reduced. Characteristically, dissonance - measured by the refusal to see immediate problems especially by those most commited to the problems themselves - can only be reduced by the introduction of more cognitive components.

This, as already stated, would include organizational measures for people to participate in, ideally instituted and measured on a local level. Here, environmental psychology could provide some meaningful help utilizing its tools of science and theory. Indeed, the studies now being undertaken in this field, taking place all over the world and exceedingly being made available in the English language, promise real hope for the future. If only mankind could find a way to make topics of the environment as modern, fun and relaxing as much of the modern technology, travel and leisure put at our disposal daily, we might find that the problems disappear by themselves. Perhaps also, we should have a second look at morality: dependability, responsibility and honor might not be such bad attributes after all and they beat immediate gratification of any and all needs at all times for providing us with a life that is more human than animal.

REFERENCES

Ehrlich, Paul, R.; Holm, Richard, W.; & Brown, Irene, L. (1976): Biology and Society. New York: Mc Graw-Hill.

Evans, Gary, W. & Jacobs, Stephen, V. (1984): Air pollution and human behavior. In: Gary W. Even (Ed.): Environmental Stress. Cambridge: Cambridge University Press, 105-132.

Hessisches Ministerium für Wirtschaft und Technik (1989): Gesparte Energie Gespartes Geld. Wiesbaden: Hessisches Ministerium für Wirtschaft und Technik.

Hillebrand, Dieter (1991): Waschtechnik im Wandel. *Strom Praxis*, 20-23.

Lennings, Manfred (1989): Energie im Blickfeld. Jahresbericht 1989, Vereinigung Deutscher Elektrizitätswerke, Frankfurt.

Middel, Bernd (1990): Energie sparen für unsere Zukunft. Frankfurt: Verlags-und Wirtschaftsgesellschaft der Elektrizitätswerke

Muscheid, Jörg (1989): Stellungnahme zum Konzept für den öffentlichen Personennahverkehr. Bremen: Angestelltenkammer Bremen.

Necker, Tyll (1989): Für eine realistische Energiepolitik – wider energiepolitische Illusionen. Vortrag beim zwölften Workshop "Energie" des RWE am 08.11.1989 in Braunlage.

O'Neill, Gerard K. (1981): 2081. A Hopeful View of the Human Future. New York: Simon and Schuster.

Samuelson, Robert, J. (1991): Tinkering with Energy. *Newsweek*, March 4, 1991, 38.

Schaible-Rapp, Agnes (1988): Das Entsorgungsproblem. In: Dieter Frey, Carl Graf Hoyos & Dagmar Stahlberg (Hgs.): Angewandte Psychologie. München: Psychologie Verlags Union, 283-297.

Schmidtz, Hildegard (1990): Elektrohaushalt. Heidelberg: Energie-Verlag GmbH.

Schröder, Norbert (1987): Die Sonne als Energiespender. *Der EAM Bote*, 2, 91, 42, Jahrgang, 4-5.

Sheeky, Noel, P. & Chapman, Anthony, J. (1984): Accidents and Safety. In: A. Gale & A. J. Chapman (Eds.): Psychology and Social Problems. Brisbane: John Wiley and Sons, 171-190.

Thurau, Martin (1991): Der Kampf gegen die Ozonbelastung verpufft im Leeren. *Süddeutsche Zeitung*, 31.05, Nr. 123, 17.

Vester, Federic (1980): Neuland des Denkens. Vom technokratischen zum kybernetischen Zeitalter. Stuttgart: Deutsche Verlags-Anstalt.

APPENDIX

INDUSTRIAL ASPECTS
OF ENVIRONMENTAL PROTECTION

Reliability Analysis V=Item Number in the preliminary questionnaire; I=Final Item Number; M=Mean; SD=Standard Deviation

Affective Reaction

| ITEM | | | GERMANY (alpha = .85) | | | POLAND (alpha =.75) | | |
V	I		M	SD	Alpha if deleted	M	SD	Alpha if deleted
9	1	I worry about environmental problems, they should concern every one of us.	5.95	1.13	.83	6.13	.94	.71
10	2	I feel our products at work could be more environmental.	5.45	1.44	.85	5.83	1.44	.74
13	3	In my firm, production already considers as many environmental factors as possible.	4.50+[1]	1.50	.85	3.83+	1.37	.74
23	4	I think the consumer should worry more about the environment.	6.14	1.04	.85	6.10	1.12	.74
24	5	When I think about the potential danger that confronts us, I become really angry.	5.59	1.44	.82	5.27	1.55	.68
31	6	Sometimes I wonder if society will survive if it stays the way it is now.	4.86	1.83	.85	4.43	1.76	.68
32	7	I am not happy with the products my firm makes, as long as I know they are not environmentally sound.	4.50	1.87	.83	4.30	1.89	.70
33	8	Sometimes I get depressed, it all seems so hard to understand.	4.23	1.60	.83	3.90	1.52	.75
36	9	The production of my firm causes environmental pollution; this is harmful to me.	4.59	1.89	.86	5.63	1.54	.75

[1] With + designated means differ from adjusted ones presented in Chapters, page , because the text of the published article was presented differently.

Reliability Analysis - Scale (Alpha)

Perception of discrepancy

ITEM			GERMANY (alpha = .18)			POLAND (alpha = .71)		
V	I		M	SD	Alpha if deleted	M	SD	Alpha if deleted
3	10	Politics and economics should be more oriented towards ethics.	4.09	1.57	.25	3.23	1.74	.57
7	11	I sometimes wonder if I am too committed to my work.	2.23	.87	.08	2.97	1.75	.65
16	12	I don't see how society can change, without threatening the advance ment that modern technology has brought us.	3.23	1.27	.18	4.47+	1.68	.66
19	13	The consumer is really the one that is responsible for what he buys, not the industry.	5.68	1.17	.12	3.87	2.06	.75
39	14	I don't know what I should give up first, everything seems to cause environmental pollution.	4.73	1.45	.16	4.97	2.19	.67

Reliability Analysis - Scale (Alpha)

Commercial Operants		GERMANY (alpha = -.05)			POLAND (alpha = .77)		
ITEM							
V	I		M	SD	Alpha if deleted	M	SD	Alpha if deleted
6	15	I am only interested in my firm, I dont have time for other things.	5.77+	1.66	.12	4.93+	1.53	.71
20	16	Only if production stays as it is, can we make a profit.	3.86+	1.73	-.41	4.07+	2.05	.77
34	17	In the firm, we work out environmental problems together.	3.91	1.51	.02	3.73	1.96	.61
35	18	I only work to make money.	2.86+	1.64	.03	3.27+	1.98	.74

Reliability Analysis - Scale (Alpha)

Singularity

ITEM				GERMANY (alpha = .18)			POLAND (alpha = .68)		
V	I			M	SD	Alpha if deleted	M	SD	Alpha if deleted
1	19	I am not interested in ethics and philosophy, I merely want to enjoy life.		3.73+	1.52	.13	3.60+	1.90	.58
14	20	I myself am for environmental protection, but my firm does not agree.		3.91	1.11	-.01	2.93	1.70	.64
22	21	Our product is dependent upon being fashionable, and must be produced regularly.		2.18	1.18	.09	1.60	1.25	.54
25	22	I feel really sad that the environment has become such a problem.		3.41	1.99	.35	2.83	2.02	.67
37	23	I am ready to quit driving a car, so that coming generations will have a higher quality of life.		3.55	1.44	.18	2.30	1.53	.69

Reliability Analysis - Scale (Alpha)

Ethical Constituents

ITEM			GERMANY (alpha = .76)			POLAND (alpha = .62)		
V	I		M	SD	Alpha if deleted	M	SD	Alpha if deleted
2	24	I am interested in culture and regularly read relevant topics and attend events.	4.45	1.37	.60	4.33	1.18	.65
4	25	To me, the question of ethics has some meaning.	4.95	1.65	.74	4.43	1.65	.53
5	26	The discussions in media and literature about ethics are interesting to me.	4.14	1.21	.67	3.27	1.48	.43
12	27	I sometimes ask myself, what I can do to protect the environment.	5.18	1.47	.79	4.87	1.78	.53

Reliability Analysis - Scale (Alpha)

Technological Components

ITEM			GERMANY (aipha = .40)			POLAND (alpha = .60)		
V	I		M	SD	Alpha if deleted	M	SD	Alpha if deleted
8	28	My work gives me a great deal of satisfaction.	3.32	1.55	.36	4.23	1.07	.53
11	29	I am often angry about the question of the environment, right away, everyone points to the big firms.	4.23	1.72	.04	5.17	1.82	.46
28	30	Environmental problems will certainly be solved by technology.	3.41	1.56	.19	4.37	1.79	.65
38	31	I would be sacrificing too much if I gave up my car.	5.18	1.62	.60	5.20	1.77	.44

Reliability Analysis - Scale (Alpha)

Commitment to Production

ITEM		I	GERMANY (alpha = .73)			POLAND (alpha = .16)		
V	I		M	SD	Alpha if deleted	M	SD	Alpha if deleted
15	32	I don't see how my firm could change products to become more environmental.	3.36	1.43	.78	3.33	2.11	-.08
17	33	Our products cannot be made better and the market dependents upon them staying as they are.	4.59	1.71	.55	3.63	1.65	.08
18	34	I often feel angry about all the discussions on the environment.	4.45+	1.57	.66	3.50+	1.66	-.11
27	35	I see possibilities of changing production, but the cost is too high.	4.36+	1.65	.63	3.50+	1.94	.46

Reliability Analysis - Scale (Alpha)

Personal Responsibility

ITEM		I	GERMANY (alpha =.40)			POLAND (alpha =.23)		
V	I		M	SD	Alpha if deleted	M	SD	Alpha if deleted
21	36	I see possibilities to decrease our waste products.	3.91	1.74	.56	2.77	1.87	.02
26	37	I really worry about the environment, but I do not know of any concrete solutions.	4.00	1.57	.38	3.47	1.55	.07
29	38	Means of transportation.	5.23+	2.09	.20	3.97+	2.11	.36
30	39	I do not worry about the environment, I leave that to political and grass-roots groups.	3.14	1.88	.03	2.90	1.77	.26